Women,

❖ • ❖

Mentors,

❖ • ❖

and

❖ • ❖

Success

Women,
Mentors,
and
Success

Joan Jeruchim
and
Pat Shapiro

FAWCETT COLUMBINE

NEW YORK

A Fawcett Columbine Book
Published by Ballantine Books
Copyright © 1992 by Joan Jeruchim and Pat Shapiro

LIBRARY OF CONGRESS CATALOGING-IN-PUBLICATION DATA

Jeruchim, Joan.
Women, mentors, and success / Joan Jeruchim and Pat Shapiro.—
1st ed.
p.   cm.
Includes bibliographical references and index.
ISBN 0-449-90448-2
1. Women in the professions—United States—Case studies.
2. Mentors in the professions—United States—Case studies.
3. Women in business—United States—Case studies.   4. Mentors in
business—United States—Case studies.   I. Shapiro, Patricia
Gottlieb.   II. Title
HD6054.2.U6J47   1992
658.4'09'082—dc20   91-58629
CIP

Manufactured in the United States of America
First Edition: May 1992
10 9 8 7 6 5 4 3 2 1

To my brother Steven and my mother, Paula;
and for my husband, Michel, and my father, Ernst,
fellow authors
—J.J.

For my husband, Dick,
and in memory of my first mentors,
Marge and Meyer Gottlieb
—P.S.

CONTENTS

Acknowledgments

No book is written in isolation, and even a collaboration is more than two people. We owe our first thanks to Kathie Lynn, who founded the Main Line Women's Network. Kathie's determination and creative leadership launched the women's networking group and drew us, a psychotherapist and a writer, together. Her conviction that working women have much to share and can help one another succeed became our modus operandi as we researched and wrote this book.

Many, many women contributed to these pages—not just those whose stories you'll read. Women all over the country welcomed us into their offices, no matter how busy they were, and shared their mentoring experiences. We appreciate their openness and honesty in sharing these experiences as well as their willingness to give us names of other women. For their generosity with sources we are grateful to Anne Angerman, Maria DiMarco, Sondra Gehardt, L.L.B., Barbara Goldberg, Gale Mendeloff, M.D., Cecil Rice, Ph.D., Susan Wachter, Ph.D., and Rhona Weinstein, Ph.D. As professional colleagues, Charles Dick, M.D., and Kenneth Weller, M.D., provided a constant sounding board.

For their thoroughness and persistence in tracking down bibliographic sources, our thanks to Lori Berninger, Bonnie Hahn, and Dan Satlow. For painstakingly transcribing our interviews, we thank Leslie Holt, Nan Nichols, and Carol Williams. Our gratitude goes to Jerry Bloom for the initial compilation of the interview data and to Bob Ray for his computer work in organizing survey data into pie charts and bar graphs.

We appreciate the commitment to this project from both our agent, Flip Brophy, and our editor, Joëlle Delbourgo. Joëlle believed in our project from the beginning and stayed committed throughout. She also believed in us and shared our conviction that women as protégés and mentors could inspire our readers. A special thanks to Joëlle for assigning editor Meg Blackstone to work closely with us on the manuscript. Her encouragement, insight, and inspiration were remarkable.

Lastly we are grateful to our husbands, Michel and Dick, and our children, Claude and Kenny, and Andrew and Margot, for their continuing love, patience, and support throughout this project.

Introduction

This is a book about women and the misunderstood, underutilized relationship known as mentoring. Mentoring *can* bring women professional success and personal growth; it offers them both power and intimacy. However, few women have tapped its potential. Many women may be put off by or uninterested in the conventional male model of mentoring: one mentor for one man in one lifetime.

We have discovered a new vision of this old relationship, one that meets the complex needs of contemporary women. Women's lives and roles are complicated; their needs are unique. Mentoring can build on their strengths and can make them stronger, more powerful, and more supportive of each other.

Our interest in women and their mentors developed out of our personal experiences, our own frustrations about mentoring, and our yearning for mentors. We wondered how typical our experiences were of women and their mentors across America. Our research project focused on professional and business women, since these were the women most likely to have mentors and to benefit from them. We selected eight professions: four traditionally male—law, medicine, academia, and corporate management; two of the so-called female professions—nursing and education; and two with mixed genders—writing and psychotherapy. In all we interviewed 106 female protégés, scores of female and male mentors, and a number of experts.

The "snowball method" was a big help locating interviewees;

we asked men and women in these fields to identify successful women who had "made it" and young women with potential. These women, in turn, led us to other women. While the interviewees live throughout the United States, we have left exact locations unidentified to respect their privacy. For the same reason we have also changed the interviewees' names and the names of their corporations, universities, and cities as well as other identifying information. The people we interviewed as experts, of course, are identified as such.

After the interviews were completed, we sent each interviewee a survey to verify the information she had given us verbally. The statistics used throughout the book are gleaned from the results of the survey (which had a 60 percent return rate). The results themselves can be found in appendix B.

The women ranged in age from twenty-four to seventy. They were predominantly white; about 8 percent were black or Hispanic. The women were raised in a variety of socioeconomic backgrounds, with many from working-class or middle-class homes. However, in terms of their professional status, income, and educational level, they would now be defined as an elite class compared with the general population. All marital statuses were represented in our sample. Almost 60 percent of the women were raising or had raised children or stepchildren while working. (See appendix B for details and conclusions of study.)

In the winter of 1989 we conducted a series of in-depth interviews that were a cross between a clinical and journalistic interview, lasting from one to two hours. We interviewed the women whose stories became the extended case histories in each chapter several times. First we screened the women over the phone; we told them we were interested in talking about their work relationships and who was helpful to them in their careers. We encouraged them to talk with us even if they had no mentors because we were also looking for a comparative base.

Our goal was to look at mentoring from four perspectives: as a woman's issue, as a developmental issue, as a relationship, and finally as a success/power issue. These themes provided the prism through which we have explored the mentoring relationship for women.

We were surprised to find far more mentors, both male and female, than we expected. Seventy-seven percent of our sample had mentors: 49 percent of those women had male mentors, 19 percent had female, and 32 percent had both male and female mentors. In fact the gender of the mentors affected their function for their protégés. Male mentors tended to give more instrumental assistance and sponsorship that helped women advance in their careers. Female mentors, who were in less powerful positions, were more emotionally supportive and gave more personal advice.

This distinction between the roles that male and female mentors played led us to speculate that other differences between men and women might also affect their mentoring. We were struck, for example, by the complexity and diversity of women's developmental stages as they proceed through adult life. In their twenties women may choose to marry and have children or they may focus on establishing their careers. During their thirties they reevaluate the work/family decisions they made in their twenties. If they gave their career top priority and put marriage and kids on the back burner, they need to reconsider having children in light of their biological clock. Or if they had the luxury of not working while their children were young, they may be ready to enter the work force. During their forties and fifties most women become more serious about their careers because typically their children are less dependent financially and emotionally. Of course at any point a woman can be divorced or widowed, forcing a reevaluation of career issues.

Because of these varied developmental patterns, women need different kinds of mentoring during different periods of their lives. Women can enter a mentoring relationship in their twenties, thirties, or forties. This is a significant departure from the male pattern—men typically follow a straight career path, and their major mentoring relationship generally begins in their late twenties. Mentors can help women formulate their work dreams, serve as role models, and help them progress in their careers.

Nevertheless, for the majority of women in our sample, mentoring did commence in their twenties or thirties. This is because these women (whom we chose precisely because they were successful) devoted their energy to their careers before starting their families. Yet for those women who were divorced or widowed or began their families before they started working, it was common to find a mentor in their late thirties or early forties. Pearl Brown (whom you'll meet in chapter 1, "Developing as Women") was a traditional woman who grew up in the 1950s. She used the women's movement as a symbolic mentor to motivate her to go back to school when she was in her midthirties. During her forties she had several male mentors, who played a purely instrumental role. Years later, when she was in her midfifties, she served as a mentor and role model for her daughters, a lawyer and a teacher, respectively, who were then in their early thirties.

Another difference between the sexes is that women typically define themselves through relationships—daughter, wife, friend, sister—and these relationships shape them and give them strength. Women have not yet been socialized to bring this propensity for relationships into the workplace. They have underutilized work relationships that can help them advance politically and succeed personally. It is time for this to change.

The reasons that women have overlooked or perhaps misunderstood this important relationship are complex. Up until now women have used the male model because they have believed it is the only model. However, because of women's complex developmental needs there were problems making the male model fit. Women also tend to be politically naive. They don't realize what mentoring can do for them, as either protégé or mentor. When women mentor other women, they can build their own power base. For example, their protégés write about them, quote them, and give them speaking engagements. For the protégé mentoring offers an opportunity to learn the profession, to connect with powerful and influential people, and to establish an intimate relationship at work.

But we believe the primary reason that women have misunderstood or overlooked this relationship is that they are a minority in the predominantly white male corporations and professions. And in the past mentoring has been an elite, white-male relationship that has shut out women and blacks.

In fact women face many of the same barriers to their advancement that blacks face. The influx of women into the work force was a direct result of the 1964 Civil Rights Act. Title VII made discrimination against women in employment and education illegal.[1] While this act forced companies to open their doors to women, once women were across the threshold, they were not so readily accepted by the white male establishment. As Hennig and Jardim, authors of *The Managerial Woman*, note, "women are beginning to discover what discouraged civil-rights leaders learned in the 1960s: you can legislate against segregation but you cannot legislate integration. In other words, saying the members of a minority can't be kept out does not mean they'll get in."[2]

And getting in does not guarantee that women won't be discriminated against on the inside. Ann Hopkins found this out the hard way. Hopkins was denied partnership in 1983 at the Price Waterhouse accounting firm in Washington, D.C., because the other partners felt she was *too much* like a man. They said she cursed, smoke, drank beer at lunch, did not wear makeup, and carried a briefcase instead of a purse. Yet she brought in more business than any of the other eighty-seven candidates for partnership—all of whom were men. Her fight ended in 1990, when the Supreme Court awarded her the partnership she wanted and ordered the accounting firm to take her back and pay her as if she had been a partner since 1983.

In an earlier sex-discrimination case, *Hishon v. King & Spalding*, attorney Elizabeth Hishon claimed that the law firm for which she worked, King & Spalding of Atlanta, had discriminated against her on the basis of her gender in denying her partnership. On May

22, 1984, the Supreme Court unanimously ruled that law-partnership decisions do fall under Title VII and cannot be based on consideration of sex or race. This case has implications for all professions that use the partnership arrangement for advancement, such as public accounting, architecture, and law. Promotion to partner must be on merit, not on gender, the Court ruled.[3]

What options does a woman have in situations like these? She can sue and fight for her rights, as Ann Hopkins and Elizabeth Hishon did. She can try to legislate for gender equality. Or she can try to find a mentor, who is usually on the inside track, to stand up for her. Ann Hopkins's so-called mentor told her to "walk more femininely, talk more femininely, wear makeup, have [her] hair styled and wear jewelry."[4] He was trying to help her assimilate into the Price Waterhouse male dominant culture, but she wanted to be respected for her abilities. If Hopkins's mentor felt strongly about gender equality, he may have been more willing to take on the "old boys" of the firm, urging them to promote her on her abilities and merit and not try to change *her* into the male partners' stereotype of a woman.

To fight isolationism and sexism, women must work harder and longer to prove themselves. Women often overlook the fact that mentors can be their allies in their pursuit to advance and crack the notorious glass ceiling. But women don't necessarily have to look to the most powerful people as mentors. They need to get mentoring whenever and wherever they can. Often it is the person who feels like an outsider himself who is willing to "risk" mentoring a woman or minority. For example, Susan Richards (from chapter 6, "The Interracial Pair") found a recovering alcoholic as her mentor. He had plateaued in his career and literally had nothing to lose by mentoring a black woman. The mentor and protégé bonded because they both felt like underdogs, on the fringes of the in-group. Having a political outsider as a mentor did not diminish the mentoring; in this case it was as sound as any relationship we found.

Women now constitute 40 percent of law school students, 37 percent of business school students, and 33 percent of medical school students.[5] But once women enter the work force, they still do not progress at the same rate as men. According to the U.S. Department of Labor, only 24.8 percent of practicing physicians are women and 29.4 percent of attorneys are women. Of those in executive, administrative, and managerial positions, 42.3 percent are women. But even this figure is misleading, because it also includes managers of small businesses (such as McDonald's franchises), not just corporate managers.[6]

At high echelons, above middle management, the discrepancies between men and women increase. Among Fortune 500 companies less than 2 percent of top executives are women.[7] And corporate women at the vice-presidential level or above earn 42 percent less than their male counterparts.[8] In a recent *Business Week*–Harris survey of 450 women executives (all working at corporations with $100 billion or more in annual sales or fifteen hundred or more employees), 60 percent of women in management identified "a male-dominated corporate culture" as the major obstacle to their success and advancement.[9]

In addition, women who have worked so hard to advance on their own merit fear that linking up with a male mentor will be misconstrued. Even in the 1990s there is still discomfort between men and women in the workplace. Men are not used to working closely with women as colleagues or collaborators. Both men and women have difficulty dealing with sexual tension and fear that sexual involvement, or the hint of it, can ruin their career. Janice Celica, a teacher in a small private school (whom we'll meet in chapter 8, "The Intimate Pair"), was ostracized by the other teachers because of their jealousy and suspicions of what was going on behind closed doors with Ed Brennan, the principal, who was her mentor. Janice and Ed learned that cross-gender mentoring is highly visible and subject to public scrutiny. They had to find ways to handle this if they wanted to reap the benefits of this liaison.

One way to cope with this discomfort between the sexes is for women to look at their mentors as father figures. Gina Carbone, a law school professor (chapter 4, "The Father-Daughter Pair"), chose three older men as mentors. This allowed her to find a safe, nonsexual way of relating to men at work. However, women who see their mentors as compensatory figures—trying to make up for what they didn't receive from their real parents—can run into trouble. For example, Brenda Marks and ad executive Bert Paley (see chapter 5, "The Enmeshed Pair") became so close that they could not separate until an outside force tore them apart. (Her psychotherapy also helped.) Only then did Brenda become independent and autonomous. Becoming too close is a risk that all mentors and protégés face in an intimate relationship (male mentors can fall into the same trap of regarding younger protégés as compensatory daughters), but enmeshment can be a particular problem for women because of their strong need for attachment. This can be combated by developing other relationships, besides the mentoring one, to balance the protégé's network.

Those women with female mentors experienced a different kind of relationship. There was more emotional support, more role modeling, and less power inherent in the role. Writer Bonnie Philpott (chapter 3, "The Mother-Daughter Pair"), for example, failed to see the power base in her mentoring—she saw it only as a relationship. There is also a competitive element present when women mentor other women, which may make some women less willing to become mentors. This type of thinking needs to change. (Unfortunately few women were willing to discuss the issue of competition among women.)

Nevertheless the majority of women today have male mentors. As mentioned earlier, there are not enough women in positions of power to serve as mentors. Because white males are the power holders in almost every profession and corporation, women who want to advance are forced to rely on men as mentors and sponsors. Although some may say this is consorting with the powerful (or the enemy), we see it as a pragmatic relationship for the politically savvy woman, one that's also an opportunity for women and men to learn to work closely and relate to each other as equals.

There's no question that mentoring from a man is different

from mentoring from a woman. Cross-gender mentoring has its difficulties (see chapter 8, "The Intimate Pair"). Sexual issues aside, women must temper what they model from a male. It is not an easy task to keep one's sense of self and femininity intact while following a male professional model. In fact this conflict cost Kathie Long her mentoring relationship with Richard Hendricks, a partner in a Big 8 accounting firm. As long as she could work twelve-hour days and perform up to his perfectionistic standards, she was the ideal protégé. But when illness forced her to reevaluate her lifestyle (she choose a more well-rounded life with husband and children), he lost interest in her. (This situation is explored more fully in chapter 7, "The Political Pair.")

Richard Hendricks was not the perfect mentor. No mentor is. But women often expect perfection because they tend to idealize their mentors. In some articles the popular press reinforces the notion that the mentor will be perfect rather than human. But in other articles, women are told not to have expectations from mentors because mentors aren't available for women. This latter view may arise because most women have received "old boy" mentoring. By contrast, the kind of eclectic mentoring we are suggesting allows for emotional give-and-take and accounts for women's different career paths at different times in their development.

Male mentors may currently be the link to power at the office, but for a woman to maintain her identity as a woman in a male-dominated environment, she must also rely on symbolic mentors or on female peers for support and role modeling. (These issues will also be explored in later chapters.) Women must be creative and invent what they can, using what one interviewee called "bits and pieces of mentoring," to their advantage. We believe that any mentoring a woman can find is potentially good mentoring. It won't be ideal or perfect, but it benefits women because it brings them closer to the power.

In the past, mentoring has been defined by men and used to meet their needs for advancement. Because of the way in which men are socialized, intimacy issues have been deemphasized.

Women's strengths have been minimized in their effort to succeed on men's terms and in their world. It's time to redefine the mentoring relationship and restructure it to meet women's unique needs— not as clones of men in drab three-piece suits and floppy bow ties, but as women who feel valued for their leadership and expertise. Women can bring a rich female perspective to the workplace. They are creative, talented, and experienced. Mentoring must be redefined so that women can express their individuality.

From our talks with over 120 women we have seen that women yearn for a life mentor (attorney Sally Enright found one in Sam Fishbine—see chapter 9, "The Life Mentor"). Women want someone to teach them how to live their lives, not just how to advance in their careers. They want a meaningful career, yet they also want rewarding personal relationships. Juggling both is the crucial balancing act of the nineties. Women want to succeed at the office, but they also want to raise healthy children and have satisfying, intimate relationships at home. Our new vision of mentoring can provide the perspective and the support that women need to succeed in both spheres, home and work.

Women,
◆ ◆ ◆
Mentors,
◆ ◆ ◆
and
◆ ◆ ◆
Success

❖ ❖ ❖

CHAPTER ONE

Developing as Women: Mentors at Different Stages and Ages

"I was complaining a lot one spring," recalls Pearl Brown, fifty-nine, a corporate officer in a Fortune 200 company, remembering an incident from her late twenties. "I was at a dinner party, and a friend and I were talking (she was a nutritionist). She was regretting that she hadn't gone to medical school and she said to me, 'Would you stop complaining . . .' and then she asked me a very good question that really started my train of thinking.

" 'What would you have done if you were a man?' she asked. And then I realized that I had always wanted to be an accountant like my father but that I hadn't known any female accountants.

"Getting my MBA began percolating in my head and it seemed like a very silly idea, because I had four children and a very traditional household. But it wouldn't leave—the idea just stuck there. I decided I'd give it a try, and I started out in business school at night majoring in accounting. I'm a night-school graduate. And as soon as I opened the book, it was a love affair, and it hasn't changed all these years."

A dinner-party conversation changed Pearl Brown's life. As a middle-class woman in the 1950s, she followed the traditional path of homemaker-wife-mother, tying her dreams to a man and marriage. Her mentors and models were her mother and her aunts. There were few models in the workplace for women then. Pearl's job—

unpaid and unrecognized—was to be a good wife, a good mother, and a good housekeeper.

But as Pearl approached her thirtieth birthday—an important developmental point for women to reexamine the choices they made in their twenties—she became aware of a restlessness within her and of a vague dissatisfaction with this traditional role. This casual conversation got her thinking: Maybe she could do more than change diapers, plan menus, and carpool kids. Like many of the women we interviewed, Pearl was initially reluctant to have an individualistic dream for herself; she didn't have the confidence to pursue her own career nor did the cultural climate encourage it.

While having an individualistic dream was new for women of Pearl's generation, today we take it for granted. Pearl's daughters, like many of their contemporaries in their midthirties, are raising families *and* pursuing careers, in part because the contemporary cultural climate has given women choices that their mothers never had.

As they progress through distinct developmental stages, women express their work identity differently in their twenties, thirties, and forties. So it's clear that women need a series of role models and mentors at different ages and at different times of their development, to help them formulate their work dreams, advance in their careers, and support them as professional women. For example, if a woman is strongly focused on her career in her twenties, she may need a gung-ho–type male mentor. As she tries to combine work and motherhood in her thirties, she may prefer an older career woman with children as a mentor. Later, in her forties or fifties, she may feel ready to pass on what she knows and become a mentor herself to an up-and-coming woman.

Pearl Brown is an example of someone who used different kinds of mentoring to meet her special needs in different decades of her life. First she used the women's movement as a symbolic mentor to help her break with tradition. When her career was established and she was near forty, she used male mentors briefly for their instrumental help. Her daughters, in turn, look to Pearl as a role model and mentor for combining their work with child care.

Such variations in mentoring are necessary for women because their development is more complex and varied than men's. While men are fathers and husbands, these roles do not interfere with their work in the same way that women's care-giving roles do. In most cases men are able to pursue their careers throughout their adult lives with few interruptions or conflicts. For women, however, every stage of adulthood contains conflicts and compromises as they balance their roles at home with those at work. Decisions such as whether to have children, when to begin a family, whether and when to work full-time, and how to find good child care must be faced and refaced. At each point these decisions must balance with career options and family situations.

Because women can and do begin their careers in almost any decade of their adult life, they can have mentors at almost any point—unlike men, who typically follow straight career paths and whose mentoring relationships begin primarily in their late twenties. Like men, the majority of the women in our study had mentors in their twenties and thirties; however, we want to stress again that we chose these women because they were successful in their careers, which often meant following the male, individualistic path of pursuing career (with family later).

Many women of Pearl Brown's generation didn't have their own dream initially but hitched their star to their husband's dream of career and success.[1] Others combined work in one of the "female" professions with raising a family. Although a few had work identities early on, many more developed their own careers later in life, like Pearl did, as they matured or divorced or their children left home.

As Carol Gilligan, associate professor of education at Harvard University, and others have pointed out, women typically define themselves through relationships—daughter, wife, friend, sister— and these relationships give them strength. It is this "connectedness" that marks women's social roles. Mentoring relationships are a particularly empowering means by which women can connect. In addition to their personal support, mentors were crucial to the women we interviewed to help ease their uncertainty and conflict, as well as to give them the positive encouragement they needed to achieve their career goals and individualistic dreams at various times in their lives.

A mentor's presence is crucial at two critical periods in a woman's career, says Ruth Halcomb, author of *Women Making It*. The first time is during the early phase of her career, when she first sees her work as more than a job and realizes that she'll be doing it for the rest of her life. She needs psychological support then, because she experiences considerable anxiety around new interpersonal relationships at work, new job demands, and new roles. The second crucial period is when she is ready for the final push to "the top rungs of the ladder," where few women have ventured and role models are scarce.[2] An important reason that women have difficulty breaking the glass ceiling is the absence of role models to guide the way. Each woman must break new ground for herself.

Halcomb points out that there are crisis points when women need mentors as well: "Individuals seem to need mentors most at turning points in their careers: a young researcher deciding on a specialty, a mature woman making a career change, a female manager on the verge of promotion. One's success or failure at such times greatly depends upon whether a mentor is present or not."[3]

Mentors are able to help shape women's professional development. They guide them in forming a work identity when they are confused or unfocused, especially in graduate or professional school or in an entry-level position (regardless of their chronological age). Jane Smythe, a forty-year-old CPA with a Big 8 accounting firm, began her accounting career in her late thirties, after raising her family. When her children were young, she ran a Montessori school because the working hours meshed with her children's school day; she had little interest in advancement, so was not tuned in to mentors then. Once her children were older, she focused more on her own goals, earning her CPA at thirty-seven. At forty she had the same need for a mentor's career guidance as a twenty-five-year-old in an entry-level position. In fact Jane was older than her male mentor, but he had far more career experience. Her mentor gave her many opportunities for advancement. Because she had the maturity to handle these opportunities and other responsibilities, she rapidly advanced to manager. She is on her way to becoming a partner, something that is still difficult for women to accomplish.

Those experts who studied mentoring, such as Yale psychologist Daniel Levinson, imply that men may miss an important developmental experience if they do not have a mentor by the time they are in their late twenties or early thirties. However, this harsh judgment is not applied to women, because of the variability of their developmental stages. The fact that many women change their identity and put their energy into work without a model is akin to having men stay at home and become "feminized," a Mr. Mom without a model. But that is exactly the situation that Pearl Brown faced; thousands of other women still face it every day. These women have few female models who combine a career with motherhood and homemaking. Betty Friedan, author of *The Feminine Mystique,* was herself constantly juggling her roles as mother and journalist. The two roles were so enmeshed that she wrote the book that made her famous on her kitchen table, from nine to three while her children were in school, rather than carving out a space of her own in which to write.

The reason men's development is a starting-off point for an exploration of women's is that most of the major adult developmental studies have been done on men. Daniel Levinson pioneered this work in the late seventies, publishing his findings in the book *The Seasons of a Man's Life.* Gail Sheehy popularized many of Levinson's concepts in her best-selling *Passages.*

Levinson's theory has been criticized by feminists because men "are taken for models of human development despite the fact that they exclude fully half of humankind." Levinson and his coauthors "seem to underscore the presumption that male equals human and female equals something else. Their insidious implication that the female is to be understood via the male can only function to take away from a deeper sense of who and what they really are."[4]

Men, for example, tend to be more individualistic in their early adulthood and then become more interested and invested in relationships in midlife. For women, relationships remain important throughout adulthood. To say that men's way is universal for both sexes diminishes the significance of women's relationships and discounts their unique way of approaching developmental tasks. This is why we believe women need their own model of mentoring, built on their unique needs, perspective, and development. The male model does not always fit women. Richard Hendricks, the partner from a Big 8 accounting firm (see chapter 7), for example, was an ideal mentor for anyone—male or female—who was willing to work twelve-hour days. However, when his protégé, Kathie Long, got married, shortened her hours, and wanted more balance in her life, Hendricks had no patience for her. At that point the male model fell short, and Kathie Long needed a woman mentor who could understand her need for balance, support her choices, and serve as a role model.

Both Levinson and Sheehy have also been criticized for not addressing the issue of parenthood in early adulthood for men.[5] Even though a book about women's adult development that ignored the impact of motherhood on a woman would be seen as incomplete, the Levinson and Sheehy books do precisely this and are still hailed as landmark books.

Nonetheless these two books were the first to highlight the notion that adulthood is not one stable era but a series of stages from which emerges a distinct and unique life. A person passes through age-related stages that represent stability or crisis, each one building on the next. Each stage is marked by key events with critical tasks to be faced and accomplished. One task is the establishment of a vocational or professional identity with the help of a mentor.

To Levinson, man's identity continues to be formed throughout adulthood as he interacts with and plays out his social roles. The wife and the mentor are the two key individuals in the man's life during his twenties. They both help him stand on his own two feet as he separates from his family of origin and grows in independence. The wife provides intimacy in his home while the mentor provides intimacy as well as power in the workplace. During his thirties he resolves the choices of his twenties and seeks greater stability. When he enters his forties, a man reevaluates his needs and accomplishments. This is the time he is likely to become a mentor to younger men and women, an important midlife task that helps him regenerate himself. Because he feels more secure at midlife, he is able for the first time to express his more "feminine," nurturing side through mentoring.[6]

Women's development is more complicated and harder to compartmentalize than men's. Four women doctoral students—Wendy Stewart, Ruth Droge, Kathryn Furst, and Diane Adams—wrote their dissertations on women's adult development using Levinson's model. They found that women progressed through the same developmental periods as men, but passed through them at different ages and approached the developmental tasks differently; therefore the outcomes were also different.[7] These differences, which this chapter explores, result from women's more complex lives and dreams and the problems they encountered in working them out.

For women, love and work—those two cornerstones of adult functioning—operate differently than for men. Traditionally a woman has shaped her identity by connecting, not by separating. Yet she, too, must separate from her family of origin to become her own woman. Ironically, in the past she has separated *through* a relationship: by finding "her special man." Being married gave her adult status and a role that differentiated her from her original family.[8]

The mentor can also be a transitional link from family to the world outside. He can help a woman feel competent as she develops an independent career.* If women would bring their knack for

*For purposes of clarity we will refer to the mentor as "he" and the protégé as "she" throughout, since in our sample most mentors were male and all the protégés were female.

relationships into the workplace more, they would find that mentoring can also be a means to personal and professional growth.

Today a woman's life is complicated because she has more options. She can still become her own person by creating a nuclear family of her own, although few women choose only this path in the 1990s. She can strive to establish her career first and forgo marriage and/or children until later. Or she can find a way to combine marriage and childrearing with work. Whichever option she chooses, she must constantly balance work and love, her need for individuality and her desire for relationships. Trying to juggle her responsibilities and achieve this balance still causes considerable tension. A woman mentor, seasoned from facing similar issues herself, can provide support and advice.

In her twenties woman's task focuses on making choices about marriage-motherhood and a career. Wendy Stewart's doctoral dissertation has shown that women who remain single and pursue a career in their twenties tend to form relationships with men and women at work who serve as role models or mentors. But those women who seek a special man—not a mentor—and marry and have children in their twenties are more highly influenced by their own mothers as models, even in adulthood.[9]

Both of these lifestyles contain a strong relational component—whether it is with a mentor, a mother, or a special man. This is consistent with the work of Carol Gilligan, who found that when women considered their own individualistic needs first, they viewed themselves as selfish.[10] By comparison a man sees individuality as his right. He, too, depends on his special woman and his mentor, but the wife and mentor are seen as helpmates—not partners—in his pursuit to become his own person. He would deny "needing" relationships. Our culture supports this denial because the pinnacle of adulthood for a man is individuality.

On the other hand, according to Gilligan and other feminist writers, women learn to know themselves through their relationships.[11] Relationships are part of the educational process for a woman. Growth need not be compromised *because* of the relationship; a woman can flourish within a relationship (just as she can be stifled). Women feel they can be individuals and maintain their identity within a relationship, but men often do not. Men tend to deny the intimacy involved in mentoring and emphasize the power/success piece while women do the opposite: They overlook the power piece and stress the support they received.

Everyone thought Pearl Brown had the ideal life. She was married to a physician and had a home in the suburbs and four adorable children, but much as she was crazy about having kids, she didn't buy the whole lifestyle. She says, "I had an awareness that I didn't fit that model in the late fifties/early sixties of what was expected of a married woman with children. That model being a mother who is at home with her children, happy baking bread and making mayonnaise, spending considerable time on her looks. There was an uncomfortable fit between me and that model. I just didn't fit that mold. I disliked it.

"I didn't have great talents as a homemaker. I wasn't interested in food. I was a crummy decorator. I didn't dress right. While I was married to a physician, I had no interest in being Mrs. Doctor."

Pearl also had a sense that she wanted to prepare herself professionally, but she didn't know how or with what. She knew, though, that "I didn't want to spend my life running a mimeograph machine and pasting stamps on envelopes." She often shared her feelings with a close group of friends who were also college educated and feeling somewhat restless. But because of the strong cultural message to be at-home mothers before the women's movement, all they did was talk. No one dared break the mold.

So Pearl Brown led the life of the typical suburban housewife: making breakfast for her husband and children, packing their lunches, changing the sheets, carpooling for Brownies and Cub Scouts. It wasn't that she disliked what she was doing but she felt that there must be more to life than this. Pearl silently asked herself the question Betty Friedan later posed in *The Feminine Mystique:* "Is this all?"[12]

Like many of the women we interviewed who are in their fifties and sixties today, Pearl felt that she had an either-or choice in her twenties: marriage or a career. Most of these women followed the traditional path of marriage and children. Very few chose a career back then, and those who did were often ostracized by their peers. It was the women's movement that gave women permission to take themselves seriously as thinking women who could be active in the world of work.

Take Paula Batoff, a fifty-two-year-old appellate judge. After she graduated from a prestigious women's college, she decided to go on to law school. "Upon graduation from college I thought I was young enough to do other things," she says. "My classmates didn't. They were twenty-two. They had to get married." They felt societal pressure to marry.

Paula always had a clear sense of where she was going as a person, even though her lifestyle remained traditional. After law school she practiced for a few years and then married a businessman. She stopped working while she raised three girls, but remained active in civic associations, making contacts that would help her later in her career. When her youngest entered high school, about ten years ago, she joined a private law firm. An important female mentor supported her working while her youngest was still at home, and then a male mentor spread her name throughout the county. She could not have advanced so rapidly without the help of both. Five years later she was appointed a judge.

Last year she was invited back to her alma mater as a guest speaker for her thirtieth reunion. She spoke about how times had changed for women. She reminded her peers of their words so long ago. " 'Poor Paula had to go to law school because she doesn't have a husband,' I said, and they all burst out laughing." Their laughter revealed the foolishness of their words in hindsight.

Young women in their twenties today have more options but

also more conflicts. They no longer have to make either-or choices—while they can choose to have only families or only careers, most combine families *and* working in some way. Today's women tend to use their thirties to look back and reevaluate the choices they make in their twenties.

They question the decisions they made so confidently in their twenties. If they gave their career top priority and put marriage and kids on the back burner, they may reconsider this decision. Those who are single may realize their prospects are narrowing and try to find a husband. Those who are married without children know they must decide about having children soon. The biological necessity of making this decision in their mid- to late thirties forces women to face lifestyle questions that will affect the rest of their lives. On the other hand, if they are middle class and had the luxury of not working during their twenties when their children were preschoolers, they may now be ready to enter the work force or go back to school.

In their late thirties, notes doctoral student Ruth Droge in her dissertation on women's adult development, women experience a shift in their identities, from being a member of a family to gaining a sense of self in a broader context. They may take on more responsibility and authority in their community, become leaders of organizations, and make a name for themselves as women.[13]

After the dinner-party conversation about getting her MBA, Pearl Brown could not let the idea rest. When her youngest child was two (and her oldest eight), she started business school at night. It took her five years to complete her degree. Although she was well organized and her mother came down on weekends to fill the freezer and watch the children so that she could study, it was a very difficult time.

"There was not a minute I didn't feel guilty," she remembers. "If I was at home, I felt I should be studying. If I was at school, I felt I should be at home."

She felt defective because she didn't fit the culturally prescribed mold of the stay-at-home mother. Pearl read Betty Friedan's *The Feminine Mystique* soon after its publication in 1963. She remembers her reaction well. "I was absolutely struck by the validity of it. It spoke to me personally. I felt like I didn't fit, and here was somebody else who didn't fit, and she said, not only do you not have to fit, it was a rather good thing if you didn't."

As she recommended the book to her friends and they talked about it, they all realized they were not alone. Nonetheless Pearl Brown had no idea this book would spark a national movement. She only knew that "other well-educated women felt in the same bind that I did and that society in essence was really very unfair to us by confining us to the role of mother, wife, and housewife when we yearned to do other things."

As the women's movement began to blossom, it created a major impact on Pearl Brown's life, validating her feelings and making her realize that she was not alone. "If not for the women's movement, which provided the climate and which made society look at women as capable and then made institutions look for women to fill slots, I would not be where I am today."

Betty Friedan and the women's movement served as symbolic mentors for Pearl Brown and thousands of women like her. Pearl had bought the cultural message about being a full-time wife and mother, but she had not felt fulfilled at home. She missed intellectual stimulation and she wanted to work in the man's world, yet she did not want to negate her role as a wife and mother. Reading *The Feminine Mystique* gave her support and made her realize that she could work and could be a fulfilled woman. The women's movement created the climate for Pearl and other women like her to break out of the feminine mystique and to broaden their definition of femininity.

On reading *The Feminine Mystique* Brown identified with Friedan as many women do with a mentor. While she never met Friedan personally, Friedan's writing was the voice of the symbolic mentor that Brown needed. They were both bright, college-edu-cated women married to professional men living similar lifestyles, both feeling restless and unfulfilled. When Friedan wrote of "this nameless aching dissatisfaction," Brown felt she was writing about her. When Friedan labeled women's problems not as personal but as a gender-related identity crisis, Pearl knew what she was talking about. Friedan wrote, "I think this is the crisis of women growing up—a turning point from an immaturity that has been called femi-ninity to full human identity. I think women had to suffer this crisis of identity, which began a hundred years ago, and have to suffer it still today, simply to become fully human."[14]

It is noteworthy that Betty Friedan's own mentor was Simone de Beauvoir, the French feminist and author of *The Second Sex.* When Friedan read *her* book, it depressed her so much that she "felt like going to bed—after I had made the children's break-fasts—and pulling the covers up over my head."[15] The message de Beauvoir espoused was that "all male ideologies are directed at justifying the oppression of women [and] women are so condi-tioned by society that they consent to this oppression."[16]

Friedan transformed *The Second Sex* and its author into *her* symbolic mentors. They motivated her to act, which led to the development of the American women's movement. At one point, many years later, when the movement seemed at a standstill, Frie-dan, seeking answers, flew to Paris to meet with de Beauvoir. "What really made me go to see Simone de Beauvoir was a feeling that *someone* must know the right answer, someone must know for sure that all the women who had thrown away those old misleading maps were heading in the right direction, someone must see more clearly than I where the new road ends,"[17] she writes. She looked to her mentor, Simone de Beauvoir, as a guru who could give her wisdom but left Paris realizing she had outgrown a mentor and needed to look within herself for answers. This led to her writing *It Changed My Life,* in which she further developed her ideas about feminism.

As Pearl Brown's symbolic mentor, the women's movement

inspired her, educated her, motivated her, and supported her—tasks a mentor often performs. Women today still have symbolic mentors, although these may not be as monumental as the women's movement itself. Writers and artists, for instance, often identify with accomplished writers and artists whom they admire. Studying the works of a Mary Cassatt or a Virginia Woolf and identifying with her lifestyle and struggles can motivate and inspire an emerging talent. Successful women in all fields, such as the ones profiled in this book, can serve as symbolic mentors for women who may not have a real-life mentor and for those who need more inspiration than they are getting from a male mentor.

The women's movement gave Pearl permission to follow her dreams and become the person she wanted to be—within the context of her marriage. Nevertheless Pearl was caught between two worlds: keeping up her traditional roles at home and then rushing off to business school at night. Her grades were mediocre, and she admits that she didn't get the most from her education because she constantly felt torn between the demands of school assignments and home. But her fight against the "defective feeling" continued as she gave up her domestic role to her mother.

Pearl Brown's husband was supportive of her going back to school in a sixties kind of way, she says, "as long as everything else in the house got done." It was fine for Pearl to go to school as long as it did not change his life at home; he did not lift a finger. Pearl's husband was an "armchair feminist"—all talk and no action. (She notes that he himself revises his role as he recalls it over the years.)

A woman's husband usually shares her dream for a family, but he may be at odds with her career dream because of the changes it provokes in the family relationships and dynamics. Ruth Droge found that the biggest handicap to a woman's growth was her husband's objections to her own plan for herself.[18] While Pearl found a way to negotiate and compromise with her husband, a marriage may be threatened and divorce can result when a husband cannot accept changes in his wife.

Jane Taylor, fifty-eight, the executive director of a nonprofit organization, learned this the hard way. Like Pearl Brown, she originally followed the traditional route, marrying her college sweetheart. But she, too, felt restless as a stay-at-home mom with young children.

When a friend took her to a League of Women Voters meeting, for the first time she met intelligent women doing volunteer work *and* raising families. By the time she was in her midthirties, she was doing volunteer work on a national level. She refused to take a paycheck, because she knew it would upset her physician husband. Her sense of competence came through community work. It should be pointed out that although society demeans this work, the competencies and networks women develop as volunteers can be important tools in their pursuit of paid work or new careers.

As Jane became more active and deviated from the prescribed feminine role, she and her husband grew farther apart. He could not tolerate a nontraditional wife, and she felt stifled in a relationship in which she had to deny a part of her real self, so they divorced.

At thirty-nine Jane Taylor went back to school. She finished her degree and landed a government job in Cleveland, a city in which she had never lived and had no contacts. Her move marked the end of her traditional life; she was now a woman on her own, forging her own identity and her own career. While she felt good about what she had achieved, she was, like many women following a divorce, lonely without close relationships.

To bridge the gap and advance professionally, Jane realized she needed a male *and* a female mentor: a woman within city hall whom she could trust for advice and information and a man to give her a beat on the male organization. Jane found both over a two-year period, and they taught her well. The female mentor, born and bred in Cleveland, introduced her to scores of people, taught her the ropes of city government, and gave her access to the powerful. The male helped her deal with professional issues at the organizational level.

* * *

Jane Taylor and Pearl Brown are representative of many women who started on the traditional track in their twenties and thirties but eventually found it unsatisfying. With an emotionally supportive husband Pearl Brown was able to pursue her career within the context of marriage, but Jane's emerging individualism threatened her husband and led to her divorce. As a divorced woman of forty who had never worked for pay, she was wise enough to know that she could not have survived in the male work world without the help of mentors. Meanwhile she also hungered for emotional intimacy.

When women become divorced or widowed in their forties or fifties, they must again face the work and relationship issues that they thought were settled in an earlier decade. They must give up their childhood fantasy of an ideal marriage, acknowledge their feelings of failure, and cope with the repercussions of this loss. They may begin dating—only this time they will need to deal with their children's feelings as well as their own. If they have not worked during their marriage, they must cope with reentering the work force as an older woman. Many women fear this, believing that they are not "good enough" or have "nothing to offer." Yet Jane Taylor's experience proves that community volunteer work and parenting experience are relevant in the world of work. Dismissing these experiences as irrelevant to a job résumé merely reflects society's prejudice against women. If women have worked but have not been self-supporting, they must view their work—whether volunteer or paid—from a different perspective. Mentors can be crucial in both of these situations.

Women in their forties have made some major, irrevocable life decisions. While they can still change careers or focus within their careers, the question of motherhood has been decided. This is the time when women become most comfortable claiming all parts of themselves. They become whole people, merging the masculine and feminine sides of their personalities and emphasizing the part that may have been repressed earlier. When Pearl Brown, for example, was a homemaker, she had to bury part of herself: she could not express her aggressive, achieving side. Working provided an outlet for expressing those undeveloped parts of herself.

When Pearl graduated from business school at thirty-eight, she took a job with a Big 8 accounting firm. Although she was fresh to the business world, her life experiences gave her a maturity that most new graduates lack. She immediately felt at home in the competitive environment.

Roland Herman, her boss, a black man five years younger than she, became her first mentor. He threw her into the pond and let her swim. "He had great confidence in me because he told me there was no mistake I could make that he could not correct. And that gave me great confidence. I went out and I performed, and I think I performed really quite well under this kind of guidance."

She handled clients on her own, consulting with Herman as needed, and she often worked jointly with him on projects. She decided not to go for partnership in the firm. Instead she worked for several small companies, gaining broad experience over a twelve-year period. When a headhunter found her a position as assistant treasurer of a Fortune 200 company, the offer was too good to turn down. As a fifty-year-old woman, she felt empowered by work. Being part of the business world energized her.

Jack Haddock, her boss and treasurer of the company, a man a few years older than she, became her second mentor. He increased her confidence even more by giving her tremendous freedom within her niche of the company. Their offices were next to each other, and they often consulted back and forth. When he traveled, he encouraged her to carve out her own role vis-à-vis the other officers, the board, and the middle managers. When he was promoted to vice president, he helped her get promoted from assistant treasurer to treasurer.

He also encouraged her to take risks in new areas, such as

public speaking. Despite her years in business she still feared speaking at board meetings. Her mentor sensed it was her inexperience—not any lack of ability—that inhibited Pearl. "Jack put his knee in my back and just kind of pushed me forward, and I did it," she recalls. The more she spoke publicly, the more comfortable she felt.

When Pearl entered the work force as an older woman, she needed mentors for different reasons than a younger woman right out of graduate school. She possessed the judgment and wisdom gained from living for four decades, but was new to the business world. She needed help with career-related and substantive issues, not with her personal development. As we have seen, she had already confronted important personal issues in her early thirties with the aid of her symbolic mentor, the women's movement, and with the support of her friends.

Pearl had difficulty giving her two male mentors credit. She spoke of them in global generalities, but could not give specific examples about how they helped her. She had a hard time admitting she needed help or was dependent on them, even though she could admit her dependence on women. While she praised her mentors, she seemed afraid to give the relationship any real meaning, as if doing so would diminish her own role in her success. Like some successful women, she wanted to appear self-sufficient and perfect. She seemed to be saying, "My mentors were helpful to some extent, but I did it myself."

It is the women's movement to which she feels she owes her career. She says, "The movement made being a professional woman acceptable and respected. It empowered me as a professional. When I first went into practice, the partners looked at me as very strange. Plus they were very worried whether I as a woman would be acceptable to clients. That nonsense would still be going on if not for the women's movement."

Now in her late fifties, Pearl Brown is building on the personal and career goals she formed in her forties. Men and women are often at opposite points during their fifties. A typical male, having worked for almost forty years, is ready to pass on what he has learned to others through mentoring or even to slow down or retire. Women who, like Pearl, have been in the work force perhaps only twenty years feel that they are just reaching a peak in their careers. They may be so involved in their own careers that they don't have the time, interest, or energy to mentor others. While Pearl works with several young people right out of business school and gladly gives them advice when asked, she avoids an intense relationship. The key relationships in her life remain in her family.

She wants to pass on the wisdom she has gained to her two daughters, who represent the next generation of women. They will be more secure because of the impact of the women's movement and the breakthroughs of women like their mother. Jennifer, thirty-three, is a special-education teacher at a private school, and Robin, thirty-five, is a lawyer. Both married professionals and have young children. Pearl Brown sees herself as a significant role model for them. Although she understands that she cannot be their mentor in the true sense of the word, she wants them to learn from her experience. She has also encouraged them to seek other people for advice and support.

About once a month on a Saturday Pearl Brown meets her daughters for lunch at a suburban salad bar. They heap their plates with salad fixings and head for a table in the corner. Their conversation usually centers on the same theme: combining work and family.

Pearl has encouraged them both to work part-time so that they don't miss their children's growing-up years, what she calls "a delicious time."

"My point of view is: What's the difference where you end up if each portion of your life has been satisfying? So you don't get to be head of a major corporation, but you have that wonderful experience of hanging out with your kids."

Robin, the lawyer, works four days a week, and Jennifer

teaches only in the morning. In fact, Jennifer turned down the principal's job last year, feeling it would be too demanding of her time.

Pearl often talks to them about balancing their lives. "If you hedge your bets across the board, you're much better off. If you put a little investment in the family, a little investment in the job, investment in a decent personal life, investment in some activities outside your work, it's unlikely it's all going to collapse."

This may sound like strange advice from someone who is part of the elite group of women executives (less than 2 percent of all working women). But Pearl Brown believes young women should have more freedom of choice than she herself did thirty years ago. When she was a young married woman raising four children in the late fifties and early sixties, society told women they were defective if they didn't enjoy staying home with their children and baking chocolate chip cookies. Today, in the early nineties, she feels there is another message, one disseminated mostly by the media. It is a very different message but just as powerful.

"The message the media sends young women is: Unless you have a big career, there is something defective about you. They are not saying you made the wrong choice, but there is something defective about you. I see women buying that message in the same way that I saw women thirty years ago buying the message that was beamed at me.

"A lot of women now think, I didn't go to law school, I didn't go to medical school, or I didn't get an MBA. There must be something wrong with me."

Pearl Brown tries to counteract this message with her own daughters and especially when she gives speeches to women's groups several times a year. She stands before them as a role model and as a symbolic mentor: a woman who has made it, who fought hard to preserve her own individuality. The women in the audience probably don't realize how much Pearl struggled throughout her adult life to become the mature, self-confident woman presenting herself before them. As we have seen, Pearl was a worried, discontented suburban housewife in her twenties. In her thirties she struggled to keep her home and family together while she went to graduate school; she then learned new skills as she embarked on a career in her forties. Finally she came into her own professionally in her fifties; only then did she approach the point in her professional career that men typically reach in their late thirties.

At fifty-nine Pearl Brown has achieved a balanced life but hopes other women can find the same harmony within themselves at an earlier age. This balance can be accomplished with more comfort and less guilt when women help other women by serving as mentors (both symbolic and actual) and as role models. If a woman has a male mentor, she can assuage his influence by finding women as secondary mentors or as sponsors, coaches, or peers (terms we'll define in chapter 2). A woman will do well to have both male and female mentors and role models in her constellation of relationships to support her as her needs evolve and change at different stages of her adult life.

❖　　❖　　❖

CHAPTER TWO

The Anatomy of Mentoring

"Hi, I'm a medical student and I'm really interested in plastics," Carol Woodman said nervously over the phone. "A friend of mine said to give you a call. I would love to do a rotation with you. Would you mind having me on rotation?"

As a fourth-year medical student Carol had heard about Peter Gibson, a "rising star" in the plastic surgery department. A clean-cut thirty-seven-year-old family man with a boyish smile, Gibson combined his time as a clinician and teacher at a prominent medical school in Milwaukee. Because no medical student had ever approached Gibson, he was flattered.

And so their mentoring relationship began; it was rooted in their mutual interest in surgery and their respect for each other. Carol loved walking down the hospital corridors with Peter and picking his brain about surgical procedures and patient diagnoses, but their banter disguised a deeper involvement. She was drawn to Peter because she longed for a relationship.

Growing up in Appleton, Wisconsin, Carol often felt isolated. She was brighter than most of the other kids and wanted more out of life than they did. She wanted someone to feel close to, to look up to, but wherever she turned, she was rebuffed. She thought her father was cold and distant, and she had no respect for her mother, who, in her eyes, had wasted her life by spending twenty years smoking cigarettes and drinking Coke. As a teenager Carol already looked to adults for companionship. She enjoyed being a candy striper in the local hospital and often followed the physicians around, asking them about their work. However, two of them misinterpreted her interest and had tried to take advantage of her naiveté.

Therefore, when she met Peter Gibson, someone who was solid and genuinely interested in her as a person, she responded with eagerness. Although she didn't realize it, she had invested both her childhood dreams and her personal goals in the relationship.

Mentoring is based on a male-to-male relationship. In the classic definition it is, at its best, a close, intense, mutually beneficial relationship between someone who is older, wiser, more experienced, and more powerful with someone younger or less experienced. It is a complementary relationship, within an organizational or professional context, built on both the mentor's and the protégé's needs. Both give and both receive. In the male model concern with power has cloaked intimacy issues. That is, men have looked at the mentoring relationship as a means to attain power. They have often overlooked or denied that their dependency needs are also being met within this intimate relationship.

The relationship constantly changes and evolves. Two people come together who idealize each other. They identify strongly with each other and become close. The protégé tries to learn from the mentor, then wants to equal him or surpass him. The mentor advises her, helps her, educates her, trains her, and then must let her go to become her own professional. Not all mentoring relationships progress so smoothly, however; there can be problems at each stage of the relationship as the mentor, the protégé, and the organization impact on one another.

The word *mentor* originated in *The Odyssey*. Mentor was a close friend of Odysseus who cared for his son Telemachus for ten years while Odysseus traveled. Mentor, as the goddess Athena in disguise, embodied both the male and the female personas. This androgyny has carried over to those present-day mentors who integrate both traditional feminine and traditional masculine qualities—the ideal mentor is nurturing, supportive, and protective as well as aggressive, assertive, and risk taking. Mentor/Athena played all the roles mentors play today to varying degrees: parent substitute, teacher, friend, guide, protector, and guru.

As we have said, we began with the classic male definition of mentoring as our base but found that it didn't fit the contemporary woman's situation. As we considered women's unique developmental paths, their strengths, and their perspective on work and interpersonal relationships, we realized that we needed to redefine mentoring. We have broadened and expanded the definition to reflect women's unique needs as well as reality factors in the workplace. For example a woman's mentor may not necessarily be older. If she enters the workplace at forty, after raising her children, she may have a male mentor of thirty-two who has ten years' more experience than she because he followed a straight career path. Or she may have more than one mentor: a primary male mentor and a secondary female or symbolic mentor, or a combination of mentors and sponsors, coaches, and peers (all of which we'll define in this chapter).

Reality factors in the marketplace also limit the availability of mentors for women. There are not as many mentors—female or male—available for women. Few women hold positions in the upper echelons of power, from which mentors are drawn. Often those women who do hold such positions do not see themselves as powerful or do not feel powerful because society devalues their gender and because they feel insecure in their position. In addition, men, who dominate the professional, business, and corporate scene, feel more comfortable mentoring other men. Mentoring a man presents less risk to them than mentoring a woman—a member of a minority with whom there may be negative repercussions because of sexual overtones.

The intellectual roots upon which our thesis is based are many and varied. Psychoanalytic theory has helped us realize the importance of early relationships with parents to our lives and relationships as adults. (We will see how these relationships replay themselves in the mentoring pairs in the next three chapters.) From feminist psychoanalysts, such as Jean Baker Miller, we have seen the social and psychological implications of women feeling inferior and realized how closely allied the political and psychological processes are. These theorists have stressed the importance of a gender perspective, in a context of political unfairness, to overcome Freud's cultural bias. Carol Gilligan's work found that women were no less ethical than men but that their ethics were based on relationships, due to cultural conditioning. The importance of relationships was reflected in our mentoring study because women tended to feel they moved ahead through support, not only through power and advancement, as men do.

Daniel Levinson, who established distinct developmental stages for men in his landmark book *The Seasons of a Man's Life,* defined a good mentor as "an admixture of good father and good friend . . . a transitional figure who invites and welcomes a young man into the adult world."[1] This to us is a life mentor; while it is certainly the ideal, in our study the initial focus was on career mentors who influenced women's professional lives. Some of these mentors did become life mentors (such as Sam Fishbine, in chapter 9) and the protégés who gained most from the mentoring relationship benefited in personal ways too.

Levinson has called the relationship "one of the most complex, and developmentally important, a man can have in early adulthood."[2] He believes the mentoring relationship is necessary for men to develop normally and usually occurs in their twenties, but this is not true for women. While we agree that the relationship is developmentally important for women, as we have discussed in the last chapter, mentoring occurs at different times and in different forms, depending on when women begin their careers and their families, their needs at the time, and the availability of mentors.

In the past, women's mothers, aunts, and grandmothers served as models for becoming wives and mothers and supported their childhood dreams of becoming like them. In the 1950s and '60s most women, like Pearl Brown, did not have dreams and visions of themselves as career or working women. In more recent years young women developed career dreams and goals, but these often conflicted with domestic roles. Female mentors can best serve as models for combining these roles because some male mentors (as we shall see in the case of Richard Hendricks, in chapter 7) may have difficulty accepting the divided loyalties of working women.

Mentoring relationships are informal and develop spontaneously at work. In the 1980s, though, many corporations began realizing the importance of mentors and instituted programs to replicate this informal relationship in a more formal, organized way. These programs pair a young professional with an older, more experienced worker. The success of these programs varies. One criticism of formal programs is that while mentor and protégé may be well matched on paper, the chemistry, which is so important for the pair to click, may not be present. Without this chemistry the relationship will not work.

A mentor usually serves first as a role model, as someone a woman looks up to and admires for his behavior, values, professionalism, and competence. This is what attracted Carol Woodman to Peter Gibson in the beginning. It marks the first step in identifying with the mentor. According to Kathy Kram, associate professor of organizational behavior at Boston University's School of Management, "It is both a conscious and an unconscious process; a senior person may be unaware of the example she is providing for a less experienced colleague and a junior person may be unaware of the strength of identification."[3] In many cases of role modeling, the junior person admires the senior person from afar, and no personal relationship develops. Not all role models become mentors; friends, peers, and leaders can be merely inspirational.

In Peter Gibson, Carol Woodman had finally found someone to look up to, and he in turn, valued her. In fact he idealized Carol, a precocious twenty-one-year-old, as much as she admired him. "I have always thought of Carol as an exceptional person," he said.

"She is very bright, motivated, hardworking, dedicated, and a very, very good people person. She was able to relate to patients very well, as well as to me, and the office staff, and anyone else we came into contact with."

Carol's family always criticized her for taking the hard way. They thought she was crazy for wanting to be a surgeon and working so hard, but Peter accepted her and valued her dedication and idealism. He had been the same way himself as a young medical student.

Carol saw herself as "a little girl from a small town who wanted to be a doctor when she grew up." Peter understood her childhood dream because he, too, had left a small town with conservative values to come to medical school in Milwaukee.

Besides their common backgrounds, they were both exacting and demanding, even compulsive. But it was their personalities that meshed so well. "There are some people you meet and you just like them. You're comfortable with them and you like the way they think, the way they do things. There's a match. That's the kind of person Peter was," remembers Carol. "From the day I talked to him on the phone, I liked the guy, and our personalities meshed.

"We would be thinking along the same lines and finish sentences for each other. The same things were important in the same way, like being really thorough with patient histories and physicals. Surgeons are known for doing this in a cursory fashion. I tend to be more to the picky side. I always want to know about my patients. I always look at the wound myself. I came with that kind of background, which Peter reinforced and encouraged."

We see mentoring as the pinnacle of relationships along a continuum of work relationships, starting with a peer and moving up to coach, sponsor, and finally mentor. Each position along the continuum has an increasing amount of power (influence within the organization), and the degree of intimacy within each relationship increases along the continuum too.

Peers are colleagues at work. Although their importance is often overlooked, they can provide a strong network for support and information. They usually have as much power as the protégé and are at the same level of the organization. They can be a sounding board and provide political information and feedback. Peers can serve as mentors when they have an expertise the protégé lacks. Two CPAs, for example—one an expert in taxes, and the other an authority on auditing—could serve as peer mentors. Each can compensate for and learn from the other, helping them mutually to advance or reach personal and professional goals. The authors of this book served as peer mentors, each bringing her own expertise, and teaching, guiding, and supporting the other to grow in new areas. By networking with peers it's also possible to find mentors.

The role of *coach* typically involves day-to-day, hands-on involvement, giving feedback and appraisals and helping the protégé improve her performance and prepare for advancement.[4] The coach encourages the protégé but also may need to give her honest criticism or feedback on her behavior or performance. Coaching is usually a short-term, results-oriented relationship. Like an athletic coach, the career coach works on building skills but also suggests strategies and moves and shares information about the key players and the political process.[5] However, coaching can become problematic for male coaches and female protégés because it requires long hours together in close proximity; the couple can easily become the butt of office gossip.[6]

Surprisingly few women talked about passes or sexual advances from their coaches. Our hunch is that it does go on but that women weren't comfortable talking about it, particularly in the context of mentoring, which many women tended to see in an idealized way. As men and women spend more time together, they will break down barriers and stereotypes and feel more comfortable relating to each other as equals and professionals.

Sponsors generally have more power within the organization than coaches do, and they use this power publicly to support their protégé. Their main function is to promote the protégé within the organization and to put her in the limelight. Sponsors place the protégé's name on a task force or a special committee or add it to a list of people with high potential. They make positive comments about the protégé to important others.[7] Sponsorship is not totally altruistic, however. Promoting a younger person can help a sponsor's own advancement because it enhances his position in the organization when he promotes someone who performs well or has high potential.

Not all sponsors become mentors, but sponsorship is a significant part of mentoring. Since sponsorship is usually linked with power, men often emphasize this aspect. A survey of 189 women physicians compared one effect of sponsorship—how quickly they moved up the ranks—between those with female mentors and those with male mentors.[8] The study found that it was the administrative or academic rank of the mentor—not the gender—that was important for sponsorship. Those in more powerful positions (mainly men) gave more career sponsorship. This included introducing the protégé to the informal power structure and power brokers of the organization, relaying behind-the-scenes information, protecting the protégé from damaging battles, and lobbying on her behalf for choice assignments.

In this study, those with low- or mid-ranking mentors (who were female) received more personal advice about balancing career and family and had less problematic mentoring relationships. These results sound stereotyped, but few women in medicine hold high-ranking positions today. The few women who did attain powerful positions used their positions to help other women move up, but will they still keep their nurturing attributes? This question will be explored in chapter 3, in which we look more closely at the unique nature of female mentoring.

When mentors sponsor, they make things happen for their protégés. It may feel like magic to the protégé, who does not yet understand how the informal power structure works. Indeed, many protégés looked at their mentors as having the godlike power or omnipotence of a godmother or godfather. In fact there *is* an ephemeral quality to the relationship that makes mentoring hard to pigeonhole with a single definition.

Bosses can fit in at almost any place along the continuum of work relationships. Because of the proximity and amount of time spent together, there is the potential for a more intense relationship, but not all bosses become mentors; some are coaches and some, sponsors. Others are facilitators, removing obstacles and making it easier for the protégé to move ahead. Some serve as guides; they may be a step ahead of you and can show you the way by sharing information about moving up, but they do not get deeply involved in a relationship. Others are expeditors, speeding up the progress but again with minimal emotional involvement.

Symbolic or fantasy mentors can also serve as inspiration to women. They may supplement a male mentor or be a substitute for the real thing. We've seen how Pearl Brown used the women's movement as a symbolic mentor; it motivated, supported, and inspired her. Symbolic mentors can be mythical figures (like Athena/Mentor), historical figures (like Joan of Arc), or pioneers (like Amelia Earhart) or someone prominent a woman admires in her profession today. When one writer could not find a mentor—male or female—she used a well-known writer whom she admired as a symbolic mentor. She recalls, "I'd open the Sunday paper and there it was again: *her* byline. I had never met her, but she haunted me and influenced my career. First it was her in-depth medical stories for the Sunday magazine, then her features in the nationals, and the latest, a book. What next? I read her articles with envy and awe. She frustrated me yet spurred me on. If she could write so well, so could I. She was my ideal, my nemesis, my mentor in fantasy."

The actual mentoring relationship itself is unique and has certain qualities that distinguish it from other work relationships. First of all, the mentor has more power within the organization than a coach, a sponsor, or even a boss does. He also has access to the most powerful and influential people and to information and resources. He can use his position and influence to empower the protégé. The mentor's stamp of approval makes her acceptable to those most powerful in the corporation, firm, or profession. "He knew all the senior people, so that if I were at one of these conventions, he might bring me along for lunch," a tenured finance professor says about her mentor. "He would never exclude me. He introduced me to everyone. This is the way mentors and senior colleagues at universities bring potential stars to light to other colleagues."

Secondly, there is a stronger degree of identification between a mentor and protégé than in any other work relationship. We think this process is very similar to what occurs between a parent and child. Just as a young child idealizes a parent and sees him as perfect, so does the protégé idealize and admire her mentor in the early stages of their relationship. This creates some distortion of reality. In talking about her first impressions of her mentor, one psychotherapist/protégé said, "I thought he looked like what I thought God looked like when I was little: gorgeous, silver hair and all." Others made such comments as "My mentor was the smartest man I ever met," or "He was secure and a genius in his field," or "My mentor was perfect." This idealization lays a fertile field for identification as well as for disappointment, for who can live up to such unrealistic expectations?

The protégé identifies with the mentor himself, admires his expertise, takes in his professional values, and models his behavior. This modeling can be as simple as noting how the mentor shakes hands or greets a salesperson or as complex as writing a scholarly paper in the university or becoming a skilled diagnostician in the hospital. One lawyer, who did not know any lawyers before she went to law school, feels she learned the law by identifying with her mentor. She said, "I learned his skills. He taught me how to write. He taught me how to deal with clients—at least his way of dealing with clients—which is very useful in certain cases."

But how much can a woman model and identify with a male

mentor? She must temper what she models. It is a very difficult task to identify with a man professionally while keeping one's own identity as a woman. Each of the protégés we profile found her own way to handle this situation, although some struggled more than others.

As the protégé develops and becomes stronger, she sees the mentor more realistically. She may take on certain qualities of the mentor and reject others. Usually she accepts those qualities that are consistent with her own values and sense of self. This period of identification, when the mentor and protégé work closely together, may span several years. Eventually, when the relationship ends, the protégé will have internalized many of the mentor's professional values and behaviors. So strong was the identification between a violinist and her mentor that after they had parted, she said, "I listened with my mentor's ears."

The third quality that distinguishes mentoring from other work relationships is the intensity of the emotional involvement.[9] Levinson says, "Mentoring is best understood as a form of a love relationship."[10] We certainly found this to be true in the protégés we interviewed. The respect they felt initially for their mentor's expertise and status gradually turned to affection and eventually love for the person himself. A woman can respect a coach or feel cordiality toward a sponsor, but she reserves deeper feelings for a mentor. Indeed many women told us that they loved their mentors. This was not a sexual love but an intense emotional attachment. When many female protégés spoke of their mentors, we perceived an unconscious undercurrent of sexuality in their language and in the emotion and intensity surrounding their talk, but they rarely acknowledged it.

This emotional intensity and closeness has its negative side as well. It can make it difficult for mentors and protégés to part company (as Brenda Marks and Bert Paley learned, see chapter 5, "The Enmeshed Pair"). Having such a close, intense relationship can also isolate the protégé from others in the organization. That's why we believe the protégé needs to develop a network of relationships. If she and the mentor then separate or the mentor falls out of favor with the power brokers, she will not be alone; she'll have a network of support.

Carol worked under Peter Gibson as a senior student, as an intern, and as a second-year resident, and she tried to scrub with him whenever she could during her third and fifth years of residency. As they spent more time together, their intimacy grew. Carol was not always comfortable with the closeness and at times needed to sort out her feelings. "I was beginning to like him as a person," she acknowledged, "and had to separate out liking him personally versus liking him professionally and what the limits of those feelings are. It takes time to straighten this out."

Since they both commuted from the suburbs to the medical center downtown, they began driving to work together. Carol's husband, who had been a classmate at medical school, would drop her off at the Gibsons' on his way to work. Carol enjoyed early-morning chats with Marta, Peter's wife, whom she admired as a super homemaker and mother of five. But strangely enough, one morning Marta, still in her bathrobe, told Carol she had just dreamed that she and Peter were having an affair. They all laughed about the dream, but it seemed to acknowledge Carol and Peter's growing intimacy and Marta's fears about it.

The dream never became a reality. Both Carol and Peter had staunch, old-fashioned Protestant values about the sanctity of marriage and realized they'd lose much personally as well as professionally if the relationship became sexual. But as their relationship developed, their conversation often turned more personal. Driving together to work, they'd talk about everything: problems with Peter's children, Carol's marriage, gossip at the hospital. When Carol became pregnant, she told Peter and Marta the news before she told even her own parents.

* * *

Although mentoring occurs within a work context, defining it solely within such a framework does not fully reveal all its subtleties. Mentoring also combines many characteristics of personal relationships. A mentor has been called a rabbi, an adviser, a friend, and a guru. The word *guru* in particular connotes an idyllic quality in mentoring. Many women *spoke* of their mentors in such idealistic terms, as we've said, but the relationship is not perfect. There are problems associated with all kinds of mentoring relationships. Nevertheless these terms add nuances to the meaning and suggest that a mentor does more than sponsor, coach, and advise. He inspires the protégé and gives her moral support and counsel. He gives her vision and shares her dream—whatever that may be—and helps her achieve it.

In many ways a mentor is like a parent—the good and the bad parent. In addition to an identification similar to that between the parent and child, the mentor nurtures and protects his protégé, just as a parent does. He may protect her from making political or technical mistakes or shield her from competitive peers. But the mentor can also overprotect, just as a well-meaning parent can. (In fact the word *protégé* comes from the French *protéger*, "to protect".) A mentor, like a parent, must also encourage risk taking. A CPA with a Big 8 accounting firm recalled how her mentor encouraged her to take risks and then protected her when she needed that. "He more or less kept me at the edge of that cliff. He's never let me fall off but he's kept me right up there. In other words, he stretched me. He let me stretch to the maximum of my capacity but he's always there to pull back on the reins.

"And he has maintained an open door to me, so that I can go in and say, 'I'm flailing. I'm really having problems and I can't do all this. I need your help.' I'm very comfortable doing that, but the other risk was that if I hadn't, I think I would have burned out and I would never have made it." In this way the mentor frees the protégé to make mistakes while she learns, so that she can become competent and independent.

The mentor is also a teacher. Not only does the mentor teach the protégé the technical skills of a particular profession, but he helps her learn the values and standards of the profession while she develops a professional identity. As we have stated, it is a difficult task for a woman to keep her feminine identity while she identifies professionally with her male mentor. One pediatrician identified strongly with her mentor professionally; however because his wife was a homemaker, the protégé felt he could not understand the conflicts she experienced from raising a family and developing a career. She says, "In the end I went in a different direction from what he expected of me, because as a man I don't think he really understood the other pulls."

This is a critical issue for women in the workplace today, because most mentors are men. Women must find a way to identify with their male mentors professionally yet keep their female identity intact. One effective way is to use women as secondary mentors or peer mentors. Another is to find symbolic mentors. These supplementary mentors can strengthen a woman's female identity in a male-dominated environment.

Carol Woodman knew Peter Gibson's routine during surgery, so it was comfortable to work together at the operating table. That's often where she learned valuable lessons. "Never trust your mother," he said one day while they were in surgery. "What do you mean?" she asked, their eyes locked over their pale blue face masks. It was then that he told her, "Never leave anything to anyone else to do. Never trust that anyone has done what you have asked them to do. You are the one who has to be responsible." That became a guiding principle for Carol.

Throughout medical school and much of her residency Carol emulated her mentor's way of dealing with patients and staff. She observed Peter, just as she watched the cheerleaders to see how they acted in high school when she wanted to be a cheerleader.

But if something didn't feel right, she didn't do it. "Peter's style is very masculine, so there are limits to how well I can apply some of it," she noted. He was always honest with patients and didn't mince words; Carol was like that, too, so she modeled how he made honesty part of his bedside manner. He also used humor liberally with his patients; when Carol tried that, it was not well received. She realized that patients wanted a woman surgeon to be serious and that they associated a female surgeon who had a sense of humor with the stereotypical "ditzy blonde."

From the day they met, Carol had looked forward to becoming a plastic surgeon like Peter Gibson. But during her final year of residency, when it came time to decide whether she wanted to receive more training in this surgical specialty, she opted *not* to go into plastic surgery.

"Was I picking the specialty because I liked the individual or because I liked the specialty?" Carol asked herself. "Some of it was that I liked the individual. This made me take my blinders off and look at why I wanted what I wanted. The reasons probably weren't right. I thought at first that if he did it, I can do it. But I'm not the same person in the same life circumstances."

It became less important for Carol to become a plastic surgeon. While Peter thought Carol had a difficult time telling him of her decision, he held no expectations that she would follow in his footsteps. He was secure enough not to need a Gibson clone. He tried to put her at her ease by telling her, "Where do you think plastic surgeons get their patients from? We always need referring doctors."

At its best, mentoring is a suprarelationship, combining parts of other relationships and becoming greater than the sum of its parts. In fact the most beneficial relationships go beyond career functions. They not only help the protégé develop a professional identity but they enhance her sense of competence and confidence and increase her self-esteem.[11] This confidence building was part of the very first meeting between a young teacher, Janice Celica, and Ed Brennan, the principal who would become her mentor. "He was the first principal who was interested in hearing what I had to say, even in a job interview," Janice says. "He was interested in my thoughts on education and on building a small school and on working with the kids. I had never had a conversation where I thought anybody wanted to hear a word that I had to say. And he not only listened to me and heard me but he made insightful comments."

But mentoring does not always manifest in its best form, nor are the people involved in it ever perfect. Like any relationship, mentoring is built on what each person brings to it. Everyone comes with his or her own personal baggage—fears, prejudices, blind spots, and hang-ups that surface in the mentoring relationship. While the relationship is ideally an enriching one, just as often it is a flawed one, with two ordinary people trying to do their best. It can also be a compensatory relationship, making up for lapses or losses in the protégé's life or development, as Carol Woodman's seems to be.

We found that people tended to play out roles from other settings in their mentoring relationship. For example, if they shun closeness in marriage, they will probably do the same thing in a mentoring relationship, or they may choose a less intense relationship, such as one with a sponsor or a coach. If they are arrogant and bossy with their children, chances are they will treat a protégé the same way. One supervisor of teachers said, "I've gone through life getting too deeply involved with people." This pattern began in his childhood, increased in adolescence when he began to fall in love too frequently, continued with his own children, and played out again when he mentored students. He admits he got too close to students, so their parents get upset.

Although typically the protégé invests more than the mentor, for both, the relationship involves trust, dependence, and caring. Building such a relationship takes time; it can last from two to ten years. Many of the relationships in our study continued after the formal mentoring had ended and mentor and protégé became collegial peers. A tenured botanist recalls how she and her two mentors maintained professional relationships after they stopped working together. "If I went to New York, I visited my one mentor and talked about what I was doing in my career. He was supportive. He did invite me to a meeting that he ran on how women are doing in science. I also stayed in touch with my other mentor in Cambridge. If we were at a meeting, we'd always get together for lunch." Most of the protégés we interviewed, however, were reluctant to call their mentors peers. Even though in reality they had become equals, the protégés continued to perceive their mentors as authority figures, just as many adults do with their parents.

The mentoring relationship can be crucial for women's career advancement. Mentors can help them progress in their profession. Mentors can also help women fight the discrimination they may feel as a minority in the corporate world, as Susan Richards, a black account executive, discovered with her mentor, Budd Churninsky (see chapter 6). Because of the minority status of blacks and women, they need mentors more than a WASP male, for example, who may be a similar newcomer to an organization.

As we stated in the introduction, women constitute between 30 and 40 percent of the students in graduate professional programs. Once women enter the work world, they still do not progress at the same rate as men. The following statistics are worth repeating. According to the U.S. Department of Labor only a quarter of practicing physicians are women, and almost 30 percent of lawyers are women. Women comprise 42.3 percent of people in executive, administrative, and managerial positions. (This figure is not as high as it seems, because it includes managers of small businesses, such as local fast-food franchises, as well as corporate managers.)[12] In many professions women can go only so far until they hit the "glass ceiling." Men still hold the positions of status and power. Women need mentors to help them crack this old boys' network and succeed professionally.

Because mentoring is a relationship within an organization or profession, however, the protégé needs to understand the organizational context before she seeks a mentor. No matter how badly a woman wants a mentor, if she is not in a corporation, firm, or profession with a climate that is receptive to promoting women, she may have difficulty finding a mentor. Each workplace has its own culture. Figuring out whether it has a cooperative, team approach, a competitive, dog-eat-dog atmosphere, or a range of climates in between will help women determine whether mentoring relationships are encouraged and will thrive.[13] Because of this and because of their minority status, women need to be creative and find mentors whenever and wherever they can. For example Susan Richards developed as her mentor a recovering alcoholic who had plateaued in his career.

As they spent more time together in and out of the OR, Peter Gibson often encouraged Carol to write more papers and present them at conferences so that she'd gain more visibility. He eagerly shared his contacts. She cites one such paper as the turning point in their relationship: the final stage when they became more equal. At the time Peter was pioneering work in breast reconstruction and wanted to write a paper evaluating women's responses to mastectomy but felt that a woman should interview the subjects. Carol volunteered, interviewing thirty women, a task requiring patience and sensitivity. She ended up doing 90 percent of the work for the paper, yet her name was listed last.

That was fine with Carol. She says, "I was almost an equal. I had done something that was a major contribution. It got his name out nationally, and I had done all of the legwork for him, and that was okay. I think what was recognized by both of us was 'Hey, I can do something for you, and here it is.' " Carol felt as though she were paying him back for all she gained from the relationship.

When Carol completed her residency, she took a position at the medical school where, as an attending physician, she now performs surgery and teaches. Gibson and Woodman both still practice and teach in Milwaukee but at different hospitals. While the intensity of the relationship has cooled, they keep in touch by phone, and whenever they do see each other, they immediately pick up where they left off, just like old friends.

It is ironic that as her relationship with Peter waned, Carol met

Dennis Oshansky, a second-year resident whom she has taken under her wing. She denies that she was ripe for another relationship. "It was not a time. It was an individual. Again, when a personality hits you or you mesh," says Carol. Although she may be young to be a mentor (she's just thirty-three), she is at the point professionally when mentoring often occurs. She has worked hard to reach this point in her career. Mentoring will give her an opportunity to sit back, reflect on what she has learned, and pass it on to another young "rising star."

Much of the popular press stresses how women need mentors and how much the mentor can help the protégé, but one of our key findings is that mentoring is a mutually beneficial relationship. The mentor also learns and grows. Although the protégé probably gains more, the mentor would not invest so much time and energy if he were not benefiting too. That's why we stress that mentoring is a *relationship,* one that meets two people's needs, with emotional and political gains for both.

The mentor has tremendous ego benefits. He feels special and wanted and wise. One executive-mentor said, "I've got a whole stack on my shelf of books people have dedicated to me." Another mentor said he felt like "a more successful teacher, someone who has tried to nurture in an educational sense and sees it succeeding. I get this rewarding feeling that you know I'm teaching my protégé. When I did teach, my favorite students were those who challenged me, and she has that quality."

Besides ego benefits, mentoring can help a mentor politically. Men seem to realize this more than women (mentors) do. Women need to use mentoring as a way to build a power base. Men, for instance, who are renowned in their careers have disciples who write about them, quote them, and invite them to speak.[14] A mentor also receives recognition and respect from his peers for choosing someone with potential and for developing this talent. It reflects his good judgment and enhances his status within an organization. On the other hand, public avowal of the protégé is a risk and can reflect poorly on the mentor if the protégé does not live up to his expectations.

In addition, mentoring is an opportunity for the mentor to reappraise his past, a central task at midlife, which is usually when men become mentors.[15] Protégés often remind mentors of themselves at a younger age, just as Peter Gibson "saw" himself in the compulsive, dedicated Carol Woodman. These ego gratifications often come at a point when the mentor may desperately need the extra strokes. The middle-aged mentor may feel obsolete and in a world apart from the young.[16] Mentoring gives him an opportunity to stay in touch with the younger generation as well as to choose and groom a successor.

At midlife, unless women have followed the "male," individualistic path, they are not at the same point developmentally. When most women reassess their past, they see years and years of caregiving. They are now ready at midlife to focus on their own needs and develop their own careers. Mentoring can help advance their careers as well as serve other purposes. For women, mentoring offers a new sense of possibility. They are no longer locked into the rigid male model of mentoring, wedded to one mentor for the duration of their careers. They are free to develop a series of eclectic relationships to meet their changing needs. This means they can explore new relationships: to mentor other women, to mentor younger men, to mentor in groups, and to develop reciprocal relationships with peers. All of these bits and pieces of mentoring allow women to fashion a patchwork quilt of relationships that can advance them professionally as well as enable them to grow personally.

✧ ✧ ✧

CHAPTER THREE

The Mother-Daughter Pair

Shawn Campbell sat in her cubbyhole, phone to her ear, checking facts. Was the date correct? Did the assistant D.A. spell Philip with one or two *l*'s? Who was the author of that book or was it an article? Each day she grew more and more frustrated with her job at *Metro* magazine—constantly on the phone, checking facts and sources, double-checking with writers. It was no wonder the word around the office was that she wasn't "blossoming." She wasn't. She came in each morning dressed in red hightop sneakers, jeans, and a T-shirt, with a scowl on her face and a sharp tongue that alienated many of her coworkers at the magazine.

Bonnie Philpott, who occasionally free-lanced pieces for *Metro,* was the only writer Shawn liked to check facts for. Bonnie, forty-four, was reputed to be a "star" at *Suburban* magazine and had sharp reporting skills. Shawn had never met Bonnie, but whenever she talked to her over the phone, Shawn thought she sounded "like she was talking from the poolside—she was very relaxed."

Shawn stayed with the job because she was broke and she saw it as a stepping-stone to becoming a feature writer. She tried to enlist several male senior editors to become her mentors, but either they were turned off because of her personality or they had sex more than her career on their minds; so her attempts at relationships ended in disaster.

After Shawn had been working at the magazine for two years, Bonnie came on board as a columnist. She wrote and edited "Inside," a weekly two-page column consisting of ten short news-breaking stories in politics, media, real estate, and retailing. Shawn remembers her first impressions of meeting Bonnie.

"Bonnie came in like a breath of fresh air. She was really obnoxious and had a terrible mouth and she would just tell people where to go in their face. It was such a relief to actually have somebody who had a mind, who was reasonably attractive. And also she really knows her job; she's a really, really good reporter. So I started to see the kind of stuff that she did and I respected it. I was drawn to her professionalism.

"And I thought, This woman knows something I need to know."

As our first mentors, both our parents teach us what it means to be women. From our mothers we learn how to be feminine and to live as a woman. A daughter identifies with her mother as a model for female sexuality, for mothering, for living and relating. She observes how her mother relates to an ever-widening circle of people: her husband and children, friends, relatives, acquaintances, and shopkeepers. Without realizing it, a daughter senses her mother's affect, emotions, intellect, and responses. Mothers also serve as models of personal qualities such as perseverance, independence, courage, and drive, which are important qualities in the world outside the home.[1]

In a girl's relationship with her father, on the other hand, she learns how it feels to be a woman in relation to a man. This relationship (which we'll explore in the next chapter, "The Father-Daughter Pair") is the model of how she'll relate to men, including male mentors, in later life. Girls who can identify with both parents are generally better adjusted as adults. They have more confidence and self-esteem and feel better about themselves as women and as individuals. How a woman feels about herself within her family shapes the sense of self she brings to the external world.

The American Heritage Dictionary of the English Language defines *feminine* as "characterized by or possessing qualities generally atttributed to a woman; womanly." Yet few people view the word simply in terms of gender. "Feminine" has become rife with stereotypes. To be feminine has come to mean passive, submissive, dependent, and weak. These are all negative attributes when compared with the connotations of masculine: strong, assertive, aggressive, and independent.

For centuries the "good woman" was the one who cared for others, especially her husband and children. She defined herself through her relationship with other people. She was "Tom's wife" or "Suzy's mother," not an individual in her own right. Being married and having children was most important. The woman was the enabler, not the doer. She looked upon herself as selfish if she pursued her own needs, because being a wife and mother was supposed to satisfy all her needs.

Many of the stereotypical connotations of femininity can be traced to Sigmund Freud. Freud was a product of his time who saw the difference between men and women as biological, one that implied an inherent inferiority of women. According to Freud, the difference in the development of boys and girls manifests itself after the age of three, when the little boy resolves his fear of castration by realizing that someday he'll grow up like his father and have a woman of his own like his mother. The little girl, on the other hand, sees that she lacks a penis and figures she has already been castrated. She then rejects her mother, who does not have a penis either and turns to her father, hoping to gain what she has lost. The boy continues to develop psychologically by identifying with his father, but the girl must wait until marriage and childbirth to continue her development, when, according to Freud, she symbolically gains the missing penis through her husband.[2]

Feminist revisionists since Freud have tried to modify psychoanalytic theory that woman's development centers around her attempt to cope with her feelings of loss (of a penis). Psychoanalyst Babette Deutsch stressed the positive value of female genitalia but defined *femininity* as the "triad of passivity, masochism, and narcissism."[3] Psychoanalysts Karen Horney and Clara Thompson took a more psychosocial view, believing that penis envy and masochism were the results of women's subordination in a patriarchal society, their lack of acceptable outlets for their aggressions, and their envy of men's power and status in society.[4]

Anthropologist Margaret Mead, who studied cultures from a psychoanalytic viewpoint, stressed the importance of women creating life and elevated the breast and the womb to a higher plane. Both she and Freud have been criticized for overemphasizing the influence of biological factors on feminine psychological development.[5] Feminist Betty Friedan, in particular, criticizes Mead for deifying woman's procreative abilities and making that her only "claim to fame."

Even developmental studies by Erik Erikson and Daniel Levinson fall into the same trap as Freud: They use the male as the prototype of humanity rather than recognizing and valuing the differences women bring to the model of human development. Psychoanalytic thinking offers a rich theory, but by making the male Oedipal experience universal, it leaves no room for social, cultural, or gender factors.

Recent studies by feminist psychologists stress that socialization and culturalization account for differences between men and women. According to Carol Gilligan, a professor at Harvard Graduate School of Education, women value relationships while men are more individualistic. "For men, identity precedes intimacy and attachment," writes Gilligan in *In a Different Voice;* "for women these tasks seem instead to be fused. Intimacy goes along with identity, as the female comes to know herself as she is known, through her relationships with others."[6] Men, Gilligan believes, have more problems with closeness and relationships, while women have difficulty separating and becoming their own person.

Women's fluid sense of boundaries also holds true in adolescence. The classic Freudian view pitted teenage daughter against mother, stressing that the daughter must sever ties with her mother to assert her own independence and form her own identity. Recent feminist theory has challenged that notion, now asserting that an adolescent girl remains connected to her mother *while* she forms her identity. She does not want to break with her mother, as previously thought, but to renegotiate the relationship and receive recognition from her mother for how she is changing and developing.

Another study by Carol Gilligan along a similar vein has shown a dramatic change in girls' development around the age of sixteen. She found that many girls around eleven years old go through a "moment of resistance." This is "a sharp and particular clarity of vision, an almost perfect confidence in what they know and see, a belief in their integrity and in their highly complex responsibilities toward the world."[7]

But as these girls get older, they lose this confidence and go through a metamorphosis. By the time they are sixteen, they have picked up a cultural message that tells them to keep quiet about what they know, almost as though they are acting out the nineteenth-century dictum for little girls, Be seen and not heard. They become tentative and lose their earlier confidence. This change in adolescents develops from their coming up against what Gilligan calls "the wall of Western culture"—the cultural stereotypes for women. Girls realize that their earlier "clearsightedness may be dangerous and seditious; in consequence they learn to hide and protect what they know—not only to censor themselves but 'to think in ways that differ from what they really think.' "[8] Gilligan wants young women to feel good about themselves as women *and* to be assertive, but this is problematic for young women at sixteen—just as it was for the women in our study who want to be nurturing *and* successful.

Maintaining their femininity is a major issue women face when they are mentored by men. In the 1970s women thought the way to get ahead was to dress, look, and sound like men. Today women recognize that this behavior does not serve them well. In the 1990s women realize the importance of retaining their femininity and being true to themselves. This is difficult in a male-dominated environment, because men determine the standards for success and control access to power and the powerful. Mentoring in the work-place, however, allows women to thrive where they feel most com-fortable: within a relationship.

A mentoring relationship helps a woman grow while smooth-ing the passage from the world of family to the larger world of work. For some the relationship is a compensatory one, making up for parents who were physically or emotionally absent. For others, whether the parenting relationship has been satisfying or not, it is what is known and comfortable and often replicated (uncon-sciously) in the work setting. Typically the mother is the model for the female mentor, just as many women tend to see the male mentor as a father figure.

When Shawn heard that Bonnie needed an assistant on the column, she realized she could get out of fact checking *and* learn from Bonnie. Shawn pestered her for weeks, and her determination im-pressed Bonnie. Even though the editor had misgivings, Bonnie decided to give her a try.

As Bonnie's assistant Shawn did all the research and legwork for the two-page column and was allowed to write one piece a week. But more important, Bonnie taught her how to be a reporter.

"I heard there's a hotel going up on the river," Shawn would tell her, not knowing if this was a big-enough deal to make the column.

Sometimes Bonnie would respond, "Fabulous, wonderful," and tell her what she liked about the idea and why it was news-worthy. At other times the idea would fall flat. Even after Shawn had made her case, Bonnie would tell her to find something better to write about.

After she wrote a story, Bonnie quizzed her: "Well, what about this? Why didn't you answer this question? Why don't you have this piece of information?"

At other times Bonnie would listen to Shawn on the phone (their desks were five feet apart) and suggest, "Try this way," or

"Say it like this." Bonnie took Shawn along to lunch when she met her sources, and Shawn would learn how to size up a person's usefulness and discern whom he was wired to, how close he was to certain situations, and how much to trust his information.

"I hadn't really been around political hacks or real estate moguls before, and she could pinpoint a lot of schtick for me," recalls Shawn. "I was learning all the time, and I was tense, completely tense all the time."

A woman's relationship with a female mentor often embodies the ambivalence she feels toward her mother. In *Between Women,* Luise Eichenbaum and Susie Orbach write of the universality of the mother-daughter relationship. "Almost all women unconsciously transfer a version of their hopes and restrictions of their own mother-daughter relationship to their current relationship. Women relating to each other see not just their friends or colleagues, they project onto them a whole range of emotions that reflect the legacy of their relationships with their mothers."[9] One protégé, a young scientist, made this connection herself in talking of her adviser, an older woman: "She is just about the first mentor, besides my mother, that I can really identify with."

Shawn felt more comfortable in a relationship with a woman because she was angry and distrustful of men. When she was eighteen, her father left her mother, an uneducated housewife whose life revolved around the family. The divorce thrust her mother into a work force for which she was unprepared; at the same time she was thrown out of the Catholic church, the one comforting force in her life. Shawn identified with her mother and expressed the anger that her mother could not. She isolated herself from her peers in both high school and college and tended to drift toward older women. She wanted nothing to do with men and had spent two years on a feminist commune in western Canada after college before coming to the magazine.

Her mentor, Bonnie Philpott, also a middle-aged divorced

woman, was an upper-middle-class, more sophisticated WASP version of Shawn's mother. She was a "tough" nurturer, a "kick-in-the-pants" mentor. Yet she truly cared about Shawn, and their views about men often coincided. Bonnie's father had deserted her mother when Bonnie was small, and as for professional men, "sex was always on the table," she said. "It wasn't that you had to sleep with the men you work with, but you had to lead them to believe that you *might* someday." (By the way, this was not Bonnie's neurotic perception but a realistic observation that other women reiterated as well.) So Bonnie preferred working with women; the relationships were more straightforward.

Although Shawn and Bonnie were only fifteen years apart, Bonnie often thought of Shawn as the adolescent daughter she never had. "There were constant battles. She was so impatient," recalls Bonnie. "She never understood that I was fifteen years older. She resented having to pay her dues. I had paid my dues, yet she wanted everything I had." Bonnie felt Shawn was ungrateful: she wanted Bonnie's salary and position without putting in her time, and Bonnie resented that.

Adolescence is frequently a time of heightened rivalry between mothers and daughters, partly because as a young girl becomes aware of her blossoming sexuality, the mother becomes conscious that hers has passed its prime. The daughter feels that her mother is holding her down, trying to keep her a little girl, while the mother feels jealous of her daughter's youth and vitality.

Psychoanalytic theory pits the mother and daughter against each other, fighting for the father's affection. The young girl, in love with her father, wants the mother out of the way so that she can have her father to herself. Nancy Friday writes in *My Mother, My Self* that the mother "began in our life as a loving friend. She became a no-sayer and rival. . . . Dad was the first man we saw. Mother was in the way. . . . The fear of competing against Mother and the guilt of wanting to beat her out spreads to the entire female sex."[10] Eventually the daughter must give up Dad, find her own man, and produce her own child.

Even if one does not completely believe the psychoanalytic interpretation, it is widely acknowledged that historically competition between women has centered on getting men's attention. Women have vied for the prettiest dress, the sharpest hairdo, the liveliest personality. It seemed that women became rivals in their fight for men. In reality, though, say Eichenbaum and Orbach, who put a feminist slant on psychoanalytic theory, "Men provided the excuse or the unconscious reason for making an effort with oneself but the real target, just as often, was for women's attention."[11] It is the approval and recognition from women—not men—that women truly desire.

They continue, "We compete about how well we are doing and we compete about how badly we are doing. The competition disguises something else—a desperate need for attention, for someone to listen to us and appreciate how it has been for us. It isn't competition per se that shapes the presentation, it is a fear that one won't be listened to that fuels the competition."[12]

Contemporary psychoanalytic theory views competition between women in a similar light, according to Friday. The contest between the mother and daughter is not only for the father. "It is the girl's struggle for recognition, for the limelight, for her place in the world, with or without daddy's presence."[13]

Competition between women, then, is really about a woman's need and desire to be recognized as a person in her own right. If Bonnie has the byline, then Shawn can't. If Bonnie wins the prize, Shawn will lose. The need and desire for individual recognition stoke the fires of competition between women. When a woman grapples with her feelings about competition, she must struggle with the cultural prohibitions against women achieving their own autonomy and gaining visibility for themselves.[14]

Very few of the women in our sample were willing to talk about feeling competitive toward other women, probably because the ethos of competition is "often at odds with the ethos of what it has previously meant to be a woman."[15] When the topic was broached, women reacted with silence, denial, and discomfort. This discomfort goes back to childhood when typically little girls are raised to be quiet, passive, and obedient. "Women are raised to be good girls, and part of being a good girl is to sit with your hands clasped on the desk," recalls Pearl Brown, the corporate officer whom we met in chapter 1. "Don't make too much noise and you will be rewarded. They are raised to be Miss Goody Two Shoes. That is just a lot of nonsense. Then they have this fantasy that you don't have to take any aggressive steps because you're going to be rewarded if you behave yourself. Well, that is the farthest thing possible from the truth."

As Pearl implies, girls are taught it is unfeminine to be aggressive, to compete and strive for what they want. When women are seen as too aggressive, they are labeled "bitches." Similar behavior in a man is not only acceptable but expected and praised. Since naked, unbridled aggression is frowned upon, men, too, must learn how to channel the appropriate amount of aggression in the corporate culture.

Taking credit for accomplishments also seems easier for men. Women tend to denigrate their accomplishments. "I was just lucky," says one woman about her recent promotion. "I don't know how it happened," equivocates another woman. "My paper just happened to be published."

While Shawn felt tension from the weekly deadline pressure and from the stress to perform and prove herself to Bonnie, it was also an unbelievably energetic time. "Bonnie and I used to make so much noise in the office. We would be screaming and shouting and falling all over the place. She would literally fall on the floor after a phone conversation, and then she would go running around the office and make a big deal about stuff that no one else understood. We would be so high energy because it was so tense. We'd have this joking, nervous thing going all the time."

Their life was a blur from Monday to Thursday, when they were on deadline, working till nine o'clock each night. When they put the column to bed late Thursday afternoon, they'd go out and have a long, boozy lunch, filled with hearty laughter and savage gossip. "We had a great sense of camaraderie at that point," remembers Shawn.

Women mentoring women is very different from men mentoring women. The nature of female bonding is different—there is more role modeling and less power inherent within the role. It would be unusual, for example, for a male mentor and a female protégé to have a lunch like Bonnie's and Shawn's. A lunch away from the office, with drinking, could be rife with sexual innuendo between a man and a woman. Not only could this situation change the dynamics of their relationship, but if somehow word of their lunch got back to the office, it's possible rumors would fly about their relationship. Neither could risk the possibility that such gossip might ruin their reputations as professionals.

This points up an important distinction between a female-female mentoring relationship and one involving a male mentor and a female protégé: There is no sexual undercurrent in the former. Nor is sexism present. "A woman might necessarily do better with a female mentor because sexism does play a role," says an editor at another magazine who has had three female mentors. "If someone is going to be the mentor, they need to have feelings of respect, mutual respect, toward each other. And if a man feels that a woman is inferior because of sexism, then I can't see how he could be a very good mentor to her."

There is more natural, uninhibited camaraderie and bonding between two women. Just as two men relate to each other in a way a man and woman cannot, so two women develop their own sense of closeness. There's an intimacy that resembles the closeness between a mother and her daughters or between two sisters. It's built on a shared gender, a feminine consciousness and familiarity, and often involves laughing at the same jokes and innuendos. Their conversation draws them closer and usually centers on their relationships, their feelings, and their perceptions—very different from typical "male" talk of sports, business trends, and the stock market.

This female bonding cements a relationship that may still have its own internal power play—despite the closeness, one woman is the mentor and the other, her subordinate. Throughout their uproarious lunches, for example, Shawn never forgot that Bonnie was her boss. Nor did she forget her hidden agenda: to remain in Bonnie's good graces so that she'd use her influence to promote Shawn to the editor. Shawn didn't realize what a burden these roles lent to their relationship until the mentoring ended and they became friends. Then they could both express the genuine warmth they felt for each other.

A mentoring relationship between women is different in other ways too. "The affective, or emotional, quality is more vital for women than for men," writes Murray Reich, who conducts workshops on careers, aging, and mentoring. In his article "The Mentor Connection," which reviews his study of the experiences of women executives with mentoring, he notes that both women and men emphasized the professional nature of mentoring, but that women were more likely to stress the caring, nurturing, and teaching aspects.[16] Men may have the same needs, but because of cultural stereotypes may not be free to express them as such and have difficulty recognizing them as important.

The difference in women's mentoring could stem from women's feminine nature, which Gilligan and others have seen as more collaborative and conciliatory, more concerned about others and their relationships. "Whereas women search for self through connection with others, men search for self through distinguishing themselves from others," write Eichenbaum and Orbach in *Between Women,* again stressing the importance of relationships to women in defining themselves.[17]

Although Bonnie could be relentless in her pushing of Shawn, Shawn never doubted her support and she understood her motivation. While Bonnie was determined to teach Shawn how to be a good reporter, the fact that she was ultimately responsible for the column is an important factor that must not be overlooked. If there were holes in the stories, they missed significant events, the reporting or writing was not up to par, it was Bonnie who would receive the editor's wrath, not Shawn. (A man would probably not think like this because he is less afraid of making mistakes.) But Bonnie did have some power at the magazine—unlike many women mentors. Although she was not the editor, she did have the editor's ear, and the column gave her status.

Because women typically do not hold the most powerful positions within an organization, they frequently give their protégés more psychosocial support; as we've noted, men offer instrumental, career sponsorship. Usually women mentors lack the power to link their protégés to important people and information or sponsor them for key committees or projects, although Bonnie could. Instead they give more advice and support. The study of women physicians and their mentors cited in the last chapter (see page 29) bears this out.[18]

Female mentors are intensified role models for professional women. Bonnie taught Shawn not only how to be a reporter but how to be a woman reporter. When Shawn first came to the magazine, she admits she was an angry feminist. She was abrupt, distrustful, and harsh. By listening to Bonnie and observing her, Shawn learned how to court people, how to talk diplomatically, and how to get the information she needed without alienating others. These qualities helped her professionally, but she still couldn't change her interpersonal dynamics. While she was able to tone down her style when working on assignment, somehow she could never hide her persistence and toughness—qualities that made her a good reporter but that continued to alienate the editor. Soon after she started working with Bonnie, Shawn also began dressing more professionally.

Shawn was determined to get ahead in her career, but feared she'd become a magazine "widow," married to the magazine with no life of her own. Bonnie showed her that a woman could be a first-rate reporter *and* have significant personal relationships and a social life outside the magazine. As an attractive divorcée, Bonnie had an active social life and often shared with Shawn details about the men in her life and the parties she attended. This knowledge freed Shawn to develop her career, although at times her zeal and impatience to move ahead alienated people.

Women protégés often look to their female mentors for advice and support in handling their multiple roles as mothers, wives, and career women. A psychotherapist talks about how she and her supervisor/mentor, a younger woman who had ten years' more clinical experience, were experiencing the same conflicts and how this drew them closer. "I think the identification was enhanced by the fact that we have very similar lifestyles. Marriage and children are a real priority in our lives, therefore we had similar headaches. She'd get a phone call in the middle of supervision about day care or struggles with an automobile. That certainly enhanced our identification."

The therapist goes on to tell how her supervisor understood "that constant struggle between wanting to be home and also wanting to be at work; feeling the need to race home when I really wanted to spend another hour at the office. And at home, having to race in where I really didn't want to leave work, but my kids needed me at that moment."

After about six months of working with Bonnie, Shawn began to relax. She had fewer questions, and her work needed to be rewritten less frequently. She realized Bonnie was not going "to eat her alive" (as she had with her very first assistant, who lasted three weeks). "She gave me a lot of running room and she was really supportive," recalls Shawn.

Once Shawn had mastered writing one piece a week, Bonnie gave her a second, and then a third. After nine months Shawn was writing almost half the column, but Bonnie was clearly in charge, making all the editorial decisions. To recognize Shawn's contribu-

tion, Bonnie talked the editor into giving Shawn a regular assistant's byline along the bottom of the page; her own byline remained
at the top of the column.

But after another six months of working together Shawn approached Bonnie about getting equal billing. She wanted her byline
at the top of the page too.

"Absolutely not," said Bonnie. "This is my column. You're not
the co-writer. You are going to take it over one day, but I'm paying
more dues than I should for this column. There's no way I'm going
to share the credit with you now."

If she couldn't have the byline, then Shawn wanted more
money. She constantly pressed Bonnie to go to the editor and ask
for salary increases for her. The first time, Bonnie spoke to the
editor and got her a small increase; but then a few months later
Shawn wanted another raise. Bonnie didn't like being the go-be-
tween and encouraged Shawn to approach the editor herself to
discuss money. That made matters worse because the editor was
turned off by Shawn's toughness and aggression.

When Shawn didn't get the byline she wanted and the salary
increases were slow in coming, she felt disappointed. She did recognize that the job would not have an instantaneous payoff and that
she was building her career. But at her lowest moments she felt
underpaid and wondered if there was a future for her at *Metro*
magazine.

Bonnie held tightly onto her prized byline, feeling that she
alone had earned the recognition and she wanted to savor it herself.
After all, she was the senior member of the team; she deserved top
billing. But because they were on the same career path (even
though Bonnie was years ahead of Shawn), perhaps Bonnie feared
that Shawn, who was naturally more aggressive, would outdistance
her and get the plum position of feature writer at *Metro* magazine
first. In reality Bonnie had been writing fifteen years longer than
Shawn and had a long string of feature articles and a book to her
credit. Yet she still felt threatened by another writer, a young,
aspiring woman, just as a mother may feel threatened by her

daughter's youth and potential. This was apparent in their clash over the byline.

Female mentors like Bonnie are uncommon, whether at a city magazine, a law firm, a university, or a corporation. In our study only 19 percent of the women who had mentors had only female mentors (32 percent had both male and female mentors). Interpersonal and internal prohibitions, such as their competitive feelings about developing relationships with other women, prevent women from helping one another. Women's political naiveté about how mentoring can benefit them (as the mentor) inhibits them from helping younger women move up.

But it is important to stress again that the fundamental reason more women do not mentor other women is that there are not enough women in senior management positions. For example, a survey by Catalyst, an organization that promotes women's leadership, found that 60 percent of the large corporations they surveyed had fewer than 5 percent women senior managers.[19] At these companies men hold at least 95 percent of the most critical and influential positions. They have access to information about job openings, pending projects, and managerial decisions, much of which is shared through the old boys' network.[20]

In the media 3 percent of television presidents or vice presidents are women, as are 6 percent of newspaper publishers and 8 percent of radio presidents or vice presidents.[21] In the male-dominated newspaper business only 7.8 percent of newspaper publishers and 16.5 percent of directing editors are women, and women are more likely to hold these positions at papers with smaller circulations.[22]

In female-dominated occupations, such as nursing, social work, and education, one would expect an increase of women mentoring other women (partly because these are nurturing, helping professions). In reality, though, mentoring has been underutilized here, too, as a career-advancement strategy.[23] Many women in these professions have seldom had opportunities for promotion, have vague career ambitions, and lack powerful women mentors as role models.

For example, it became clear during our interviews that some nurses feel confused about the place of mentoring in their careers and uncomfortable in the mentoring role. While one nurse selected a lawyer as her mentor, another chose a hospital administrator who was a former nurse. They were drawn to women in powerful positions. In another instance two nurses, Carol and Lottie, did form a relationship, but Carol was not sure who was the mentor and who the protégé. While Carol started as the younger woman's preceptor, once Lottie received her doctorate, Carol felt Lottie became *her* mentor because Lottie encouraged her to do the same.

Some of this confusion about a nurse's role as mentor stems from the precarious position of nurses in a hospital, but a larger part of their difficulty is generic to women. Women's culturally prescribed role as nurturer makes them particularly vulnerable to becoming enmeshed in a mentoring relationship, as either mentor or protégé (we'll explore this further in chapter 5). The dean of a nursing school recalls how her early mentoring relationships took over her whole existence. "They were ridiculous. They got in the way of my life. My husband used to go crazy over them. I would get so many phone calls from troubled women. I was not able to separate or really be clear about what the differences were between the psychotherapeutic role and the educational role, which is a problem I see around me all the time, here as well as anywhere else."

Nationally almost 68 percent of the nursing profession, which is almost 97 percent female, work in hospitals. Only 1.8 percent are in nursing education, considered the elite.[24]* Practicing nurses are clustered at the bottom of the hospital pyramid. Those nurses who move up into administrative or teaching positions give up what

*The breakdown of other settings includes 6.6 percent in nursing homes, 6.8 percent in community centers, 7.7 percent in ambulatory care, 2.9 percent in student health services, and 1.2 percent in private duty.

drew them to nursing in the first place: hands-on patient care. Many say they do not want to give up their staff positions for that reason, but how many more nurses would *elect* to move into more powerful positions if they were given the opportunity or if they had female mentors as role models to show them the way?

Many nurses feel uncomfortable assuming power in the workplace because the hospital hierarchy is dominated by white male physicians who serve as administrators. Being in such a tenuous, deferential position does not foster a climate for helping others climb the hierarchical ladder. While nurses can serve as models for younger nurses, teaching them how to become better on the job, they are not in positions to help newcomers politically because they do not hold the power within the hospital. Thus the traditional business model of a mentor as a powerful political adviser does not hold in nursing. The nursing mentor is more of a teacher and role model.

In education only 24 percent of principals are women, and female superintendents constitute a mere 4 percent.[25] Many women choose teaching because the hours and vacation schedule coincide with their children's, allowing them to work and raise their children with minimal conflict. Others like working in a classroom with young children or at the secondary level, teaching a particular subject.

Teachers are not the only ones desiring and choosing positions with more flexibility. This is a high priority for all women with families, particularly younger women who have rejected the Superwoman concept of the seventies. Corporate women are selecting the so-called mommy track and flextime as ways to cope with family pressures.[26]

In addition more women are opening their own businesses. The total number of women-owned sole proprietorships increased 62 percent between 1980 and 1986, according to the National Association of Women Business Owners. A major reason women open their own businesses is to have more flexibility and control over their lives. Although starting a business requires sacrifices, hard work, and long hours, women like being the masters of their fate. They can choose to attend a PTA meeting on a Thursday afternoon and then make up the time whenever they see fit. Balancing work and family time is emerging as a major trend in the 1990s for both women and men. We feel this is a positive direction, because it encourages both women and men to become more well rounded and to share responsibilities for child care and breadwinning.

It's still unclear whether the majority of women teachers, whether novices or old-timers, remain teachers by choice or are not interested in moving up because they feel these positions are beyond their reach or would interfere with their family life. More women hold leadership positions today than twenty years ago, but they still remain the minority.

A Santa Fe principal talked about how difficult it was for her to find a more experienced principal as a mentor. "I can name only one woman who has been a mentor. I've sought others and I've tried to develop them, but the research will tell you that women are not very good about helping other women. Those who have made it are not real gracious in helping others. They feel, 'I've done it, you can do it too.' "

Those women who've made it into the top rungs but don't help other women are called queen bees. If they've succeeded on their own, despite prejudice and chauvinism, they reason, why can't others? Rather than helping young women move up, the queen bee is threatened by bright, young women and resents that they are given opportunities that she never had.[27] Consequently she doesn't put herself out for other women. The queen bee fears she will lose what she has fought so hard and long for if she gives it away. We hope this situation will change as more women move into positions of power and begin to shatter the glass ceiling.

However, some experts dispute the queen-bee theory. Agnes Missirian, in her survey of one hundred top corporate women, found that 13 percent of those who responded had had women mentors. Considering that few women are in a position to mentor other women, Missirian believes that this figure is a high percentage of women mentors.[28] The queen-bee concept needs further study, particularly in relation to other minorities.

What the queen bee and other successful women often don't realize, however, is that mentoring can help their careers as well. Mentoring is reciprocal and benefits the mentor as well as the protégé. Women tend to see mentoring as only giving, and a giving that, if anything, takes away from their own careers. This reflects a shortsightedness that women often bring to the workplace.

For example one woman cited in *The Managerial Woman* complained about having to complete a complicated report for the president of the company on short notice and wanted to do her "assigned" work first. She completely overlooked the fact that if her work was good enough to merit the president's attention and approval, it would enable her to have a personal, working relationship with him. When the authors pointed out the possibilities for advancement, growth in status, and influence as well as in skill and expertise, she replied, "My God, I never saw it."[29] This woman is not atypical: women tend to be preoccupied with short-term planning rather than seeing the long-term implications of their actions.[30] Mentoring is a long-term relationship with long-term growth and advancement for the mentor as well as the protégé.

Even when women do hold positions that would enable them to mentor others of their gender, they frequently choose not to. Others may see these women as firmly established in their upper-management positions, but they don't feel secure. They recognize that they are a minority in business, corporate, and professional settings. This minority status and lack of power breed insecurity. Women face some of the same issues that blacks face in the workplace, including perfectionism to make up for their reputed "inferior gender," stereotyping, isolation from the mainstream, and bicultural pulls.

Some women who make it to the top feel they must keep their hands clean, that they will endanger their own career if their male colleagues see them as prejudiced in favor of women—that is, mentoring other women.[31] They need their male colleagues' approval to maintain their position so they don't want to rock the boat by doing something—such as mentoring a young woman—that might jeopardize it.

Women, regardless of age, also feel they are struggling to survive and prove themselves, as any woman would in such a tenuous position. As underdogs they feel stressed and often become perfectionists. They believe they must constantly work to maintain their position by putting in long hours, attending meetings, and keeping up contacts. All this takes time, and many women don't feel they have the extra time or energy required to mentor a younger woman.

And of course if they do have extra time, most women choose to spend it with their families. They are already stressed from juggling family and work responsibilities. How can they justify giving a young manager extra time when they already feel guilty for not attending their ten-year-old's school play?

Women also do not have the same generativity needs as men. At forty or fifty, when middle-aged men typically mentor, a woman has already raised her family. Her nurturing and generativity needs have been met at home with her own children. As one psychologist said, "They're just worn out mothering the world. They don't have enough left to give to a protégé." A woman in her forties may still be moving up the ladder herself; she wants to focus on developing her own career, not on cultivating a twenty-five-year-old's career. A man at forty-five, however, has probably plateaued or risen as high as he can. It is a time for him to reevaluate his life. He may realize he has been so busy pursuing his career earlier that he missed forming close relationships with his own children. He may have a greater need for relationships at midlife to compensate for what he missed earlier, and use mentoring to meet that need.

When Bonnie was promoted to feature writer, Shawn was put in charge of the "Inside" column. "I was glad for her and glad for me," says Shawn. "It was a promotion for each of us, and I was

THE MOTHER-DAUGHTER PAIR 63

glad not to be under her tutelage anymore."

But the editor was still leery of giving Shawn the reins, so he asked Bonnie to help Shawn choose her assistant. The first person they hired lasted two weeks. Trying to find someone else heightened the tension between them. Bonnie was constantly on edge because she wanted out of the column and feared that she would be dragged back into doing it again if they did not find an assistant soon. Shawn was tense too. She was so impatient to move ahead, she wanted to do the column now. She wished Bonnie would move on; she was ready to be free of her and on her own.

The tension led to constant bickering. In addition the editor had refused to give Shawn the top byline until he was certain the column would work out and decided to keep Bonnie's byline for a few weeks—even though she was not working on the column (she was only helping Shawn choose her assistant). When Shawn heard this, she thought this was Bonnie's idea and became enraged. They had a huge fight, which escalated into a screaming match. When they realized that everyone in the newsroom had stopped working and was listening, they went outside but continued yelling. Both strong women, neither backed down, and their relationship cooled.

They were civil to each other and eventually hired a young woman to assist Shawn. Bonnie was finally free of the column and could devote all her energies to her new position as feature writer. They ignored each other for a while and then slowly started chatting. Without the strain of working together, they gradually renewed their friendship. Each made an effort to reach out because they genuinely liked each other and wanted to remain friends. Without the demands of churning out a column together each week, the warmth they felt for each other surfaced more easily, and much of their old camaraderie returned.

After a year on her own Shawn felt the "Inside" column had become drudgery. The payoff—the byline and prestige—paled in comparison to the burden she felt psychologically. Although the editor could have found a feature spot for her at *Metro,* he could no longer take her constant demands and grew tired of her feistiness. Shawn eventually realized there would be no feature-writing position for her there.

Shawn stayed at *Metro* magazine for another six months while looking for a job. Recently she accepted a position as a political reporter for a national news magazine. Although she is not doing features, she finds the work exciting, with many options for advancement. She and Bonnie still talk by phone and often meet for lunch, gossiping and laughing like two old friends.

Separating from a mentor can be painful and can arouse a range of emotions in both the mentor and protégé. Although both Shawn and Bonnie were advancing and moving into positions that they desired, the change was still stressful. Eichenbaum and Orbach describe what typically happens: The protégé feels "deserted, left, abandoned, as the other woman moves on and develops. It feels as though the successful one is turning her back, leaving her friend to stay stuck in the space they once shared. At the same time, the woman who is a success feels alone in the new and unknown space. She may feel guilty about her achievements."[32]

Bonnie and Shawn's anger surfaced around the tension of choosing Shawn's assistant and when Shawn learned that she would not get the byline during the transition. Since Bonnie was no longer writing the column, why *didn't* she go to the editor and fight for her protégé to be given the byline? Bonnie had simply grown tired of fighting for Shawn. Her personality, demands, and impatience had worn Bonnie down. Bonnie was no longer willing to risk losing favor with the editor by sticking her neck out one more time for Shawn. She was ready for Shawn to grow up and fight her own battles. She had groomed her successor; she considered her work finished.

Many mentors continue to promote and sponsor their protégés even when they are no longer working directly together. Bonnie chose not to do so for political and psychological reasons. She felt competitive with Shawn and feared she would endanger her own career and future if she continued to ally with her protégé, someone whom the editor disliked. The formal mentoring functions ended when they stopped working together, so their intense relationship ended abruptly, lasting only a year and a half. Most male mentoring relationships last at least three years, according to psychologist Daniel Levinson.

For many mentors and protégés separation is a necessary part of the relationship. They both need to grow and gain their independence. But a conflictual separation is not always necessary for two women. Instead women tend to renegotiate the relationship. Many of our female pairs did not formally separate. Some grew apart or moved away; others remained friends after the mentoring ended. The protégé may still call her mentor a mentor after the formal mentoring has ended, but the relationship is in fact more collegial. Because women have more fluid boundaries, they often choose to stay connected with other women. This connection does not stop them from growing and developing, and in fact the enduring nature of the relationship enriches their lives.

It *is* difficult to develop mentoring relationships with other women. And some women never found the mentor they yearned for. Aretha Brown, a fifty-six-year-old black woman who does training and development for an educational institution, still grieves for the mentor she never found, years after one would be helpful. "One of the reasons this whole discussion of mentoring threw me into a tizzy is that I was feeling a kind of grief when I started to think through this issue, because I needed a mentor," she said. "I needed someone who was close and would follow me along." Many of our interviewees who were successful expressed similar sentiments, believing they would have achieved even greater heights with a mentor.

Women can help one another fulfill their dreams. If women can see mentoring as reciprocal and mutually beneficial, they may feel more at ease in the role of mentor. As more women move into positions of power and become more comfortable with that, we hope they will choose to mentor younger women. This will give more women an opportunity to experience the special nature of women's mentoring. A psychologist/protégé eloquently describes what she sensed as the heart of woman-to-woman mentoring: "I think part of the essence of healthy mentoring is shared femininity. The senior partner allows the junior partner to partake in her strength, wisdom, and confidence. Slowly the strength, wisdom, and confidence are absorbed by the junior partner and made her own."

Shared femininity is a gift women can give to each other. Yet some women shun such generosity, feeling that they'll lose a part of themselves if they give too much away. But in truth a woman is enriched by sharing and giving to other women. A parent discovers that she has a bottomless well of love for all her children, and the more she gives, the more she reaps in return. Mentoring is like that too. When a woman shares her strength, wisdom, and confidence with another woman, she herself becomes stronger, wiser, and more confident.

CHAPTER FOUR

✧   ✧   ✧

The Father-Daughter Pair

At one p.m. every weekday one articulate middle-aged woman and nine elderly men meet for lunch at a long rectangular table in the corner of the faculty dining room. It's a plain, nondescript room with Formica tables and metal chairs, except for a speck of color from the fresh red carnations on each table. But the dynamics at the Law School Table, as it is known, are far from ordinary. The table looks like any other table in the room, but it is not. Everyone who sits there is a tenured professor who wields power and influence in the law school of this prestigious West Coast university. No one simply walks in and takes a seat there. That would be unthinkable, a terrible intrusion. A professor must be asked to join by another member already seated at the table.

"Did you see the article in the *Times* this morning?" someone asks while another complains about his wife's arthritis and asks for the name of a good rheumatologist. "Mitchell Beame is coming up for tenure," says another professor and leads the discussion about his credentials. The conversation, lively and insightful, wavers between vaguely confidential professional matters and personal concerns of the men.

Gina Carbone, forty-two, a tenured associate professor in the law school, is the only woman who ever sat there—because Stan Risosky, her second mentor, brought her. She was still untenured six years ago when Stan, like a caring father, initiated her into the elite world of tenured male professors.

* * *

As men and women work together more and more—sitting side by side in the conference room, discussing projects over dinner, traveling to meet clients—it's natural that they develop positive feelings for one another. They respect each other's expertise, grow to like each other, and feel a warm affection for each other. With increased contact and closeness an intimacy often develops.

Intimacy, which forms the core of mentoring, creates special feelings on the part of the protégé toward the mentor, who is an authority figure. Such figures lend themselves to an identification with a parental figure. Some of this is conscious, such as when the mentor is an older man, but much is unconscious. A woman may not recognize that she perceives her mentor as a father figure. She understands only that she's relating to an authority figure of the opposite sex in a way that feels safe, comfortable, and nonsexual. Perceiving the mentoring relationship as a father-daughter pairing makes a sexual liaison unthinkable because of the incest taboo.[1]

Just as a young girl's relationship with her mother is the prototype for her future relationships with women (as we discussed in the last chapter), so her relationship with her father is the model of how she'll relate to men in later life. If her father values her and approves of her, this will increase her confidence in all spheres of her life. Fathers have often served as a "bridge" for their daughters into the adult world outside the home.[2] For the women in our study, and for most women (only recently have two-career families became more common), fathers modeled work roles.

Many of the women in our sample who followed the individualistic path identified with their fathers, not their mothers, and remained allied with them throughout adolescence. Most of their mothers did not work outside the home, but they felt comfortable as models of marriage and childrearing. The women in our sample clashed with the prescribed norms of their day and often played the role of the son for their fathers. This is unusual for teenage girls, but then the women in our sample were extraordinary. They were highly motivated, achieving women who attained professional success, sometimes at the sacrifice of their personal lives.

Margaret Hennig and Anne Jardim, authors of *The Managerial Woman,* found similar adolescent backgrounds in their study of successful women. Their subjects, all presidents or vice presidents of large financial and business corporations, identified more with their fathers during adolescence. Their fathers encouraged them to ignore the cultural stereotypes restricting girls from certain activities. These fathers did not treat them as boys, nor did they reject their femininity. Instead they emphasized their abilities and skills.[3]

For instance, as a teenager, Gina Carbone loved it when her father, a police officer, picked her up from school and took her over to the union hall. She'd sit in the corner, sipping a Coke and observing the men. Her mother, a homemaker, encouraged this behavior, even though no other girls did this kind of thing. She did not want Gina to lead a sheltered life or to grow up like many other girls in their Italian neighborhood—married and pregnant at eighteen.

Many of the women in our study spoke spontaneously of their fathers as their first mentors. We were surprised that these grown women still glorified their fathers. Sylvia Lubin, a psychotherapist in her early seventies, spoke with awe of her father, a rabbi, now deceased. "My father was a very, very unusual man. He was a scholar in the truest sense and he lived the genuine philosophy of Judaism, the real true content of it."

As adults, these women continued to idealize their fathers and in some cases overidentified with them. Society's patriarchal system reinforces the father's larger-than-life role, because in reality men still have more power and higher status. This is one of the reasons so many women have male mentors: Men hold the positions of status and power today.

For now women must find a way to work comfortably with men in power. To do this, women often bring familiar roles from the family into the workplace. Just as women transfer patterns of interacting with their mothers to their female mentors, so they bring the father-daughter roles with which they are most familiar and comfortable to the office. The protégé who is used to being a "good little girl" with her daddy at home will reenact that role in the office without even realizing it. However, this role can be limiting at work: If she's worried about keeping the mentor's approval, she won't be free to express herself honestly or to differ with him. Psychologically women have been trained to say yes to men and to authority figures and to seek their approval.

The mentor who is accustomed to being the strong, protective father will tend to shield the protégé in the same way he would a daughter. He will provide coaching and advice but try to protect her from the harsh realities of organizational life. This behavior may be fine for a protégé who is most comfortable in a dependent role, where the woman is expected to defer and is thus guaranteed protection. Some young women like the feeling of acceptance this offers and may continue to act as though they are dependent and incompetent—even when they are not. They feel safe and don't have to risk much, but they probably will not advance far professionally. Independent women would feel inhibited and hampered by this type of control.

The parenting role meshes naturally with mentoring because traditionally both roles involve an older person, usually a male, guiding a younger or less experienced one, typically a female. In the best possible scenario he promotes her growth and encourages her to become her own professional and her own person—just as a good parent would. But mentors—and fathers—can also be disappointing for women, because they can be selfish, egotistical, and sexist.

In Gina Carbone's case it was more than her three mentors' advanced years that made them father figures. They each had a daughter about her age (although none of their daughters went into the same fields as their fathers), so they were comfortable in a paternal role. "They were fatherly," explains Gina. "There was no hint of anything sexual about their help. I think they saw that women needed help, because their daughters were already out working."

The psychological process Gina experienced is common to all mentoring relationships. Although the age span of thirty years or more between Gina and her mentors was atypical, it made it easier to build a nonsexual relationship. She also thought her married status made her more acceptable to her mentors. From her viewpoint her marriage announced publicly that she was a normal, sexual woman, not just an intellectual. Thus her mentoring relationships were intimate but nonthreatening both to her and to her mentors, because she was already "taken" by a man.

Richard Tyre, assistant director of the Uncommon Individual Foundation, a group that sponsors mentoring seminars, says that like parenting, mentoring involves "a kick in the pants and a shoulder to cry on. It's all the gestures that say, 'You're a human being, I affirm you, your likes, your fears, your loves, your hates.' This is a delicate balance between support and challenge, and successful mentoring is a mix of these two. Parenting and teaching is a mix between affirming the person and challenging him, pushing him."

The nurturing mentor, like the nurturing parent, supports and affirms the protégé, and this gives her confidence. Sandra Young, a young biologist working on her Ph.D., speaks of her adviser/ mentor, who saw her potential, in this way: "She was treating me as an equal, someone who is developing in science. I don't know as much as she does, but she very much considered my capacity to know. It was a completely novel experience for me to be taken seriously." Because of both gender prejudice and their own inexperience in the work world, being taken seriously can be a new experience for women.

The nurturing mentor also protects the protégé. He may protect her from premature or untimely contact with superiors or take the blame—or credit—in controversial situations.[4] At other times he may act as a shield against clients or colleagues who are threatened by a capable or attractive woman. Richard Hendricks, the partner in a Big 8 accounting firm whom we'll meet in chapter 7, protected his pretty twenty-eight-year-old protégé from a chauvinistic supervisor while at the same time he "tested" her ability to handle him. Hendricks sat in the next office listening to their conversation, ready to barge in if the supervisor crossed the line of decency. The protégé passed the test: she held her ground without angering the supervisor. In corporate settings protégés are often watched through layers of bureaucracy; a powerful sponsor can intervene only when needed, giving protection and direction at judicious moments, allowing the protégé to act independently.

Knowing how much to protect is a delicate judgment call because excessive protection can smother the protégé. A judge recalls how her mentor, her first boss after law school, found the right balance. "He told me, 'Go and do whatever you think you should do, because there is no mistake you make that I cannot, in some way, correct.' And that just gave me a lot of confidence. Instead of always looking over my shoulder or being nervous about whether the i's were dotted and the t's crossed, I just went out and performed. I think I performed quite well under this kind of guidance."

In work relationships, particularly those between male mentors and female protégés, finding the appropriate amount of protection may be difficult. A young female may feel that she is being deprived of opportunities for advancements by her older male mentor, who may in turn feel that women are weaker or have less experience and therefore need to be protected. His feelings can be due either to the real difficulties he foresees in the workplace or to a stereotypical way of relating to women. According to Kram, "Excessive protection reflects a basic discomfort with the unfamiliarity of working closely with a manager of the opposite sex."[5]

However, for some women, nurturing and protecting create so much comfort that they do not want to leave this warm cocoon. These protégés become too comfortable and need "a kick in the pants" so that they can grow as professionals. This kick can come in many different forms: through challenging the protégé, giving her criticism and feedback on her work and behavior, and encouraging her to take risks.

Maria Stappone, a thirty-nine-year-old chemist, recently

started on the management track at a large pharmaceutical company—only because her mentor encouraged her to break out of the laboratory. She had worked in the lab for several years when her mentor, Sarah Medhart, a fifty-five-year-old chemist, began encouraging her to consider a management position. Maria says, "I was in terrible anxiety for the last year and a half. Sarah was very patient and very encouraging. She'd say, 'You'd do great outside the lab. You've had a lot of fun in here and you've done some good work. Now go on to something different. Otherwise, the alternative is, if you don't leave the lab at a certain point, you can never leave.'

"I would say, 'No, I don't want to hear it anymore. I'm not leaving the lab. I'm not doing that job.' Then she'd say, 'This job is up on the board.' 'I don't want it, I'm not ready.' And eventually . . ."

Maria knew Sarah was right: It would be almost impossible to leave the lab after she had worked there for many years, yet the laboratory setting had been her love and her security since she was thirteen. Sarah had reached the point where she herself could no longer leave but, like a caring and unselfish mother, wanted Maria to benefit from her hindsight, even if their relationship changed. In one sense she was protecting Maria from making the same mistake she had made; but on the other hand her encouragement allowed Maria to risk and try something new.

Balancing "the kick in the pants" with the "the shoulder to cry on" is tricky. If given appropriately, criticism can motivate the protégé and inspire her to change and improve. On the other hand, if the feedback is too harsh and excessive, the protégé can become consumed with the negative and become immobilized. A 1987 study of top women managers by the Center for Creative Leadership implied that one of the main reasons *some* women fall off the "success track" was that they denied critical feedback. They ignored the negative comments, rather than learning from them; this made their superiors believe that they were unwilling to change.[6] We could not verify this assertion in our interviews because we did not discuss criticism. But the results of this study reinforce our belief that women in leadership positions feel insecure; they may be so threatened by criticism that they ignore it rather than risk changing.

Support and challenge must be balanced. Jack Tabson, Gina's first mentor, tipped the scale. He supported her only as long as it served his purposes. He was the type of boss who could be used as a mentor in certain circumstances but who was not a natural facilitator. His challenge became too controlling, and in Gina's mind he became an authoritarian, tyrannical father.

When Gina's paper, titled "U.S. Drug Agents in Foreign Countries: Does the Fourth Amendment Prohibition Apply?" appeared in the *Journal of Criminal Law and Criminology,* Jack Tabson, director of the legal research center at the university, was impressed and called her to work on a project quantifying the involvement of U.S. agents overseas. She hadn't met Jack personally but knew he was a full professor with a big name in his field.

At the time Gina was twenty-nine and a faculty member, teaching part-time in the law school. Contracting some of her time as a researcher in his center appealed to her because she could pursue her research interests and get paid for it. After graduating from law school she had spent a few years teaching in England, where she met her husband, a management consultant. When they were both twenty-eight, they came back to the States, and Gina began teaching at the West Coast university where she had attended law school.

Jack ruled with a rod of iron. "He doesn't work with people, they work *for* him," says Gina, adding that he often put his name on other people's work. She and the other researchers felt exploited by this and some of his other tactics. "He was the most bizarre person I ever worked for," she recalls. "He was outrageous. He'd listen in on phone conversations, open people's mail, look in your trash can. He once stole data from someone else's tape. There was nothing that was too low for Jack."

Much as she disliked his ethics, Gina had to admit that Jack wielded power because of his position. He had many corporate connections and often took Gina along when he taught corporate seminars, introducing her to the power brokers. He also introduced her to her third mentor, Melvin Moore. He advised her on how to write articles and obtain grants as well.

But Jack wanted total loyalty and total control. After four years of working at the research center, Gina realized she had to leave or she would become consumed by Jack and his research projects. She was grateful for all he had done for her but could no longer put up with his domineering personality and unethical standards. She had to leave to grow emotionally and professionally. "I very much disagreed with his ideological stance. I would have found it very difficult to stay without completely selling out," Gina says today.

Gina remembers well the day she resigned from the research center. She wrote Jack a letter of resignation and handed it to him in his office. He read it and didn't say a word; he just stared at her. He was livid, but he didn't yell because he didn't believe in raising his voice to women. Later he accused her of being ungrateful and unappreciative. This time it was Gina who remained silent.

Their relationship ended abruptly the day she left the research center. Although they exchange Christmas cards, Gina believes her mentor has written her out of his life.

"I feel like a child who has died," says Gina.

Conflicts between mentors and protégés are as inevitable as conflicts between parents and children and are just as stressful, but most women did not feel comfortable discussing them. In some businesses and corporations the protégé's transfer to another department deflects the conflict. In other cases the mentor or protégé moves to another company or another city to take advantage of a new opportunity. In these cases a separation occurs, but the conflicts are never stated, nor do they always emerge. Gina needed to clash with her mentor in order for her to leave the research center.

According to Kram, separation is a crucial stage in the mentoring relationship, "marked by significant changes in the functions provided by the relationship and in the experiences of both individuals."[7] However, she goes on to say, "if the separation is untimely for either individual, feelings of abandonment, anger, or resentment dominate the experience during this phase."[8] Both Gina Carbone and Jack Tabson encountered these feelings.

Over the years Gina's resentment and anger at Jack had built up. Much as she claims she abhorred his ethics and disliked him personally, she stayed for four years. (It is true that she also needed a job.) Something drew her to him; she was more involved than she lets on. This situation is similar to a child who still loves a cruel parent no matter what he does. True, she gained politically from the alliance, but more important, she needed him psychologically. She felt passive and impotent alone; he motivated her. For her to say, "I felt like the child who died" implies a far deeper relationship than she admitted.

When Gina left, Jack felt angry and betrayed, like the parent who had provided for a child. She took the provisions but rejected him. If he had yelled at her, perhaps he would have said, "How could you? After all I've done for you!" Jack knew he had empowered Gina, but he felt Gina minimized him; she didn't need him anymore. Because mentors have invested so much, they often feel hurt and threatened when their protégé needs them less.

Tabson's indignation typifies how the mentor feels when the protégé wants to end the relationship so that she can become independent. Due to his domineering personality and need for control, he took her leave-taking more personally than others might. He saw his way as the only right way; when Gina left the research center and went back to teaching full-time, he felt rejected.

If a mentor identifies with or invests too much in the protégé, she cannot be independent. The protégé can also feed into this because of her own needs (we'll explore this pattern in the next chapter). On the other hand, if a mentor or parent encourages independence, the child can separate gracefully from her mentor. The most giving mentor, like the most giving parent, must be able to let the protégé go freely. Then they must both readjust their roles. The protégé may want to become a friend or colleague, but the mentor may have difficulty with a relationship of equals and may indeed cut it off if he can't continue on top.

That's what Jack Tabson did. Gina needed to break with him to become her own person and her own professional, just as a child needs to separate from a parent to grow up. She wished Jack had treated her as the good father who would make her feel special, but she paid a price for his help and admiration. Ultimately, because of the invisible strings attached to his power, she could not be the good daughter and he the good father. Gina refused to give up her independence for harmony in the relationship. Her papers, her research, her reputation had to be her own. She had to leave.

But Gina had difficulty expressing her anger, as many women do. According to Harriet Lerner, Ph.D., author of *The Dance of Anger,* our society discourages women from "the awareness and forthright expression of anger." Lerner also notes that women who openly express anger at men are especially suspect. They turn men off and are seen as unloving and unlovable, devoid of femininity.[9] Then what of the woman who expresses anger at the male authority figure, the man who holds the power, like Jack Tabson? Gina says she felt silence was the most effective way to handle her first mentor. Was that a cop-out or was it truly effective? She had no difficulty clashing with her mother as a teenager, but her mother was not a man nor an authority figure in the same way as Tabson. Women are used to deferring to such authority figures.

Women also have trouble expressing anger toward people on whom they feel dependent. For years women have been economically dependent on men; this may have produced a psychological dependence as well. Some choose to be economically dependent on their husbands for a while while they are full-time mothers; today more women support themselves financially, but the remnants of the psychological dependence remain. Our culture has encouraged women to rely on men in personal as well as professional relationships. But according to Colette Dowling, in her book *The Cinderella Complex,* many women like being dependent and, deep down, want to be taken care of.[10] In point of fact everyone wants to be taken care of to some degree, although men's dependency needs are usually more hidden and less acceptable in this culture.

Some form of dependency is present in all relationships, regardless of the genders involved, and the mentoring relationship is no different. Gina depended on her second mentor, Stan Risosky, an adjunct professor who had been dean, as she would a nurturing, supportive parent, and he enjoyed this paternal role. He was sixty and she thirty-two when they met. Gina was still working in the research center, so the beginning of their mentoring overlapped with the last year of her relationship with Jack.

On her way in each morning she'd pass Stan's open door. He'd be sitting at his desk smoking his pipe, newspaper on his lap, ready for conversation. She'd sit down in the easy chair across from him and they'd talk. Sometimes they'd discuss current events or news of the department. At other times the talk centered on mastering the university hierarchy.

The first time she stopped in with a question about the teaching schedule, she realized he reminded her of her father—same age, even the same physique. As they talked, she found she and Stan had more in common: They were both from the East, now settled on the West Coast, and they were both non-WASPs (Stan was Jewish and Gina Italian) in a predominantly WASP university. "I found what he had done fascinating, his insights interesting, and him humorous," Gina recalls. "I felt very much at ease with him very quickly and I think that was mutual."

Stan was impressed that Gina had knowledge of the real world from visiting the union hall and hearing her father talk about his work. So many young people were too theoretical, came right out of the ivory tower, he thought.

As her parents' daughter, Gina was used to doing what they expected and easily fell into that role with Stan. During those early-morning talks he taught her about the informal power structure at the university. When he advised her on how to negotiate for a higher salary or how to prepare for getting tenure, she listened carefully and followed his advice.

One morning, after she had known him only a year or two, he asked her who she was planning to approach as references for tenure.

He said, "Which professors are you going to put down? Who are the leaders in the field?" Gina thought about it and gave him names and he said, "Okay, how are you going to come to their attention?"

This was five years ahead of the time she would come up for tenure. Gina thought, This is wonderful—it's not unplanned. Most women think if they work hard enough, they'll be noticed. Boy, are they in for a surprise.

The climax of their relationship came four years after they met, when Stan took her to the Law School Table, that plain Formica table in the faculty dining room reserved for the most powerful men in the law school. Eating lunch with these men gave her access to power and information.

After cracking the old boys' network and receiving tenure the following year, Gina relaxed more with Stan. She thought of him as "a favorite uncle" and began to return some favors. When he died a few years later, she spoke at his funeral and called him "a perfect mentor." To this day she remains the only woman to sit at the Law School Table.

It took four years for Gina's initiation into the private club of tenured males, the Law School Table, and with good reason. This was a tribal rite of passage, and female initiations are much riskier. The mentor faces disapproval or criticism from his colleagues because his choice is outside the old boys' network. Gina acknowledged this herself: "It's not that women have a hard time getting mentors particularly, but the mentors have a hard time persuading the colleagues to accept the women. There is more resistance." But none of the male faculty members objected. Gina joined the tenured male professors. But to reconcile this with her feminine self, she needed to see herself as the professional daughter and Stan as her father. In this way she could become one of the boys without losing her femininity.

Unfortunately Gina's success in cracking the old boys' network is the exception, not the rule. According to the National Center for Educational Statistics, 38.5 percent of all college and university teachers were women in the 1985–86 academic year, but of these, nearly 44 percent were instructors, the lowest rank. Only 11.6 percent were full professors, the highest academic tier.[11] Those who do hold top professorial ranks usually do so at teaching colleges, not at the more prestigious research institutions.[12] These statistics reinforce our conviction that women as a minority need mentors to help them advance in male-dominated academia.

Risosky, a tenured professor with a brilliant career as dean of the law school, was powerful and secure enough in his own right. He could take the risk of taking Gina to the table and could stand against the male tide if need be. But that never happened—instead, Gina's status was increased because, according to Ruth Halcomb in *Women Making It,* "A man has more power and prestige of his own so that he can be more effective in enhancing the prestige of a protégé."[13] Because she received the stamp of approval first from Stan and then from the other men, Gina became a more acceptable colleague. By taking Gina to the table, Stan publicly announced his alliance with her: others could see she was his protégé.

Through this alliance Gina became empowered—both politically and psychologically. Psychologically Stan's help was very much like a parent's: He had confidence in her, which made her feel special. This confidence as well as his gentle prodding enabled her to achieve more than she would have alone. Gina's difficulties in tooting her own horn began in childhood, when her mother would tell her she had a swelled head if she complimented herself. But Stan helped her promote herself. The men at the Law School Table accepted her because she was a brilliant, outstanding professor, not because she was the token woman. As her self-esteem and confidence grew, she achieved more, both personally and professionally. (However, never once in our interviews did she talk of her accomplishments.)

Stan also empowered her politically. A cadre of senior professors saw her as someone other than one of those faceless people who probably wouldn't get tenure. Because of her association with Stan and the men at the table, these senior professors perceived her as having more potential. Once she received tenure, one professor even said to her, "Now I'm going to bother to learn your name. It's so much effort. These young people come and go so fast."

After the senior professors accepted her, her reputation grew, and the results of this snowballed. Other people in other departments in the university knew her, she was appointed to committees, and she became chairperson of some committees very early in her career—all moves with political implications.

If Gina saw Stan as the nurturing parent and Jack as the domineering one, then Melvin Moore, an internationally renowned criminologist and her third mentor, was a patriarchal figure. A secure man, Moore was generous and giving, with a national reputation for fairness, justice, and due process. Ironically Tabson, with his questionable morals, introduced her to Moore, whose ethics were above reproach. Tabson recognized Moore as an important person for Gina to know and he "forced" her to show Moore a chapter of a book she had written. "I would never have gone and knocked on the door of an internationally renowned figure and said, 'Here, read this chapter,' " says Gina. But Jack ordered her to go over to the College of Arts and Sciences, where Moore teaches, and even phoned Moore to alert him she was coming.

Gina's relationship with Moore also began in the last year of her mentoring with Jack and coincided with her mentoring with Stan. Women often have parallel or overlapping relationships with their mentors. For clarity in writing, we have examined each of these relationships separately and labeled Stan as the second mentor and Moore the third.

When, despite her misgivings, Gina walked across campus, she found an elderly man in his midsixties who was cordial and respectful, immersed in an office filled with books. A true scholar, he loved nothing more than discussing ideas and philosophies and stimulating young people to think. He spent hours with Gina going over that chapter, which was the first of many intellectual sessions they enjoyed together in their ten-year relationship.

He told Gina about his seminar on the impact of the drug culture on Americans abroad, and she asked to sit in. Since she knew more than the students on the subject, the seminar became a mini-dialogue between the two of them, and their intellectual mentoring became solidified.

"He developed my thinking," says Gina. "If you give a young scientist ideas, you help his career. Melvin got me thinking about models in my field. Through our discussions he enlarged my vision of models I could propose."

From a very early date Moore introduced her to people with international reputations in her field who came to town. Interestingly Gina believes he did not introduce her to these people to advance her career, as Jack Tabson and Stan Risosky had done. He had no political sense, she says, and thinks he did it to stimulate her intellectually.

She and her husband often attended dinner parties at Moore's house with men whose names filled *Who's Who*. The conversation always centered on academia and scholarship, so she knows very little about Moore's personal life. "Does he believe in God? Does he go to church? Who's his favorite painter? His favorite musician? I have no idea," she says. Moore did not make small talk. "He's a classic professor who thinks only of developments in his field."

After she received tenure, Moore asked her to edit a journal with him. They now give the drug-culture seminar together. "We are now seen by some people in the field as something of a team with a senior and junior member," notes Gina. Her association with Melvin Moore has increased her credibility and visibility.

By virtue of his age and status Melvin Moore also served as a father figure for Gina, but in different ways from her two other mentors. He was first of all a patriarch, someone worthy of respect and reverence because of his age, position, and dignity. He was a godfather, a special person who cared for Gina in a unique way. And he was a rabbi, a scholar removed from the mundane world who influenced Gina's thinking. He had strong ethical standards and guided her intellectually. Although neither Gina nor Melvin was Jewish and the subject of their study was not Judaism, Moore's mentorship followed the Jewish tradition of reading the Talmud with a personal tutor. He stimulated her thinking by creating a dialogue, also reminiscent of the Socratic method from her law school days. These methods provoked Gina to question her previous beliefs. Moore was more of a symbolic father than the other two mentors.

Moore enjoyed helping Gina flourish as a teacher and seeing her develop as a scholar in her own right. He experienced the pride a parent feels when his child has turned out well. As with parenting, though, mentoring is not all giving. The mentor also gains something. Levinson writes, "The mentor is doing something for himself. He is making productive use of his own knowledge and skill. He is learning in ways not otherwise possible. He is maintaining his connection with the forces of youthful energy in the world and in himself. He needs the recipient of mentoring as much as the recipient needs him."[14] The protégé, the recipient of his knowledge, helps him stay vital. Mentor and protégé give a gift to each other, both receiving one in return.

Midlife mentoring is part of the developmental process that psychoanalyst Erik Erikson called "generativity," helping create a new generation of offspring.[15] People typically serve as mentors in middle age when they are already successful in their careers or are at a turning point in their lives: they can turn inward, rest on their laurels and call it quits, or they can turn to the next generation and pass on what they know and whom they know. While Gina's mentors were all past this point—they were closer to retirement age—they received the same benefits as younger mentors.

Although women can create "new life" biologically, men cannot. Mentoring allows men to regenerate themselves through their work, which their protégé carries forth. This may be another reason that there are not more women mentors: Most women have already regenerated themselves with their own children, so they don't have the same unfulfilled generativity needs that men do. At midlife women want to concentrate on developing their own careers.

Gina's mentors, all older men, chose generativity, although they expressed it in different ways. Jack Tabson cared for Gina in his own way and, through her work in his research center, helped her career advance. But his ego interfered with her development, so she needed to part company in order to fully develop as a person and a professional. Stan Risosky was the caring, supportive parent who nurtured Gina. Through his contacts and his caring, he helped her make a name for herself in academia. She received the respect and trust of the tenured professors much faster than she could have done on her own. Melvin Moore, the more distant patriarch, influenced Gina intellectually and morally by his high standards.

Gina often wonders why she was so fortunate to have three mentors when many women can't find one. "I don't think of myself as extraordinary, and I don't understand why I was able to have mentors. Am I doing something different from other women or am I just truly lucky?" She concludes, "I was lucky."

In many ways Gina *was* lucky: She is in academia, which is somewhat less pressured and less bottom-line oriented than a business or corporation. But we feel calling her lucky does an injustice to her own attributes and makes her success seem accidental. Even though her gender and personality tended to minimize her talents, her brilliance and important contributions to criminal law impressed the tenured male professors. That she was one of the few women in the law school and may have reminded these men of their daughters were important factors too. She also felt comfortable with older people. She treated them with deference but was not submissive. She could debate with them and hold her own. She was not offended by cursing, off-color jokes, or references to sex. And she didn't take herself too seriously; she could laugh at herself. Lastly, when opportunities to advance her work or herself presented themselves, she seized them.

Like Gina Carbone, many women choose to relate to their male mentors as father figures. This is a safe, comfortable way to relate to men in the workplace. It allows both men and women to avoid uncomfortable sexual issues. However, it also prevents them from relating to each other as full human beings, because in many cases the father/daughter roles can be limiting, as we've discussed. Although it is natural to bring ways of relating from the family to other relationships, our hope is that as men and women work together more frequently as colleagues, they will become more comfortable together. Then they will have less need to rely on these familiar roles and will become freer to relate to each other as full, authentic human beings, acknowledging all parts of themselves.

CHAPTER FIVE

❖ ❖ ❖

The Enmeshed Pair

Brenda Marks did not know how she was going to get through another day. Out of work for six years with a preschooler and a toddler at home, she felt like she was the lead in *Diary of a Mad Housewife.* She had to get back to work but didn't know if she could pull herself together enough to do her résumé and write a cover letter.

She had had an impressive career with a prominent L.A. advertising agency, but since moving to San Francisco, she was known only as Josh's mother or Harvey's wife. Tired of hearing her complain, Harvey finally suggested she use his business contacts to find a job. She spent the next week at the typewriter, working feverishly in her bathrobe, and sent out letters to six ad agencies. She received six phone calls; everyone was impressed with her L.A. agency experience.

She was particularly interested in working for Bert Paley, forty-eight, a tall, lean man with a thick head of gray hair and a full beard, who was president of Paley Advertising, because he had told her to bring the kids if she couldn't find a sitter.

Brenda recalls their first meeting. "When we met, we knew we simply had to find a way to move forward together. The man is just charismatic. He has a personal magnetism that's very powerful. There just was an immediate, compelling quality to our reaction to one another. It did not develop incrementally over time. It was there in the first seconds and it never went away."

Bert, too, remembers that initial meeting. "Brenda is so different in so many ways and very bright. She's very creative and has a rather unusual, perhaps unique, knack for grabbing hold of a moment in dramatic and memorable ways. She's not always appropriate, but she positions herself as different, and that difference was very interesting to me.

"I offered her a job as my assistant, without any real job description or anything else. I just wanted her to be around."

Everyone brings her or his psychological needs into the workplace. It is unrealistic to expect men and women to leave their psychological baggage at home when they go to work. If a man needs to be loved and adored at home, he will bring those same emotional needs to the office. If a woman is used to relating to men socially as a dependent, helpless female, she will relate the same way to men at work.

Both women and men bring to the workplace ways of reacting that are typical and comfortable for them. The reactions, feelings, perceptions, and ideas that make each person unique accompany her wherever she goes. These patterns develop from relationshps with spouses, children, and friends. But the genesis of most of these patterns goes back many years to the family of origin. As we discussed in the two previous chapters, the way we learn to relate to others is modeled after our parents. Many therapists and popular theorists have commented on the tendency of people to repeat the themes and patterns from their early life in their later intimate relationships.[1] "To some large or small degree when we attain adult status most of us have not put our childish things behind us," writes Maggie Scarf in *Intimate Partners*. "We are deeply influenced by the patterns for being that we observed and learned about very early in life and that live inside our heads."[2] In mentoring, just as in marriage, men and women replay old themes, patterns with which they are comfortable.

Psychodynamic therapists refer to this phenomenon as transference, when people transfer their feelings from early familial relationships to people with whom they are close today. Why did Brenda and Bert respond so strongly to each other? Did they remind each other of someone else and transfer those feelings to each other? Did they trigger an emotional reaction from another situation? They both admitted the rapport was instantaneous. The chemistry was right. There was an immediate identification and attraction that was so strong that they simply had to work together.

Once within the relationship, the mentor and protégé must define themselves. Like two people in any intimate relationship, each participant must define his or her personal boundaries. Each person wants to become close without losing his or her sense of self. They must keep their uniqueness yet bond in a way that makes the relationship whole. They must remain separate while being united. If they become too close, as Bert and Brenda eventually did, they each pay a heavy toll psychologically.

Psychotherapist Althea Horner, in her book *Being and Loving,* writes of this conflict, which begins in infancy and continues until adulthood. "The pull of the yearning for the blissful union rhapsodized by poets is a threat to their sense of being, to their sense of self or identity. They express fears of disappearing or of being swallowed up. Yet staying separate confronts them with the anxiety of the loss of sense of connection, and they feel abandoned and depressed. They experience the full force of the conflict between being and loving."[3]

In a healthy mentoring relationship the mentor and protégé relate to each other in positive ways; however, if carried to an extreme, these can become negative. For example, the protégé must identify with the mentor in order to develop a relationship, but overidentification, where the protégé can lose herself or become a clone of the mentor, is a danger. Kelly Green, a twenty-four-year-old management consultant who had little sense of self, was groping for a professional self as well and latched on to her mentor, Sharon Stafford, forty-five, a well-established consultant with a national reputation. During a joint interview we saw Kelly look at

Sharon to see how she was sitting and cross her legs in the same way. She used her hands like Sharon did and copied her mode of dress. Every time Kelly spoke, she glanced at Sharon for her reaction. In her private interview Sharon talked about how Kelly followed her around like a puppy dog. Even though these are all fairly superficial, outward signs of becoming a clone of the mentor, they do reveal an internal process as well.

In the beginning of a mentoring relationship the protégé usually idealizes the mentor. He is a role model, the ideal professional who has many of the qualities the protégé desires for herself. But as they work together, a protégé's idealization usually begins to fade, and she sees the mentor in more realistic terms. Sandra Young, the graduate student in biology we mentioned in the last chapter, who had little confidence, spoke glowingly of her adviser. "I consider her a role model and I've always tended to idealize people. I tend to see only the best in other people. I think, to a very large extent, the more critical you are of yourself, the more willing you are to see other people as better than you." This protégé's low self-esteem and her continued idealization of the mentor locked her in a subservient, childlike position. By keeping her mentor on a pedestal, the protégé also keeps herself in the "lowly" student role, while the mentor, an untouchable, remains on high.

This graduate student also became overly dependent on her mentor, a situation that can be stifling for women. But dependency is not a sign of weakness unless it becomes overdependence and enslaves the person. Everyone needs people to care about them, support them, and understand them. Men have dependency needs, just as women do, but these are deemphasized by our culture. In reality, however, men are extremely dependent. They depend on their secretaries and their old boys' network at work and on their wives at home. However, they would never label these relationships in those terms.

For both Kelly and Sandra a positive characteristic has been carried too far, causing the relationship to go awry. The protégé usually suffers the consequences most, both professionally and personally, because she is the more vulnerable one. But when the relationship becomes unhealthy, both mentor and protégé are responsible for the course of the relationship.

Brenda spent at least three-quarters of each day in Bert's company for the first three years of their relationship. She sat in his office while he made phone calls; she accompanied him on calls and meetings with clients. In the beginning she carried his briefcase and made the coffee. She read all the files, took notes, and memorized what Bert said and did.

But their time together was not all business. Brenda had a million problems she wanted to discuss. She'd plop herself down in Bert's office, say, "I feel lousy; I want to talk," and stay for three hours. Bert almost never lost his temper; he'd stay quiet. Sometimes he'd recommend classical Freudian psychoanalysis for her problems. Occasionally he'd say, "Stop it. That behavior is just not acceptable."

"I was a neurotic mess," recalls Brenda. "Very busy debasing myself and being abject and crying and God knows what." She goes on, "But Bert's a revealer. He's a sharer too. He was foaming at the mouth and spilling his guts too."

Brenda learned the business quickly, so Bert started sharing tasks with her. Then he assigned work to her independently: "Plan the association luncheon," he'd say. "Negotiate this contract." "Manage this project."

Brenda was scared and reluctant to handle projects by herself. In addition to being a "neurotic mess," she had lost a lot of confidence in her abilities from staying at home with the children. She wanted to run back to Bert's office every five minutes to tell him what she was thinking and planning, but he refused to see her. He had confidence in her abilities, far more than she had in herself. In the end whatever project he gave her was a huge success. With each success he gave her another project, larger and more complex.

"He was Elmer Gantry, and I was sitting in the tent chair, and whatever the hell he said was fine with me. I went up and threw myself on the floor and spoke in tongues," Brenda says, recalling her adoration.

The initial attraction Brenda and Bert felt for each other never left. The more they got to know each other, the more time they wanted to spend together. If a one-hour conversation was good, then a two-hour talk was better. They'd come in on weekends to work on a special project and instead spend hours just talking. They each had spouses and kids at home, but that didn't matter; they just had to be together. Their relationship never became sexual, despite the intensity and intimacy of their involvement; yet there may have been some sort of substitution going on, making up for a camaraderie they missed at home.

Bert Paley was meeting Brenda's "ministration needs," which, according to psychologist Harry Levinson, include the need for gratification, closeness, support, protection, and guidance.[4] These are often the first needs that are met in a relationship within an organization. By listening to her and counseling her, Bert also tried to meet Brenda's basic needs, but they were monumental and seemed insatiable.

Once the ministration needs are satisfied, the relationship usually moves on to a different level. But in this case it seems that Bert was compensating for what Brenda hadn't got from her parents: She never felt loved for herself. The only child of working-class Jewish parents, Brenda said she had "a kind of tortured, special childhood. I was special in school. I was special on the violin. I was this messianic thing in ribbons and bows." She wanted to be like everyone else and do "normal things" that kids do, like be a cheerleader and just hang out, but she had to perform and be special in order to receive her parents' love. Their love was conditional, based on her behavior, grades, and performance. She was looking for unconditional love and acceptance and a sense of herself.

Bert gave that to her. He was attracted to her brilliance and creativity, but he loved her for herself, not only for her achievements. Bert had also been an only child but, unlike Brenda, he grew up in a home with few demands and little affection. His father died when he was three, and he was raised by a mother who had severe emotional problems. He yearned for someone to care for him, give him guidance, and listen to him, but he never found that at home. Instead he ended up mothering his mother; he took care of an incapable parent.

Here are a mentor and a protégé who came to each other with tremendous needs and, through the relationship, satisfied them for each other. Althea Horner identifies some of the dynamics in such a relationship. "It is a kind of reenactment of the relationship with the early attachment figures as the individual experienced and interpreted it through the mind of the child," she writes. This is an unconscious process in which adults bring expectations, demands, and reactions from their childhood to present intimate relationships.[5]

Bert Paley and Brenda Marks are not alone. Other mentors have told us of their overinvolvement in their protégés' lives and careers. Thelma Rice, a television producer who is committed to helping young people advance, told us about how she pushed Lori Wilson, a young assistant, up the ranks faster than she wanted to go. Lori, who had a small child, was continually complaining about being stressed. One day Thelma came in and found her sobbing at her desk. "I just can't do it anymore," Lori moaned. "I don't want a high-powered career. I want to be home with my baby." Thelma had got so much gratification from feeling important and needed and helpful that she ignored Lori's feelings and pushed her into a situation in which she couldn't cope.

James Friar, the middle-aged teacher who said, "I've gone through life getting too deeply involved with people," finds this happening with young teachers and students whom he has mentored. "I get too close to students, so their parents get upset. The moment the kid says at the dinner table, 'Mr. Friar this' and 'Mr.

Friar that,' the parents want to know 'Who's this Mr. Friar?' What they're saying," Friar continues, "is 'You're being disloyal to the family. This outside person is corrupting you.' " James Friar is aware that overinvolvement is a problem for him, but he can't change it, even though *his* mentor pointed out the dangers. He says, "I've been saved each time because they graduate. They have to leave. That's what saves me. They go away to college or graduate school."

Psychologist Anne Alonso writes, "Everybody needs to be admired, loved, sought after, validated and even feared."[6] But in Bert Paley's case his need to be loved and admired became excessive. He saved every note Brenda wrote to him, whether positive or negative. "I need to be liked and respected and admired," he admits. But when the mentor's needs become exaggerated and the protégé has monumental needs of her own that mesh with his, difficulties within the relationship result.

Why was Bert willing to put up with Brenda's zaniness? Because she was a quick study, a hard worker, and a brilliant, creative woman. But there was another reason: She was meeting his needs as no one else had. She adored and admired him and could listen to him for hours ("I was mesmerized by him," she said), just as he would do for her.

Despite the problems within the relationship itself, it must not be forgotten that this was a highly successful mentoring relationship. Bert was a terrific teacher and Brenda an apt student. Brenda feels he taught her everything she knows about the advertising business. "I would say that he taught me technical and operational components of the business," recalls Brenda, "and on the other track he taught me behaviors: an elevation of standards, an uncompromising demand for excellence." In her interview Brenda did acknowledge the duality of their experience. "It was mentoring because of his capacity and desire to teach and my capacity and desire to learn. Without that I just think you would have been looking at two lunatics who absolutely were stroking each other's violins."

*   *   *

Bert continued to give Brenda more and more responsibility. He asked her to create a public relations profit center and then run it. He appointed her creative director. Eventually she became vice president of special projects, a catchall title that, according to Bert, meant that "Brenda does everything better than everybody else."

With each new project Bert had to push her to take the risk and then control her when she became too full of herself. They spent less time together than during the first few years, but they were still together almost constantly. Even though she had many successes under her belt, it took her years to feel confident in her abilities. "No matter how much I was learning and building myself up, I never believed there was a life after Bert. I thought that if I left him, it would be like pulling the plug on a respirator. If it weren't for Bert, I wouldn't have the work to do. And I wouldn't have the clout, the authority, and the respect. If all of that was taken away from me, there'd be no me."

Aware of her low self-esteem, Brenda entered psychotherapy and after a number of years says, "I began to have a self. That self began to have an ego, and I began to need some privacy. As I began to need less, say less, tell less, share less, it strengthened both of us."

As she began developing more confidence and more of a sense of herself and her boundaries within the relationship, Brenda began to criticize Bert publicly. "I think Bert doesn't know what he's talking about," she'd say, or "He's doing this and this and that's ridiculous." Her behavior shocked her and everyone else in the organization. However, she began to realize that she could think for herself and that *maybe* she could survive without him.

We've seen how, as Bert and Brenda's relationship developed, he gave her more difficult projects and she did them more independently, but they still remained close. With each new project she'd rant and rave that she couldn't do the work until he calmed her down and gave her assurances. Each time she succeeded but didn't feel successful. She needed his approval again and again to validate her behavior and herself.

In many mentoring situations the protégé becomes less dependent on the mentor as she grows more competent professionally. Usually, once the protégé's career is launched, the mentor's emphasis shifts to professional development. In some cases the relationship can break down at this point, because the protégé becomes more competent and needs less guidance.[7] In Brenda's case she was achieving outstanding accomplishments on her own, yet the mentor and protégé remained enmeshed. She couldn't separate from him. When she thinks of that era today, Brenda says, "I'm in tears for myself. I'm sad to see a girl who had so little ego, so little capacity to set up some boundaries." Brenda could not break out of the enmeshment until she developed a sense of self through therapy; then she could attain some distance and eventually criticize him.

Although Bert's needs also kept them together on a personal level, professionally he was acting as an effective executive. Bert was encouraging Brenda's "maturation needs," the next set of needs to be met after "ministration needs." "Maturation needs act to prevent intellectual and competitive scrawniness," writes Harry Levinson. "Fulfilled, they increase the potential of both the person and the organization. Unfulfilled, they deprive both the person and the organization."[8] Bert fostered Brenda's creativity but then needed to put in reality checks to control her. He says mentoring her was a matter of "expanding her and controlling her." He gave her the freedom and encouragement to express her ideas. At the same time, because her ideas were sometimes off the wall, he needed to contain her and rein her in. But he was not molding her into a Bert Paley clone nor into an image he desired for her. He allowed her to develop and blossom into her own person.

Mentoring has often been connected with the legend of Pygmalion. The king of Cyprus, Pygmalion carved a woman out of stone into the image he desired and then fell in love with the statue;

Aphrodite brought her to life as Galatea. But mentoring is not shaping, according to Charles Dick, senior attending psychiatrist at the Institute of Pennsylvania Hospital in Philadelphia. "Shaping is not done to people. People shape themselves. The skill in mentoring or treatment therapy involves presenting the opportunities for people to shape themselves. Both parties are influenced by the process. It's not a one-way street. Shaping implies that the master sculptor takes this shapeless lump of clay and crafts a Michelangelo. It's just not the way it is."

Bert was not molding Brenda into a specific image. Nevertheless, when she criticized him publicly and loudly, everyone, including Bert, was shocked. He wondered if he had created a Galatea. Her behavior was not acceptable. Protégés do not talk negatively about their mentors. Their loyalty is expected. It is part of the trust that is implicit and essential in the mentoring relationship.

But what if the mentor betrays this trust or exploits a protégé's loyalty? In more extreme instances a protégé's unfailing loyalty and blind trust can lead to her betrayal. When Elizabeth Kahn was a medical student in St. Louis, she thought Dr. Smithson was the perfect mentor. "He was like a father to everybody. We particularly hit it off and had a lot of common values in terms of the practice of medicine, the way we treated patients and cared about them." For a fleeting moment she wondered how he could afford such an expensive home and several cars but dismissed the thought because he was so ethical at the hospital. "His technique was like a symphony to me," she says. "When I'm in the operating room and it's a difficult situation, he's standing there right behind me, guiding my way." Her fantasy was to be in practice with him one day.

After her internship she and her family moved to the West Coast, and she went into practice with an HMO. A year later Dr. Smithson called and asked her to go into his industrial practice with him. It was a dream too good to be true. He told her he'd pay her moving expenses and her malpractice insurance, and she'd earn what the HMO was paying her plus benefits. There was some vague talk about putting everything in writing, but, says Elizabeth, "we never made a big deal about this, because it was like dealing with your father." And what kind of a daughter, she questioned, would need to put a father's promise in writing?

Elizabeth uprooted her family, her husband gave up his job, and they all moved back to St. Louis. But Dr. Smithson was never around to train her. His practice consisted of doing evaluations for people filing for disability claims. The lawyers with whom he worked always expected a favorable result for their client, and Dr. Smithson gave it to them. When Elizabeth questioned some of the diagnoses, Dr. Smithson cut her out. He scheduled no patients for her and never paid her.

In the end Elizabeth sued Dr. Smithson for her moving costs, her malpractice insurance, and the salary he owed her. "Here was this guy whom I loved and trusted, and every day was like getting stabbed in the back," she says. "I felt like I was failing him, like it was a father and I hadn't met his expectations. I felt awful." In her mind her mentor had become her father and she assumed he would take care of her, like a father, so she would not have to look out for herself. But this was fraud; she had been swindled. Anyone would have difficulty dealing with a betrayal like this, but Elizabeth's overidentification with her mentor made it worse. Elizabeth went into a deep depression and needed psychotherapy to help her put the ordeal with her mentor in perspective.

The impact of an unethical or dishonest mentor can be devastating on a protégé, as Elizabeth learned. Donald Myers and Neil Humphreys state, "Mentors are often selected because of their technical expertise or leadership skills; little thought is given to their personal habits or ethics."[9] Mentors who discriminate, misuse funds, or cheat on their taxes are poor role models, but protégés often deny these qualities because of their blind loyalty, trust, and idealization.

Although it happens less often, mentors, too, can be betrayed by their protégés. Tim Wolff, a partner in a management consulting firm, worked closely with his protégé, Sondra Dayton. They became good friends as they traveled together, put on seminars together, and collaborated on various projects. Tim often played the third-party negotiator between Sondra and another partner for whom Tim had a long-term dislike.

"I spent hours and hours and hours of my time, between the two of them, negotiating points, making sure they listened—like a marriage counselor," he recalls. After several months of this he learned through the office grapevine that Sondra and the partner were having an after-hours affair, while he was negotiating their fights on office time. "I felt abused, used, cheated, and angry," he says. Sondra left the company shortly thereafter. This situation is akin to what family therapists call triangulation, in which two people resolve their stress by bringing in a third party. His partner and his protégé used Tim to diffuse the tension in their relationship. He thought he was being helpful; in reality he was being used.

When Brenda had been working for Bert for ten years, he suddenly sold the company. Bert did not tell Brenda until the papers were signed. "That's when I realized that he had a separate life from mine," she recalls. At first she was furious, then she felt sad and abandoned—how would she survive without him?

About six months later she made a comment to the new owners about Bert that he could not forgive. She didn't deny it when he confronted her, but it caused both of them to contemplate life without each other. She says, "I felt about as bad as you can feel, but I didn't feel alone. I didn't feel panicky or desperate. I felt if it turned out that I would have to be without Bert, I would be sad, there would be a great loss, but I would survive." Bert's anger and hurt were so intense that he could hardly be in the same room with her.

Bert left the company about six months after that, and Brenda stayed on for two more years as vice president for client services. Then Brenda opened her own advertising agency and experienced three years of "incredible freedom and exhilaration."

She and Bert went through a slow, difficult healing process. The incident is behind them, and they are now able to put their mentoring in perspective. "I discovered, to my shock and guilty horror, that I was damn glad to be rid of Bert. I was really ready to stop being mentored. Until I left him, I did not know how heavy the mantle was, how intrusive it had become, and how blind I had become to those intrusions."

Today Brenda feels she and Bert are peers. She has moved on to a prominent position in another San Francisco ad agency, and he has become a consultant. She sums up her feelings today: "I think he loves me. I know I love him. All of the anger, the resentment—not just from the incident, but from the separating—all of the crap is behind us. And so I feel now the way a kid does at twenty-two. He graduated from college. He loves his mother again. I feel just terrific about him and the way he's in my life."

It took a force from the outside—Bert's selling the company—to cause Bert and Brenda to separate. Would they still be together if he hadn't sold the company? Regretfully, she admitted, "I'm sorry to say that I honestly think I'd still be there." Although Brenda had grown stronger and was developing a sense of self, she could not have voluntarily separated from him. They were too enmeshed. In retrospect she knows that it was time for their relationship to end and for her to move on. But she could not have done it herself.

Brenda needed to separate to become her own person. The separation allowed her to appraise her accomplishments and take credit for them. When she saw that she could indeed take them with her, she realized how much she had internalized what Bert taught her. That the new owners offered her a position as vice president and that she could thrive at her own company are tributes to how far she has come.

Brenda had reached the third and final stage of needs Harry Levinson has delineated: the gratification of her mastery needs. She had mastered enough of the world to survive on her own. Levinson

writes, "Ministration needs require supportive and facilitative efforts that come from outside the person; maturation needs require
conditions for the natural unfolding within the person. When both
needs have been sufficiently met at each step of the person's development, the conditions are created for the next stage: the gratification of mastery needs."[10]

But to master the world, she needed to separate from her mentor. Any separation involves a loss: it is giving up the known and
moving toward the unknown. In this separation there were feelings
of anger and betrayal as well as feelings of relief and freedom.
Resolving these emotions has taken a healing period of almost five
years for Bert and Brenda. They are both able to see the relationship realistically and acknowledge how they have grown and what
they have gained.

"Even the best of all outcomes will not be without some pain,"
writes Gail Sheehy. "Just as child must inevitably see parent as less
than the repository of all the world's wisdom, so must the apprentice eventually repudiate the mentor in order to believe in her
independence. What small corner of his heart dies when she slips
away? Will she honor him, ridicule him, immortalize him in her
memoirs, dissect him with her psychiatrist, or will she simply leave
him to his sunset years forgotten?

"It is possible, of course, that after a predictable period of
strain during which the seeker is distancing herself from her former
guide, the two will find their way back to a footing as friends. This
requires an exceptional degree of sensitivity on both their parts."[11]
Brenda and Bert were able to do that and today see each other as
peers and friends.

Could their enmeshment have been avoided? "Although developmental relationships require a certain degree of interaction and
intimacy, the two must be balanced to avoid an excess or dearth of
either element," write James G. Clawson and Kathy Kram. To
avoid enmeshment, they suggest offsetting attractions by identifying the other person's shortcomings, avoiding discussing personal
matters, and striving to maintain a professional, platonic relation-

ship. They also recommend that the mentor and protégé assess and discuss the consequences of growing too close.[12] However, in light of the length and intensity of Bert and Brenda's relationship, these recommendations seem impractical if not downright silly. Often the mentor and protégé don't realize the potential for enmeshment until they *are* enmeshed and the damage has been done.

Perhaps Brenda would have been less enmeshed if she had seen the mentor as a transitional figure, which is how Daniel Levinson originally conceptualized him. For the male the mentor is a combination of parent and peer, someone who helps the young man make the transition from childhood to adulthood.[13] This theory cannot be applied strictly to women because of the different developmental patterns, as we've discussed. But if women like Brenda were to view the mentor as a transitional figure and see the relationship as impermanent, perhaps they would have less likelihood of becoming enmeshed.

However, mentoring, to be successful, requires intensity and involvement and even, to some degree, intimacy. This can result in more of a problem for women. In general, women have more difficulty being autonomous than becoming attached; they tend to be happier within a relationship than without one. Once in a relationship, it's easier for women to become too involved than to pull back and separate. Knowing this about themselves may help women try to keep some distance between themselves and their mentors.

CHAPTER SIX

❖ ❖ ❖

The Interracial Pair

Susan Richards likes to call herself an acceptable black. In high school, when clubs needed a token black, she was it. Her English was impeccable and she got along with everyone. She learned that from her grandfather, a mailman who was the state's first black justice of the peace. His small office off the side of their house drew people of all races and cultures, from college professors to murderers. He taught Susan to talk to them all and to treat each one with dignity.

Susan never knew her father. When she was a baby, her mother moved to Baltimore to get her nursing degree, so Susan's grandparents raised her in nearby Hightstown. They made her feel special even though she was forced to live in Ward 6, where all the blacks were segregated. Because of her grandfather's status the Richardses were looked upon by the other blacks as "uppity" and "well off." In fact they weren't richer than anyone else, but they always held their heads high when they walked down Main Street.

The white community perceived the Richardses as acceptable blacks for the same reasons other blacks shunned them. Nevertheless the white community was too prejudiced to include them in their social events.

So Susan grew up within the black community yet not really a part of it. Her huge extended family, which congregated in Hightstown to celebrate every birthday, graduation, and funeral, provided her with support. The clan even had family reunions annually from 1915, with handwritten minutes to prove it.

Susan had a rough adolescence. She got pregnant twice in high school, yet her family supported her and cared for the infants so that she could get her high school diploma. She didn't let two children hold her back. She was determined to make something of herself. Her mother, who worked as a nurse in Baltimore, took care of Susan's infants so that she could go to college. Susan completed two years and then dropped out to get married. She and her husband got a small apartment in Baltimore.

Ten years ago, at age twenty-three, she began working as a typist at FFT Corporation, a giant food conglomerate. Early on, she made no secret of her career goals: to make $100,000 a year by the time she reached forty and eventually to become a vice president for strategic planning for a major corporation.

Like Susan Richards, most blacks live in a bicultural world. They grow up among a black family and friends in a black neighborhood; their churches and community organizations are also black. However, the dominant culture around them is white: the schools, health care systems, and businesses and corporations. A career-oriented woman must straddle both cultures. She lives in a black culture but enters the white world every day to work. She often experiences tremendous stress in balancing these two parts of her life.[1]

As a minority in American society as well as in the professions and corporations, blacks are frequently on the fringes.[2] Like women, they are not part of the old boys' network and face similar problems in being integrated into corporate, professional, and academic cultures. Because of their minority status, they must work twice as hard, be extra smart, and be especially pleasing to get the approval of the white male majority. Like women they, too, can move ahead only so far, until they hit a glass ceiling and then are shut out of the upper echelons.

Is it an advantage to be a black woman or a double negative? In reviewing research on black women's career experiences, David

Thomas and C. P. Alderfer note that one researcher found black women in a unique position, because there are no prescribed roles for them in corporate America as there are for black men and white women. Some may say that would give the black woman greater flexibility, but this lack of roles could also be the basis for racial and gender discrimination. She may also be preferred for hiring because her status as a black and a woman gives a "two-for" for affirmative action.[3] On the other hand, a black woman may feel doubly stressed because of both gender and racial discrimination. In addition a black woman must constantly balance the strain between the black culture where she grew up and lives with the white world in which she works. Two studies revealed that black women registered higher stress levels than those reported by the general population; this often stems from their sense of lack of control over their lives. Another study of over five thousand managers cited that black women expressed more criticism of their work experience than any other race or gender group.[4]

A mentor can help a black woman manage this stress by easing her integration into the white corporate culture. He can serve as her coach, sponsor, or mentor by teaching her, advising her, and paving her way in a predominantly white male environment.

In this chapter we will be speaking of the interracial pair as a white male mentor and a black female protégé, since that pairing is the interracial one most typically found today. Although our sample of interracial pairs is small, it does illustrate well the findings in the literature on the effect of race on career mobility. Mentoring for blacks, like mentoring for women, has grown out of affirmative action programs that are an attempt to reverse discrimination. Despite these programs, though, studies on developmental relationships for racial minorities have not increased in the last two decades.

However, a review of the research literature does show that capable and talented black women have found mentors. Malone (1981) found that 82 percent of black female administrators she studied said they had mentors. Ford and Wells (1985) found that 65 percent of eighty black public administrators and executives had mentors, and Murray (1982) found that 51 percent of her study of black middle-class men working in a predominantly white corporation in the Midwest had mentors.[5] In our sample 75 percent of black women had mentors. Of those who had mentors 66 percent had white mentors, 17 percent had black mentors, and 17 percent had both a black and a white mentor. The women we interviewed were all professional or managerial middle-class women, although some grew up in working-class families, like Susan Richards. Most of the research has also been done on this population.

The day Susan punched in as a typist for administrative supervisor Budd Churninsky, she knew she'd like working for him because he was so outspoken and outrageous. Everyone in the office was surprised they hit it off, because Budd had a reputation for being prejudiced. "He *is* a prejudiced person," says Susan. "He can't deal with people who slough off their capabilities and don't perform. It doesn't matter if you're white, red, or blue." Budd's reputation stemmed from an incident involving someone who was incompetent who happened to be black.

"Get your butt in here and take a letter," he'd yell to her from his side of the partition separating their offices.

"Cool it. I'm coming," she'd shout back. This constant yelling back and forth went on all day. Eventually the other workers, each partitioned off in the huge room, grew accustomed to the loud banter and even ignored Budd's cursing and crude language.

Susan found Budd's zaniness refreshing in the conservative, uptight corporate environment. She felt she was just as crazy as he, but she tended to conform more, not wanting to jeopardize her job or her future at FFT. She often wondered how he dared say some of the things he did.

Although they joked around a lot, Budd was quietly observing Susan's work, demeanor, and style. He noted her efficiency and her flexibility and congeniality and began thinking about helping her get ahead.

"What do you really want to do here?" he asked her one day.

She told him that she wanted to be an account executive. Although other people in the organization had laughed at a secretary (she had her first promotion in six months) wanting to get into the management ranks, Budd took her goal seriously and set about to help.

But first he told her, "You're lazy. Get off your ass and go back to school."

In many ways interracial mentoring is like any mentoring relationship. It involves an intimate relationship that goes through the same stages as one in which mentor and protégé are of the same race, and it contains many of the same dynamics. But an interracial mentoring relationship is much more complicated one. The powerful difference in race, which cannot be overlooked, leads to other ramifications.

In cross-racial mentoring relationships, the initiation phase is longer. This is the stage when the mentor and protégé are getting to know each other; the protégé idealizes the mentor, his skills, and his potential for help; and the basis for identification is established.

While this process does occur to some extent in cross-racial relationships, the context in which it occurs is more charged. David Thomas, an assistant professor of Organizational Behavior in Human Resource Management at the Harvard School of Business who has written widely on interracial professional relationships, has defined this as "the *reconnaisance period* of the initiation phase" in "which the mentor and protege *begin to explore the potential for a relationship*."[6] They first must each resolve their inhibitions in order to find a common meeting ground for their feelings and then for their identification. This is a much more cautious and thought-out approach.

Typically the mentor gathers information about the protégé and watches her from afar (without her knowledge), to assess whether his initial impressions are correct and whether he wants to become involved. Since mentoring someone of another race is a risk for him, he wants to make sure this is the right move before he commits himself publicly, even though he may have supported her privately. When the mentor offers the protégé public support, it signals to her that the mentor has chosen her as a protégé. She then begins to develop her own expectations for the relationship.[7]

But, unlike in *intra*racial mentoring relationships, in *inter*racial mentoring the protégé doesn't develop an expectation about the mentor's willingness or ability to help with her career—until there is concrete evidence of this.[8] In other words the protégé does not get swept up in a dream of how the mentor will transform her career, although she may idealize him to some degree later on. This realistic perspective has a positive aspect: By not idealizing the white mentor and, in a sense, waiting to bestow her trust, the black protégé protects herself from becoming more vulnerable.

Identification is complicated by differences in race and gender. The people involved come from different spheres with different perspectives and often have preset notions and stereotypes about each other's worlds. Budd, for example, had little contact with blacks as he was growing up. His father was an officer in the National Guard, and they moved frequently, as often as every six months. He tended to keep to himself because he knew his friendships wouldn't last more than a few months. When he was ten, they settled in a small town in Virginia. His father went overseas (it was during World War II), and he was raised by his mother. In his high school class there were a handful of blacks in a class of four hundred. "Prejudice was not in my vocabulary," he says. "I'm a goal-oriented person. Let's get the job done. I don't care what color you are."

Susan, as we described, grew up without a father in a warm, loving extended family. However, she experienced prejudice first-hand in her community. As a young girl she became aware of the need to put whites at ease in her presence and had developed the skills and street smarts to do this gracefully.

The mentor and protégé must find a basis for their identification. Since they may not find a common ground in terms of cultural or ethnic background, religion, or socioeconomic class, interracial pairs need another basis for their identification. According to Thomas, technical competence is the major source of identification in the cross-racial mentor-protégé relationship.[9] Technical competence comprises professional ability, knowledge, and skills. The protégé sees the mentor as someone who has the qualities she desires; she admires them and needs this information for her professional growth.

In *intra*racial mentoring relationships, the mentor often "sees" himself in the young protégé, almost in a parental way. He recognizes in the protégé some of the same qualities he possessed as an up-and-coming professional. This identification creates a bond and makes the mentor want to help the protégé.

However, this psychological identification does not happen as often in interracial mentoring; when it does, it may take longer or it may be denied. Susan and Budd's case was one of the minority of interracial relationships where a strong identification took place. In Susan, Budd "saw" someone who was lazy about her education, as he had been. Budd, who had wasted his own talents, thought she was headed in the same direction if she was not pushed. "I could kick myself for not pursuing my education when I was younger. I could see a waste of talent if she didn't get off her tail. She had the ability, and the corporation would pay for it," stressed Budd. He had joined the army after high school and then took ten years to get his associate degree at night.

People involved in interracial mentoring do not usually use parental metaphors to describe the relationship. "It is more difficult for me to see a senior white male, given all the baggage that comes with racial history in this country, as a parental figure. He doesn't remind me of my father," notes Tyrone Jones, a black professor.

White protégés may look at the mentor as a parental figure, but blacks cannot, agrees Veronica English, thirty-nine, an assistant to the commissioner for the Department of Human Services for the state of Illinois. "You are not this person's son or daughter. And even if *they* choose to forget it for a moment, you cannot."

She goes on, "I know who my parents are. In a very real sense my parents raised me to have a particular view of the world and to understand the world is dangerous; it's majority white and you have to cope with that. To take on someone white—even if it was the commissioner, whom I work for now—and use it like a father-daughter relationship isn't going to work. His view of the world is different from mine, and the things he's going to advise me to do are not going to work for me because the larger world is still remembering that I'm black, whether he does or not."

She concludes, "It would be dangerous for me to say, 'Yes, I have a father-daughter relationship with this man. Wherever he goes, I can go.'"

A bond does form in interracial mentoring, but not because the relationship is consciously reminiscent of parent and child. The bond may be because both mentor and protégé feel they are underdogs, on the fringes of the in-group. In the early stages of their relationship Susan had not learned why Budd was an underdog and was willing to risk his reputation by allying with her. All women are underdogs and outsiders to the white male establishment, but this is particularly true of black women. In fact far more black women verbalized this in our discussions than white women did, perhaps because white women were quicker to identify with the larger culture.

With white male mentors and black female protégés there are other factors that could be barriers to identification. There is a long history of sexual taboos between blacks and whites, which could make white men reluctant to pair with black women and to publicly support and promote them. A simple act, such as going out to lunch together or stopping for a drink after work, can create office gossip about sexual involvement. Susan Richards and Budd Churninsky never went out alone. If they went out to dinner or traveled for business, it was always as part of a group.

The mentor's own experience with race affects the identification process as well.[10] His experiences outside of work will determine the mind-set he brings to his work relationships. Budd, as we've seen, had little contact with blacks growing up. It wasn't until he joined the army that he met blacks, but he denies having preconceived notions about them. For protégés, too, their past experiences with whites will have an impact. Tyrone Jones recalls his days as a doctoral student writing his dissertation with a white professor-mentor. "That relationship was in its fourth year before I would allow anything that would actually make me emotionally dependent with my mentor to come out. The other black males I knew allowed less of their dependency to come out than the white male grad students."

All black males may not have the same experience, but this professor avoided being in a dependent position because it brought back collective memories of being subservient to whites. Veronica English had the same reason for refusing to get coffee for a white female boss.

Jones is now tenured at an Ivy League university. He recalls his students' reaction on the first day of class. "Whether we admit it to ourselves or not, we walk into organizations with preset views about who belongs where. My students, black and white, come into my first-year introductory core course, which means they have to take me. If you don't take me, you don't get out of undergraduate school. They're shocked, black and white. Why? Because I'm black. Ninety percent of my students have never had a black person in authority in their lives. Never." At the end of the semester many students thank him for changing their perceptions.

Racial differences can impede identification between mentors and protégés. These differences also make trust a continual issue in cross-racial relationships. Black protégés have told us it is important that they never forget where they came from and that their world is different from the white world. One black protégé said bluntly, "Fundamentally I don't trust white people to have my interests continually at heart." Because of this distrust (which is not often articulated so blatantly to whites), mentor and protégé typically keep their distance and rarely get as close as a mentoring pair of the same race. Both are aware of certain boundaries that they are not comfortable crossing. For example, while many white mentors and white protégés told us of having dinner at each other's houses and meeting each other's spouses, interracial mentoring pairs rarely did this. A black protégé will receive plenty of instrumental career guidance, but the intimacy may not be as deep as in an *intra*racial relationship.

One Monday morning Budd gave Susan a pile of letters to be typed. One in particular, about an Alcoholics Anonymous meeting, caught her eye. This bit of information surprised her at first, but then it made sense of Budd's behavior. He was a recovering alcoholic, she thought, and no doubt had plateaued at FFT. Now she understood how he could risk his reputation by helping her— he had nothing to lose. She later learned that FFT had agreed to keep him on at his current level if he would go for treatment that they sponsored.

Susan and Budd never discussed this letter, but her knowledge of Budd's problems drew them closer. "By virtue of the disease and the recovery process," says Susan, "you hit rock bottom where you no longer look down at anything, including a roach. Either you become a very real person or you don't survive." Knowing they were both underdogs in a sense tightened their bond, and Budd worked more openly to help Susan meet her goals.

Because of FFT's elaborate hierarchical system, Susan needed to pass a number of steps over several years to get into the management track. First she had to be promoted from exempt to nonexempt, and then she had to go through sales training. Budd made her appraisal 110 percent higher than the person with the most seniority, which automatically promoted her to the job right under sales trainee. He pushed her through and then created a job on his national account team for her to work for him as a manager.

The team often went out to lunch together and traveled en masse to other states to service their accounts. Susan and Budd continued to work closely together for another year. Their banter continued, and Susan felt more at ease in sharing in the repartee. The next year, when Susan's teenage son had drug problems, she turned to Budd for advice. He listened to her and counseled her, which seemed to draw them even closer.

Budd continued to pull strings for Susan, so that within three years she had her foot in management ranks. She says, "If I had not had a Budd Churninsky, I'd still be in the clerical ranks. It took somebody who was not afraid to continue to push. Many other people who had career aspirations of their own would have backed off. I feel he had my best interest at heart. Many times you get a manager who won't fight that hard because of the repercussions for his own career—or the perceived repercussions. Budd didn't care."

As Susan and Budd got to know each other better, the initiation phase melded into the cultivation phase, the longest stage, during which the mentor and protégé are engrossed in working together. A deeper intimacy and attachment develop as the mentor and protégé feel more comfortable together. The mentor encourages the protégé, teaches her and promotes her, as Budd did. Budd had a great sense of fun and saw life as a game. He enjoyed getting the upper hand and maneuvering the numerical ratings in Susan's favor so that she could move ahead.

In this stage and the ones that follow, the interracial mentoring relationship follows the same process that all relationships follow. In fact by this point Susan and Budd identified so much with each other that they denied each other's races. "I don't care what color you are," says Budd. "If something needs to be said, I'll say it." Susan laughed when Budd said things like this, because it reminded her so much of her grandfather. While most black protégés may not allow themselves to see their mentors as father figures, in this case Susan's identification with Budd became so tight and so color-blind that she consciously identified him with her grandfather.

A mentor with a protégé of a different race is sticking his neck out because he is allying himself with someone outside the accepted (white male) corporate culture. The protégé must be exceptionally competent or show unusual potential for the mentor to risk his reputation. While having a protégé usually enhances the status of the mentor, mentoring a minority member can be fraught with difficulty. What if the protégé does not measure up? Or worse yet, what if she pulls the mentor down with her? If the mentor's peers do not accept the protégé, the mentoring relationship can isolate the mentor from his colleagues, those with power and influence.

According to Professor Thomas, the man who would choose to mentor a woman of a different race has certain qualities that distinguish him. First, he is someone who is socially marginal himself.[11] As a white male he may be part of the old boys' network, but he is not a leader. There are a number of reasons that he is on the fringes of that network. Perhaps his career has peaked, or he has overpowering personal or personality problems. Because of his marginal position he may not have many relationships at work and may feel safer choosing a black woman, who is unlikely to reject him, to mentor.

Budd Churninsky fits this definition perfectly. As a recovering alcoholic he had plateaued. The corporation had seen him through his rehabilitation. Budd knew he was not going to progress any further, but he also knew the corporation was not going to fire him. His position thus provided a security that allowed him to do as he pleased and say whatever entered his head. Ironically Susan Richards benefited from his position and modeled his behavior. She herself became more like him as she moved up the corporate ranks.

His marginal position also made him a risk taker. He did not have as much to lose as someone who is completely ensconced in the ruling body. Actually Budd had nothing to lose, and Susan had everything to gain. But their relationship made him feel more powerful because he was doing so much for her.

Interestingly a man who mentors minorities may not do it because he is a strong proponent of affirmative action and may not be willing to put his career on the line behind his beliefs. Instead, mentoring an unconventional professional appeals to his maverick nature. Budd relished thumbing his nose at the white corporate establishment. So did Susan, and this tightened their bond. They were two mavericks bucking the white corporate structure: a black woman and a white male recovered alcoholic with a dead-ended career. Hearing of cases like this may encourage women to look for mentors in nontraditional ways and unconventional places.

Like all mentors a person who mentors minorities must also be a good developer of people and have influence within his work unit or company.[12] "When I'm with my peers," notes Budd, "and we're evaluating a multitude of people, I will fight for and get my people positioned in their appraisal process so that they get the attention of higher people. When I recommend someone, no one complains. No one comes back and says, 'You gave me a turkey.'" This behavior, typical of strong corporate mentors, is particularly important for a white man mentoring a black woman, because he must justify this unorthodox relationship to his colleagues. Nevertheless, Budd says, "I got no credit for promoting a black person."

The interracial mentor, then, is typically someone who is an iconoclast, willing to go against the corporate culture, or someone who has little to lose professionally. His career has leveled off, he can't progress any farther for various reasons, or he does not care whether he advances. Thomas writes, "Persons who were plateaued but viewed as influential were those most likely to have mentored a black person in an area of the company that was felt to be hostile to blacks. However, none of these mentors voiced that part of their reason for sponsoring was to promote integration or affirmative action. Each stated that his primary motivation was that the individual was competent and deserving."[13] Some people may mentor to promote affirmative action, but they are in the minority.

That still doesn't completely explain why a white male mentor chooses to mentor a black woman. If he's not doing it for ethical or judicious reasons and it's not going to help his career because his career has already peaked, then why does he put the time and energy into such a risky endeavor? The relationship may give him a feeling of acceptance that he doesn't have in other relationships at work. Because of his marginal position the white "wounded" mentor may feel a bond with a black woman; they are both underdogs in a white corporation. This creates a strong point of identification for both of them. Lastly he may get the same sense of satisfaction that all mentors receive from guiding a protégé, particularly one with two strikes against her.

A mentor is especially important for a black woman because he can increase her prominence within an organization, especially her visibility to other departments. "You can become invisible as a woman or as a minority because you are not a member of staff hired by that particular division; it is very easy for them to overlook you," said Veronica English, who has started her own mentoring programs for minority women and men in the Department of Human Services. Professor Thomas has found support for English's feelings in his study on the impact of race on managers' experiences of gaining mentoring and sponsorship. "Blacks are frequently on the periphery of the information and social networks which emerge naturally in organizations," he writes, noting that blacks need to look outside the formal network and to other blacks for support.[14]

Ideally a black woman should have two mentors, each with a different function: a powerful white male mentor to help her progress in her career and move up the corporate ladder, and a black mentor, preferably female, to give her someone to identify with and to provide support in struggling in the white professional world. The black female mentor could help her developmentally, and the white male mentor's sponsorship could help her gain more power and combat discrimination. This is also our recommendation for white women: that they find a powerful male mentor as well as a powerful female mentor or supportive peer.

Lucinda Broom, a thirty-eight-year-old divorced black woman who is a researcher at a pharmaceutical corporation, was fortunate to have both a black and a white mentor. Both men, they performed very different roles for her. Her first mentor, John Carsen, was part of the white establishment; he pushed her to try harder and take risks. When she worked the night shift, he encouraged her to read technical manuals rather than popular magazines. He'd say to her, "Why don't you read this?" or "Why don't you go do this study for a while? They need help over there." He increased her visibility by bringing her successful projects to the attention of others. Her technical competence also grew under his guidance.

Her relationship with Wes Brown, her second mentor, a black man about twenty years older than she, was very different. By now Lucinda was more established in her field, so she no longer needed the same kind of guidance and encouragement. Wes gave her the support she needed at this stage of her career.

Relationships with other blacks can provide more emotional support than cross-racial ones. Veronica English yearned for a black female mentor, but since there were none in positions of power in the state office where she worked, she was pleased simply to have a close black peer. She says, "You need someone else in the corporation who can validate or affirm that what you are seeing is actually what is happening or not. At meetings I've been asked for my opinion about music. For example, I'm expected to speak for all minorities. I can't speak for all minorities. If you tell a white peer about this experience, they say, 'You're making it up. I never noticed that.' "

Colleagues of the same race can provide this validation and are important as support for blacks in an all-white organization, but they do not serve the same function as mentors. In predominantly white organizations blacks are not usually in positions of power, so they lack the status to serve as mentors. Black professionals, businesswomen, teachers, and nurses must then rely on whites as mentors.

With Budd's help Susan Richards has continued moving up the management ranks. She is currently an account executive and industry consultant. They worked together for about three years. When she stopped working directly for him, the mentoring part of their relationship phased out. They no longer had day-to-day contact because she did not need the same kind of help from him. They continued to talk by phone, but more as equals.

Last fall, upon reaching fifty-five, Budd Churninsky chose early retirement. Susan and Budd still keep in touch, only now their conversations focus on Bud's pension plan as often as on Susan's career. They see themselves as friends. For the first time Susan's mother invited Budd for dinner to thank him, as Susan says, "for holding up the work end while she held up the personal end." Budd and Susan both came with their spouses. It was pleasant, but they probably will not see each other socially again.

Some of Budd Churninsky has rubbed off on Susan Richards. She, too, has become outspoken because, she now feels, she has nothing to lose. "People don't believe what I do. I'm finishing my master's on June third, and I've told my manager that I'm going to get the hell out of here and my reasons why and what I want to do with my life. I don't see that happening at FFT.

"I think I'm extremely marketable," she continues. "The most they can do to me is fire me, and I don't particularly give a damn about that. In that respect Budd and I are alike. Because if you fire me, it may give me the impetus I need to get my life in the direction I need to get going. So I'm subject to say anything, but not in as crass a way as Budd did."

Although Susan and Budd considered their relationship a close one, the end of mentoring was not painful for either of them. "Cross-race relationships are less likely than same-race relationships to end acrimoniously," write Thomas and Alderfer.[15] In some mentoring relationships the termination stage, when the mentor and protégé separate, can be traumatic because of their deep emotional involvement (as with Brenda Marks and Bert Paley in the last chapter). In this case, although they both call each other friends, Susan and Budd classified their relationship as more work-related than personal.

In fact Budd did not see himself as doing anything extraordinary. "If you had to label what I did," he says, "I was just the boss doing my job. I don't push dum-dums. She had the ability to get something done and on time. She was the exception. I was the facilitator, but I needed something to facilitate. I had a job to get done, and she was the one to perform it. A perfect match."

Because cross-racial mentoring relationships require mentors with special characters, minority protégés typically do not find their mentors in the usual places. Here again Susan Richards was unusual, since her boss became her mentor. It is more common for black protégés to cross traditional hierarchical boundaries, skip levels, or go outside their departments to find a mentor.[16]

When Yvonne Brown, thirty-three, now a personnel manager in a predominantly white male big-city hospital, sought a mentor, she did not approach her white boss. She went beyond the immediate line of command and sought Doris Bailey, a former nurse who was the hospital administrator. She chose Doris, an older black woman, because of her reputation for helping young women of all races move ahead.

Yvonne started at the hospital nineteen years ago as a nurse's aide with a high school diploma and three college credits. She met Doris after she had been there about five years. Doris took her under her wing. She let her sit in on meetings and observe how she handled what Yvonne called tough males. Yvonne continues, "She has a very unique, very assertive management style, and she pointed out a lot of tips on how to survive in a predominantly male organization."

Under Doris's tutelage, Yvonne received thirteen promotions. But Doris also kept long-term goals in mind and encouraged her to complete her college education. "Why should I go back to school when I am moving right along without the benefit of the paper?" Yvonne had asked. "You will receive more respect, more recognition, and besides, the dollars are going to be there for you," her mentor told her. "I'll help you, whatever it takes, you have access to me." The birth of her son interrupted her studies, but Yvonne is now finishing the remaining credits for her bachelor of science degree.

The protégé must be exceptionally competent for the mentor to support her and endorse her publicly.[17] Generally speaking, all blacks and all women must be so superior that they stand out. Blacks often feel they can't make mistakes and must be perfect; they feel that their behavior is being scrutinized and will reflect— either positively or negatively—on the whole race. A mentor does not want to be associated with someone who is less than competent, particularly someone who goes against the corporate culture. If the protégé has not yet proven her competence, then the mentor will choose someone who has high potential, so the risk of sponsorship is less (for the mentor).

In addition to technical competence, the black protégé must also have interpersonal competence, according to Thomas.[18] She must get along well with her coworkers. Blacks need considerable interpersonal skills because they are often put in the position of having to put whites at ease in their presence. An overtly angry black, no matter how competent, is going to have a difficult time finding a mentor in a corporation or institution. One of the things that impressed Budd Churninsky about Susan Richards was her ability to handle people from all walks of life—what he called her flexibility and street smarts. She could talk black jive or elegant finishing-school English as the situation demanded. When she had to travel to Dallas for a project, she went with two strikes against her, as a black and as a woman. Not only did she get the job done, but she received kudos for her performance and courage.

It's difficult for both blacks and whites to let go of stereotypes and past experiences and perceptions and relate to each other as authentic individuals, but Susan Richards and Budd Churninsky achieved that. White mentors can provide black protégés with technical knowledge and skills and help them find their way in a white organization. The mentor himself gains the satisfaction of having guided and advised a capable woman who probably would not have progressed so far without his help. But usually neither mentor nor protégé in an interracial pair experiences the same closeness and bonding as an *intra*racial mentoring pair. When the relationship does succeed, against so many odds, it is a growth experience for both.

CHAPTER SEVEN

❖   ❖   ❖

The Political Pair

Richard Hendricks: his name alone made Kathie Long tremble. Kathie had heard Hendricks's name during her first week working for the Big 8 accounting firm. Rumor had it that he was one of the most powerful partners and that he could make or break you. He was head of the bank practice in the Denver office and, to the young class of new recruits who got the word from the staff accountants, a godlike figure who could do no wrong.

Since Kathie was right out of college and feeling insecure and unconfident as an assistant accountant, she thought it best to avoid him. She had heard that his first impressions were impossible to shake, even when those select few whom he trusted tried to change his mind. She decided she would concentrate on doing the best job she could.

But Richard Hendricks, always on the alert for bright young recruits to sponsor and promote, heard about Kathie anyway. She was "spectacular," said one of his confidantes. Yet another partner, Frank, told him she was "terrible" and was not working out at all. These conflicting reports intrigued Hendricks, who thrived on a challenge. "I was going to get to the bottom of why one person whom I trusted said this person was so good and another person whom I also trusted said she was terrible. She seemed to have it all—great college grades, had traveled a lot, a strikingly pretty person—and was not using the skills she had available to her."

Without speaking a word to Kathie, Richard Hendricks, forty-two, began working behind the scenes to see if she merited an investment of his time and energy.

To advance, women need political allies—mentors. Although the popular press often claims that mentors don't help women or make a difference in their careers, we have not found this to be true. Mentors can and do help women advance.

Mentors like Richard Hendricks are part of the dominant male culture. Does allying with a mentor mean consorting with the enemy? Or is mentoring simply an instrumental relationship that can unlock the door to the corner office? If the organization itself is sexist—as in the Supreme Court case involving Price Waterhouse's denying Ann Hopkins partnership because they felt she acted "too much like a man"—what is the role of the mentor? The mentoring relationship is more complex today because so many forces affect women in the workplace. Women need to know and understand the politics of the organization; they need to be aggressive in the best sense of the word. Both of these things are new for women, so they need someone to guide their way.

As we've stated, women in graduate professional schools now constitute 33 to 40 percent of the class.[1] They've made it to "the starting gate," as one college professor called it. They have even reached a critical mass in the white-collar professions, say trend forecasters John Naisbitt and Patricia Aburdene, authors of *Megatrends 2000: Ten New Directions for the 1990s.*[2] This can lull women into a false sense of security because they then think there's acceptance for them in the workplace. But getting in does not guarantee their success or their advancement.

In fact women are not advancing at the same rate as men. They earn 71.8 cents for every dollar a man makes. In addition they earn significantly less even when they do the same job and have the same experience as or *more* experience than men. This is true whether they are assembly-line workers or partners at a prestigious law firm. A 1990 study by the *National Law Journal,* for example, found that "women lawyers at major law firms get fewer choice assignments, earn less money and still face heavy sexual harassment by their male superiors."[3]

Pundits in the popular press could point to Labor Department statistics—specifically that women hold 42.3 percent of executive, administrative, and managerial positions—to support the "critical mass" argument.[4] It is therefore necessary for us to restate that many of these female managers are clustered in smaller firms and less prestigious businesses. Less than 2 percent of top executives at Fortune 500 companies are women.[5] More upsetting is the fact that as women advance, the wage gap increases. A report done by the U.S. Chamber of Commerce in May 1987 found that corporate women at the vice-presidential level and above earn 58 percent of what their male counterparts earn.[6]

So where are all these educated, competent women going after graduate school? Why can't they advance on their abilities, as men do? After all, this is 1992, not 1972. Isn't America supposed to be a meritocracy, where people of all genders and races advance on their own merit?

Richard Hendricks sat Kathie Long down in his office. He gazed out the floor-to-ceiling windows overlooking the Denver skyline and then told her, "I don't know whether you're going to make it here or not. Frank doesn't like you. You know I have confidence in Frank's judgment. Frank and I are tight. So I'm going to give you one year, and in that one year you must prove to me that you are good, or you get out."

Kathie nodded and secretly quivered, her stomach in knots. She knew that her immediate boss, Roger, a manager, would be supervising her, but she had no idea that he would be giving Richard monthly progress reports on her.

When the reports came back, they were excellent. Frank had told him her work was a "2," so Richard expected maybe a "6." Instead he got a "10." He was delighted: he had found a woman who was bright and motivated. She was willing to work twelve-to-fifteen-hour days, and the clients loved her. She developed a specialized niche in loan loss reserves with their major banking client. Richard was used to sending the gruffest male accountants to these tough banking clients to get the necessary information, but they often came back empty-handed. When Kathie went, she charmed them. The loan officers were dying to answer her questions and even volunteered information.

Richard Hendricks had found someone as driven as he. She would be worth his time and energy because she was definitely partnership material. After a year of observation he was ready to draw her into his inner circle—his family, as it was known—but first he needed to test her himself.

He spent a full day grilling her on one particular area of an audit related to loan loss reserve. He walked around the conference room, papers in hand, and fired question after question at her. The other assistants, seated around the oblong mahogany table, were awestruck and sat there silently. She answered each question thoroughly, and if she didn't know an answer, she told him so. She appeared confident and well prepared, but inside she quaked and her stomach churned. From that day on he trusted her. She became part of his inner sanctum, and he began promoting her to his peers, the other partners. Kathie knew she had Richard's confidence after that grueling session, but knowing what power he wielded, she still couldn't relax in his presence.

The realities of the workplace support the need for mentors for women. According to the Cox Report, a study about American males' career advancement done by businessman Allan J. Cox and a sociologist, 85 percent of top male executives say their companies are eager to promote women to *middle*-management positions, while only 68 percent support women moving into *top* executive slots. Furthermore 40 percent of top executives and 43 percent of middle managers agree that women are likely to advance more slowly than men with the same qualifications.[7]

People today joke about the unsophisticated women of the forties and fifties who sipped sodas at Schrafft's in L.A. waiting to be discovered for a part in the movies. In fact this passive waiting-to-be-called mentality is still alive in the business world in the nineties. It's time women realize that they may need to consort with the powerful—that is, men—if they want to succeed. Most women still believe, as Kathie Long did, that if they do a good job, they will be rewarded. They realize they must be superior to stand out, but naively believe that's all they need to do. A male mentor commented about the naiveté of his protégé, an intelligent young woman. "We talked about situations, because I don't think she had a lot of aggression. It would never occur to her to think through how tomorrow's meeting might go and who would do what and how to be persuasive and who would win. I don't think she had that notion of winning. She thought everything was a nice, fair fight and the brightest person would win." In fact it's usually the most political one who wins.

Although women are networking more than ever, they usually network with other women, not with the men who hold the power. Within the organization they tend to isolate themselves. They don't realize that they are part of a larger organization, nor do they see themselves as integral to it. As a consequence women fail to play politics, observe hidden agendas, delegate, and use their power. "Without cooperative teamsmanship," writes executive consultant Allan Cox, "no woman ever can expect to be promoted."[8] Being part of a team means being able to accept criticism without taking it personally and being able to risk making mistakes—two areas where women and other minorities have difficulty.[9] Women are unaccustomed to seeing political relationships at work as helpful in a sponsoring, reciprocal way—even though they are very open to relationships in their personal lives.

However, Srully Blotnick, author of *The Corporate Steeplechase,* feels that teamwork is overrated. "Although Americans may greatly admire a well executed move made by a team on the playing field, at work different rules apply," he writes. "Money and promotions are at stake and only a fool would risk it by being too cooperative."[10] Teamwork has its place, but so does competition. Women need to distinguish when to be part of a team and when to be more competitive. Mentors, as more seasoned professionals, can help make this distinction.

If women are disenfranchised to this extent, then certainly they can't see themselves as powerful in a positive sense or as power holders. Traditionally women have been taught to use power negatively by manipulating men by mothering them, seducing them, or acting childlike and helpless. But if women bring these tactics into the office, they can destroy their potential collegial or mentoring relationships with both men and women. Women who recognize the behavior will mistrust one another, and men who have been manipulated by women all their lives will fear it will happen again.[11]

Women who realize that these old techniques will not work in the workplace can feel helpless and powerless. They're unsure of what to do or how to act. They know they must constantly prove their competence. While they want to advance and make a name for themselves in their careers, they don't really know how to go about it. They may realize they are dependent on the men who hold the power but often fail to see the positive implications: for instance, the fact that they are once more dependent on men can obscure the opportunity that a higher-up interested in their career presents.

Again, this is why women need mentors. In most instances women cannot advance alone. They need to form relationships at work—with both men and women—which will help them progress and give them an understanding of the powerful dynamics propelling the organization. While we stress that women need mentors in a male-dominated environment, we must emphasize again that women need not resort to the traditional male model of mentoring. Women need a series of mentors, sponsors, and peers at different periods of their adult work lives, because of both their varied developmental paths and the political realities that we have mentioned in this chapter.

Every corporation, law firm, and university has within its structure two parallel organizations: one visible and one invisible. The visible organization is described in flow charts, newspaper articles, and reports to stockholders. It is definable with projects, statistics, and reports, and it is quantifiable.[12]

The invisible organization is what author and consultant Michael Zey has labeled the shadow organization. There are no statistics to analyze it, no charts to illustrate it, and no reports to describe it. Yet it makes things happen. This is the political arena where the drama of power is enacted: the secret networks, the old boys' club, the insiders and sponsors, the mentors and protégés.[13] Richard Hendricks's real work was accomplished within this invisible organization—not at formal meetings in boardrooms behind closed doors, but in whispered conversations in hallways, over lunch or cocktails, or on the golf course. "None of the formal structures are even adhered to," complained a female corporate manager. "Jobs that are available are posted on the bulletin board. That is so fake. I've applied for three or four jobs and never been contacted. I've never been told I was turned down for a job. I've never even been interviewed for a job. Nothing."

Most women can understand the visible, functional organization. They can read the annual reports and minutes of board meetings, follow industry reports in the trade papers, and figure out the organizational hierarchy. But by virtue of their gender and minority status, they are not a part of the shadow organization, and thus they have difficulty understanding it.

In a culture dominated by men, a fear of possible sexual involvement or innuendo may hold women back from making the necessary social contacts. They may excuse themselves from social occasions because they are aware that appearing friendly may be misconstrued or be interpreted as being too familiar (these issues will be explored more fully in the next chapter).[14] Working women who have learned to draw boundaries on intimacy issues may need to reconsider them in light of the importance of these informal networks for their career progress.

Since men inhabit all areas of the power structure, women as a group will be more easily integrated into every part of the corporate world if they are mentored by the holders of power in that world.[15] Once women have mentors and are admitted into the invisible network, these all-boys' enclaves will be transformed. The resulting coed groups will give women more visibility, more clout, and more access to the most powerful. The ideal coeducational group, says Mary Patterson McPherson, president of Bryn Mawr College, "is a group of very able women working in a community of very able men who are not threatened by bright, articulate, strong-minded women."

"Don't worry about promoting yourself within the firm," Richard told Kathie during one of the long conversations they'd started having. "Just do a good job and I'll take care of it."

Kathie knew Richard was influential, but she never knew exactly what he did to promote her within the firm. She realized Richard put her in charge of meetings and projects where she had to write memos to partners and they would have to respond to her personally; he did this so that she'd develop a personal relationship with the power holders. At other times he took her to meetings with top executives. He'd introduce her as the senior accountant on the engagement (an accounting term for the account). At first she merely sat in, but once she was familiar with the client or had done the accounting research, she participated.

In addition Richard promoted her in ways unknown to Kathie. "I made sure she worked for several people, so other people could see what a wonderful job she does," he says. "When the opportunity exists where I can describe how the person is doing, I tend to use superlatives about the person. I make sure the person's pay raises are at the top of the scale. Sometimes I will ask the person to do a job that she is not prepared to do." Under his direction

Kathie succeeded when Richard took risks with her. Then Richard made sure her "name was all over."

The feedback from others made Kathie realize Richard's behind-the-scenes sponsorship must have been significant. "The other partners had confidence in me before I even worked for them. They knew my name and reputation. And other managers too," she recalls. "It was very subtle. Just looking at where I am today, I know he must have done something."

During her four years with the firm Kathie progressed from assistant accountant to staff accountant to senior accountant to manager. Today she manages audit engagements and has from ten to fifteen people working for her. She entered the firm with forty others, about half men and half women, all right out of college. She was told that only one of them would become partner (in eleven to twelve years) and that half would leave the firm. Kathie always had her sights on partnership and, with Richard's backing, felt it was within her grasp, until she realized the knots in her stomach were not just nervousness. When she got sick, everything changed.

As a mentor Richard Hendricks performed powerful sponsorship activities for Kathie—what every woman needs who wants to move ahead in her corporation. He introduced her to influential people in the company, advised her about how the system works, and gave her highly desirable assignments, and then promoted her and her achievements to the other partners.

One protégé, a sales manager from a large communications corporation, recalls how her mentor not only talked up her name but got her the support she needed to complete her projects successfully. "He made sure that the right people heard about what I was doing," she says. "He made sure that if we were working on critical sales with a customer, we got the type of support from headquarters we needed."

There's another benefit when the mentor sponsors the protégé: she can bask in "reflected power." Just by being associated with

such a powerful person, the protégé's status increases in others'
eyes. They know the protégé has the mentor's backing and resources. This in turn increases the protégé's own power and influence.[16] This "halo effect," as author and consultant Michael Zey
calls it, extends the mentor's influence far beyond his physical
presence. Even after mentors have died, the benefits of their association with the protégés live on. For example we saw in chapter 4
how Gina Carbone continued sitting at the Law School Table with
the tenured male professors after Stan Risosky died. *His* peers
included her and treated her as though he were still alive—indeed
his influence was.

The halo effect benefits the mentor too. When mentors choose
protégés with high potential and the protégé lives up to his expectations and succeeds, the mentor earns a reputation as a "people
picker." Other managers may seek him out for advice on new
employees, and his status within the company improves.[17] Richard
Hendricks developed a reputation for excellence, so that when he
nominated new partners, his endorsement of the new partner was
a "done deal." "When I put a person's name on the table, they
know pretty much what that person is like," he says. "I cannot
recall in the last five years long discussions about any of them. It's
not usually 'Who is your candidate?' It's 'Fine, next.' It's almost
that fast."

Richard Hendricks was a powerful man and was comfortable
with his power, a word that often has negative connotations for
women. But the word has many positive meanings: the ability to
get things done; the capacity to act and to mobilize resources and
people; access to resources such as time, money, and information
and to other people who hold power.[18] Power lies in the person's
title and rank in the organizational hierarchy. Who becomes powerful within an organization, according to Rosabeth Moss Kanter,
depends on the way "personal characteristics and background
combine with the way an organization distributes scarce resources
through positions to give people differential opportunities to
become influential."[19]

Mentoring usually occurs where the powerful reside—in the

middle and upper echelons of a corporation, not in the lower ranks. According to Agnes Missirian, an associate professor of strategic management at Bentley College who surveyed the one hundred top businesswomen in America, the higher up the corporate hierarchy one goes, the greater the likelihood that one has or has had a mentor. Mentoring, then, is an elite concept.[20] It is only for those who hold the power or for those with potential who want to become power holders.

However, if women are not part of this elite class and do not have a significant male mentor, they can still learn and grow and progress. One woman told us of how she got "bits and pieces" of mentoring from different people. Another woman, the president of a small college, said that she tries to learn from everyone she meets. Others use peers for support, advice, and networking. This is how mentoring is for most women today: they invent it in whatever form they can and use it whenever possible to benefit their careers.

Mentors can initiate women into the invisible political organization where business gets done, deals are made, and promotions are decided. By sharing "state secrets," as Zey calls them, mentors reveal information to protégés that would not ordinarily be shared with a subordinate.[21] When Gina Carbone sat at the Law School Table with her mentor and his male colleagues, she learned inside information about tenure decisions that would not ordinarily be discussed with an untenured person, especially a woman. Her acceptance at the table meant that her mentor and his peers considered her trustworthy, that she had potential and would eventually be moving up to join their ranks. Unfortunately, however, Gina was the exception; other women did not follow her to the Law School Table.

Do mentors really make a difference in the careers of successful women? Do they help them move up the corporate or professional ranks or crack the glass ceiling? Studies have shown that women involved in mentoring relationships have greater job success and satisfaction than women who do not have a mentor.[22] In our study of 106 women 23 percent said they did not have a mentor. Even though they achieved their success on their own, most felt they would have moved ahead faster with a mentor. From those who did have mentors, we heard again and again the same refrain: "I owe my career to my mentor" or "I would not be where I am today without my mentor." Ninety-eight percent of the women who had mentors said they were better off professionally, and 95 percent said they were better off personally because of this mentoring relationship (see appendix B for details).

While studies on women and their mentors are rare (perhaps because this is an area that is just beginning to be recognized as important for women's advancement), the ones that have been done support the importance of a mentor for a woman's career progress. Nancy Collins surveyed over four hundred professional women in the San Francisco Bay area, publishing her results in *Professional Women and Their Mentors.* She found that women were not as sophisticated in seeking mentors, and over half reported that they "fell into" the relationship. She also felt that women did not really understand the mentoring concept and were not comfortable being coached.[23] Despite that, Collins reports that 75 percent of her sample had male mentors. In asking her sample to list three ways in which their mentors helped their careers, they most frequently cited that their mentors "taught them corporate rules, provided opportunity and increased their self-confidence."[24]

Agnes Missirian, who published the results of her survey of top businesswomen in *The Corporate Connection,* found that 85.7 percent of the women who reached the top management ranks had had a mentoring relationship of some kind. However, she discovered that the channel of advancement for women was different than that for men. Women reach the top management ranks through staff positions, which are appointed and where power is a function of personal influence, whereas men reach the top by climbing up the ladder through line positions, where power is inherent in the hierarchy and title, as in the army.[25] This means that staff positions are a more accessible way for women to advance for now, possibly because these positions are regarded as secondary power positions and therefore more appropriate for women. With time we hope that other routes to advancement will open for women and that staff positions will lose their secondary status and be regarded as an excellent training ground for leadership positions.

In a third study of women executives drawn from a number of networking groups in New Jersey, Murray Reich found that 77 percent of his 353-woman sample had mentors who influenced their career development. He then compared the women's experiences with men's experiences with mentoring. The women felt their mentors aided them by assigning them special projects and granting them autonomy for difficult tasks. Female protégés also felt that the emotional quality of the relationship was more important than male protégés did. Yet some of the women he interviewed argued that mentors are not necessary for advancement, that they can hurt a career, and that they must be chosen very carefully.[26] We agree that mentors should not be chosen casually and we will discuss the negative side of mentoring later in this chapter.

After a series of tests Kathie was hospitalized with bleeding ulcers. Richard visited her every day, bringing her a Walkman and tapes. The three people who influenced her most—Richard, her mother, and her boyfriend, Scott—sat together around her bed.

When Kathie came back to work after a month, she was a different person. Not only had she lost thirty-five pounds, but the hospitalization had given her time to rethink her whole life and she realized how unbalanced it had become. She accepted Scott's proposal to get married and she no longer felt as driven. Her mother had told her that the illness was caused by career pressures and working twelve hours a day, six days a week, and deep down she knew her mother was right.

One of the biggest changes after her illness was that she was no longer afraid of Richard and she felt comfortable expressing her feelings to him. "I still wanted to do a good job, but I realized that there were other things and that I had to reprioritize my life. If it meant I couldn't get things done, then I couldn't get them done. It was sad for Richard. It was as if the old Kathie had died and there was this new Kathie that he didn't quite know."

Richard was deeply disappointed in the change in Kathie. "When she became ill and returned, I got upset with her because she was not one hundred percent in her career anymore, only eighty percent," he recalls. "The person she reported to told me he wasn't sure how committed she was. I told him, 'I think we ought to terminate her.' It really upset me that she had these skills and she wasn't going to use them. It bothered me enough that I thought of pushing her out of the circle and putting her back in the fishpond."

Richard tried talking to Kathie. "You are bright," he said. "You are beautiful. You dress well. You are physically big. You have what it takes to be successful." He went through a laundry list of her attributes, trying to motivate the old Kathie. Then he reminded her that she wasn't the same as she used to be. "You're right," she'd respond. "But I don't want to be that way, Richard."

Now she knew what she wanted: She wanted a balanced life. She was twenty-seven; she wanted to get married and have a family. For Richard that was heresy; she had deserted ship. With a snap of his fingers he explained how fast he lost interest in her and her career. "I have difficulty mentoring a person who does not ultimately want to be a partner. If you can be a ten, I don't understand people who are satisfied with a seven. If a person doesn't want to be a ten, I don't want to help her be a seven. I don't know why. It's such a waste."

Kathie had become the black sheep in Richard's family: she no longer met his standard of a driven accountant, just as Ann Hopkins, the accountant who sued Price Waterhouse for not making partner, did not meet the unspoken expectations of her firm. He was so disappointed in the changes in her that he pulled back and lost interest in her career. He felt angry that she had found meaning in her life outside his "work family," and yet he was still drawn to her. She sensed his disappointment, but she could live with it. She had her own priorities now, and if Richard didn't like them, that was his problem. She wasn't sure she wanted to make partner anyhow, if it meant giving up everything else in her life.

This is a good example of male mentoring clashing with female developmental needs. As Kathie got closer to the milestone of her thirtieth birthday, she heard her biological clock ticking and responded. She wanted to lead a balanced life: she wanted to marry, have children, and spend time with friends as well as to work. But this was not acceptable to Richard: he wanted all of her energy invested in her career.

Richard was not a perfect mentor. He said he wanted the best for her, but he had difficulty understanding the personal influences on Kathie's life. He had treated her "like a man," as she requested, and now she asked him to understand her feelings as a woman. In fact Richard did understand intellectually what Kathie was experiencing. He had gone through a similar situation with Susan Thomas, another protégé, who chose her child over her career and left the accounting firm after she made partner—something that was virtually unheard of. But Richard could not understand emotionally the personal pressures on a woman.

He could identify with Kathie only as long as she was as driven as he. When she admitted she needed balance in her life, he lost interest. He felt angry and betrayed and showed it by disinterest. The mutual identification, so important in mentoring, disappeared with the snap of his fingers. He could only mentor someone who was totally dedicated to her career and her career alone.

It is interesting that attractive women, such as Kathie Long and Susan Thomas, intrigued Hendricks. He had no time for "tekkies," as he called the women who were plainer in appearance and more technically oriented. Yet with both Kathie Long and Susan Thomas, he had a hard time relating to them as women who want full lives as wives, mothers, and professionals. Perhaps he would be better suited to sponsor men—so long as the men were not "new men," who wanted to take time off to be with their children.

Like any relationship, mentoring can go awry, no matter how

powerful and wonderful the mentor may seem. If a woman puts all her political eggs in one basket, this can lead to disaster. What if the mentor falls out of favor? Fails to protect the protégé? Leaves the corporation unexpectedly? Or, as in Kathie Long's case, loses interest when she chooses a path different from his wish or the dominant corporate culture?

A critical problem for women today centers on where the mentor fits in if the organization is sexist. Does the mentor help the protégé assimilate, as Ann Hopkins's mentor tried to do, or does he champion her and take on the sexist system single-handedly? Then if the woman doesn't advance, do you blame the organization or the mentor? It's a very complicated situation. Both the mentor and the protégé are caught in a Catch-22. A woman is damned if she is too aggressive and damned if she is too "feminine." Richard Hendricks's protégés told him, "I want to be treated like the men. Don't hold anything back." So he gave them what they wanted: He treated them like driven males. But he was then accused of not understanding their needs as women. When Kathie decided she wanted to escape from the rat race, he couldn't relate to her. He couldn't understand how she could jump off the partnership track when she had so much potential. It seemed that Kathie had given him a double message. In reality, many women yearn for the same balance in their lives that Kathie Long strived for. If their mentor is a single-focused male, conflicts can result.

Just as the positive effects of being closely associated with a mentor can have far-reaching implications, so can the negative effects. When it is widely acknowledged that the mentor and protégé are a tight pair, whatever happens to the mentor will affect the protégé. Women in particular seem to be more vulnerable to negative mentoring outcomes, because they are in a minority status and can become overly dependent on their mentor to help them progress in their career.

When the mentor falls out of the good graces of the powers-that-be or fails at an important project, this can adversely affect the protégé and her career. If she has not developed an identity as her own person, when the mentor falters, so will she. Zey calls this the black halo: the wide-reaching halo effect that was so positive suddenly turns negative for the protégé.[27]

This situation can be prevented. If the protégé keeps in touch with other people and keeps tabs on the political climate in the company, she may have advance warning when something negative is going to happen. She can then fortify herself by either putting distance between herself and her mentor or developing other alliances, so she is not seen as only in her mentor's camp.

In other situations a mentor may fail to protect a protégé from organizational pressures. This can happen if the mentor is blind to the protégé's work problems. If the mentor still idealizes the protégé, he may not see her situation realistically or may fail to see the real problems she is up against. Or, because of his own problems or weaknesses, he may fail to perceive the organizational changes that are creating these problems. At other times he may be so involved with his own agenda that he misses what is truly happening. In these situations the protégé is left vulnerable.

If the mentor leaves—whether because of promotion, relocation, or retirement—the protégé who is unprepared can feel abandoned and isolated.[28] Their intense involvement can isolate her from others and give her a false sense of security. If he has protected her from the political realities of corporate life, she will feel lost when he leaves, not knowing where to turn without him. Ideally the mentor should help the protégé become integrated within the power structure and she should make contacts and allies of her own. However, if the mentor leaves unexpectedly or should suddenly die, he may not have finished his "work" with the protégé and she will be left on her own.

The preceding situations are further reasons that a protégé should develop her own support system and not rely totally on the mentor for everything. Allying only with a mentor does not make good political sense. Working women need other relationships, particularly female ones. They also need peers, colleagues, and other senior people in their support system. If Kathie Long had other supports, perhaps they would have helped her see Hendricks more realistically at an earlier point in their relationship.

Nevertheless this can be difficult. Because of the protégé's alliance with the mentor, her peers may see her as "the chosen one," which may cause resentment. Mary Mitchell, a second-line manager at a large electronics corporation, talks about her peers' reaction to the special attention her mentor gave her. "There is definitely peer competitiveness and it's difficult. There is some resentment from some peers, like, 'What's so great about Mary? Why is she the chosen one?' " Her peers felt she had been given a special status with special privileges. Her favored position created jealousy and competition. If they truly resent her being chosen as a "favorite," they may even try to sabotage her by not answering her memos or ignoring her suggestions.

To assuage her peers' resentment, a protégé needs to work at developing peer relationships. She needs to continue interacting with her peers and demonstrate her competence to recapture their confidence in her. It would also be helpful for her to downplay her relationship with the mentor when she's with her peers; at the same time she should let her peers know that she can be a source of information for them as well as a conduit for taking their ideas to her contacts farther up in the organization.[29]

This is a very delicate situation, however, because there may be situations when the protégé will have to choose between her peers and her mentor, as one businesswoman did. "I made a very conscious decision and a painful one, but I was ready for it, that I'd rather go to lunch with [her mentor] on a regular basis than go to lunch with 'the girls.' I really would rather grow and move forward than pay a regressive price." Once "the girls" recognized that her loyalty rested with her mentor, they no longer asked her to join them for lunch. She chose her relationship with her mentor over her relationship with her peers, which may not always be the right choice. To make this decision, she needed to weigh the support she felt from each and evaluate her priorities.

* * *

Ironically Kathie got promoted six months after her illness and in spite of Richard's pulling back. Because of Richard's earlier sponsorship and her fine performance, she had made a name for herself at the firm.

But her relationship with Richard disturbed her. They never fought, because he was slow to yell at women and she often still held her tongue. The week before her wedding Richard had not responded to the invitation, so she remarked casually, "My mom hasn't heard from you, but I told her you were coming because I knew you wouldn't miss it." He looked at her askance. The next day he sent his regrets.

Kathie was crushed. What could be more important than her wedding, she wondered? She refused to return his phone calls and avoided him for two weeks after the wedding. When he finally cornered her and they talked, he explained he had had to work on an important project. Kathie still hasn't forgiven him.

Last year she received her own office, right next to Richard's. Although she never goes in and chats with him, they have a more casual rapport now because they are neighbors. She feels like more of an equal and is not as dependent on him. She knows she would not be in her present position without Richard Hendricks's mentorship and feels deeply indebted to him, but their relationship has changed. "I used to rely totally on him. Whatever he said to do, I'd do. Now I look to others for advice as well. Richard knows me from a work perspective, but he doesn't know all the pressures on my life anymore. I tell him, but he doesn't always listen." Then she speculates, "I wonder how he'll react when he finds out I'm pregnant?"

Like any relationship, mentoring has its benefits and drawbacks for both the mentor and the protégé. But mentoring is not a relationship in isolation; it develops within an organization, and because of this the organization also benefits when mentoring succeeds.

Mentoring helps integrate the protégé into the corporation, gives her a sense of belonging, and creates a loyalty to the company. Kathie Long would not have come back to the accounting firm after her illness if it weren't for Richard. His concern and special treatment had created a loyalty to him, to the corporate family he had created, and to the firm. He cared about her and may have even felt jealous of her relationship with her fiancé. When a woman feels a part of the company, her productivity increases; she's less likely to leave and more likely to make important contributions to the corporation. Mentoring also enhances the communication among all levels within the corporation and contributes to the process of managerial succession.[30] These are important reasons for a corporation to encourage informal mentoring relationships and to create a climate in which they can flourish.

Realizing the value of informal mentoring, many companies are now going a step farther. As many as a third of the country's major companies have set up formal mentoring programs. These programs, at such corporations as Johnson & Johnson, AT&T, Colgate, and Pacific Bell, pair a senior manager with a younger, less-experienced employee and provide personal counseling and career guidance.[31] Linda Phillips-Jones, author of *Mentors and Protégés,* has researched formal, assigned mentoring relationships. Some programs appear to be more superficial than others, and some are more public relations tools than substantive programs. Phillips-Jones suggests the criteria for a successful formal mentoring program: clearly defined purpose and goals and careful selection of the mentor on the basis of interpersonal skills, interest in developing employees, and accessibility. She feels the mentors should be trained and the organization should require weekly meetings between the mentor and protégé[32]. (No research has focused exclusively on the involvement of women in these formal programs.)

Women can use these programs as a jumping-off point to get involved in the corporation's informal network and to develop their own personal network. Formal mentoring programs help women become socialized into the corporate culture, train them to do their jobs better, and help them develop professionally. However, because the mentor and protégé have not personally selected each other or initiated the relationship, there may be personality conflicts, resentment from other workers, a lack of personal commitment on either's part, or other problems.[33] Formal mentoring programs fall outside the realm of our research, but there is a need for further studies here.

For working women, any opportunity to become a part of the shadow organization is an advantage. We can't stress enough how any mentoring a woman gets, including formal mentoring, is advantageous: It expands her network, exposes her to new relationships, and brings her closer to the power holders. The more relationships a woman builds, the more she can advance her career and enrich her life.

CHAPTER EIGHT

❖   ❖   ❖

The Intimate Pair

Janice Celica sat on the floor of the big, old Victorian house, drinking beer and eating a sandwich, and marveled at the group collected around her. They felt like family and yet the twelve of them had met just six months before. She thought Ed Brennan had recruited a wonderful group of young teachers to start this small private school for emotionally disturbed youngsters in Burlington, Vermont. A teacher and coach for ten years, at thirty-four Ed had a sound educational background but was also accessible, and he listened—unusual qualities for a headmaster, Janice thought. She noticed that the door to his office, the old living room, was always open.

Tonight they gathered for a light supper. At dinner they discussed their educational philosophies, how the school was running, and how to handle some of the children's special needs. They ended up talking and laughing and telling stories until three a.m. Janice went home feeling good, hoping things would never change.

But they did. After two years Ed felt the school needed to expand. They needed more students if the school was to thrive. He started assigning administrative tasks to each teacher. They were assigned to curriculum, directing the lower, middle, and upper school, athletics, and so on. Ed put Janice in charge of admissions, because she was so energetic and outgoing and had the kind of personality that got kids excited about learning. When she did reading testing, for example, she had a knack for putting the kids at ease.

At first Janice was apprehensive about taking on such a responsibility, but Ed assured her he would hold her hand through the
entire process. She was the only one who needed grooming, he
thought. The others could manage on their own.

Mentoring is an intimate relationship. Being intimate means being
close, familiar, informal, private, and personal—qualities usually
associated with family, close friends, and lovers, not with the workplace. But mentoring occurs in the workplace, and therein lies the
rub: men and women are used to relating to each other as men and
women, not as colleagues, coworkers, or collaborators. "The
kicker," as Gail Sheehy notes, "is that the relationship of guide and
seeker gets all mixed up with a confusing male-female attachment.
And it is this mysterious, ambiguous, potentially enriching but
possibly crippling attachment with which many successful women
and their mentors must cope."[1]

The number of women who work full-time continues to rise
each year. According to the Bureau of Labor Statistics, 36,605,000
women were employed in the work force in 1989. The total number
of men and women working was 84,553,000.[2] That means that 43.2
percent of the work force consists of women. In education alone 69
percent of the public-school teachers and 76 percent of the private-
school teachers are women. Yet the majority of their bosses, superiors, and mentors are men: 76 percent of the principals and 96
percent of the superintendents.[3]

Since men and women are working together more than ever
before, they both want to build and maintain effective relationships
with each other at work. However, they're unsure of how to relate
to each other in a work environment. This is not surprising considering how men and women were raised. Growing up, boys tended
to play in competitive team sports, but girls were never part of their
teams. If girls were involved in athletics at all, they played solo
sports, such as tennis or gymnastics, but did not compete with
boys. (In recent years girls' soccer and softball teams have become

more common.) Later on men related to women as their girlfriends or lovers or, in work situations, as their secretaries. In many of these cases the women were helpmates; they had no real identity of their own. This way of relating, which may seem more true of pre-feminist days, is beginning to change, but remnants of it still linger.

Men and women now find themselves in new roles in the work force, uncertain of how to act and unsure of how they feel about working together. According to Kathy Kram, "Both men and women allude to sexual tensions and fears of increasing intimacy that cause anxiety, ambivalence and confusion in their relationship with colleagues of the other sex."[4]

To relieve this anxiety, men and women tend to rely on prototypical ways of relating to each other. These are familiar and comfortable for both but may be limiting. For example, when the mentor acts as a father figure and the protégé, a daughter, the mentor can overprotect his protégé and keep her dependent. The protégé, if locked in this role, must act helpless and incompetent. This can compromise her growth and her advancement. (Nevertheless, relating as a father and daughter can also be an authentic way of relating, as it was for Gina Carbone and her three father-figure mentors in chapter 4. They reenacted their family roles in the workplace.)

Mary Patterson McPherson, president of Bryn Mawr College, explains, "If a young boy grows up seeing his mother as a respected partner in the home, that's the way he's going to look at women. If, on the other hand, the mother is there to do for everybody and is never supposed to have an idea and is really not listened to or taken seriously in anything but domestic matters, then that's the way he sees all women too."

McPherson goes on to conjecture how a man might think when he works with women on an equal basis for the first time: "I understand how I handle women. I have a mother. I have my daughter. I know what their roles are. Now suddenly I have a woman who's a colleague. I don't know how she wants to function and I certainly don't know how I'm supposed to function vis-à-vis her. I'm not used to that. I don't understand it. I don't know how it's done." Therefore he relies on ways he has related to women outside the workplace. Acting as a father is a safe, comfortable, and nonsexual way of relating to a member of the opposite sex.

If a male mentor and a female protégé do not enact the father-daughter roles, Kathy Kram, Rosabeth Kanter, and others believe they collude by playing other stereotypical roles. We do not always see these as stereotypes but as authentic, though perhaps misguided, prototypical ways of relating to the opposite sex that people bring unconsciously to the workplace. For example, if the man plays the "chivalrous knight" and the woman acts as a "helpless maiden," we do not believe they are always consciously choosing to don these stereotypes.[5] Rather, this may be the way the man relates to all women, including his wife and daughter, and he treats his protégé the same.

This is how Richard Hendricks, Kathie Long's mentor in the last chapter, often related to women. He tested Susan Thomas, another protégé, by watching discreetly to see how she handled a chauvinistic coworker in the next office. "He went past the line of decency, which he always does," says Hendricks. "He sat down so that he could get a better look at her legs. I noticed that Susan immediately knew what he was doing, because I could see her pull her skirt down. She said, 'Look, Mr. X, I understand what you are saying, but please help me here. I've got a job to do and I've only got so many hours to do it. I need to have answers to these things now.' " Hendricks was ready to charge in and "save" his protégé if need be. The protégé proved to him that she wasn't a helpless maiden. Hendricks's actions were based on his cultural training and his unconscious feelings about being a male.

Another male-female pair may act as the "tough warrior" and the "nurturant mother."[6] Here these roles allow the man to maintain the image of the tough, rational male to others while he unloads his problems to the empathic woman, who serves as his listener and provides psychological support. A third pair, that of "macho" and "seductress," relate to each other in a sexual, game-playing way.[7] Suzy Daley, a marketing manager of a large corporation, is a tall, attractive blonde. She relates to men at work flirtatiously, because that's how she always relates to members of the opposite sex, whether socially or at work. She is highly competent and aggressive, but her sexuality masks these qualities. Some men in the corporation are attracted to her but then feel threatened. Others try to ignore her appearance and sexuality and concentrate on what she has to say. Both men and women can find this style offensive in the workplace.

Each of these prototypical ways of relating allows men and women to communicate with each other in a traditional male-female way. Sometimes the participants are not conscious of what they are doing. They both unconsciously collude by bringing their way of relating to the opposite sex into the workplace. Problems can arise when either the mentor or the protégé feels locked into these roles; feels that these roles limit their effectiveness, growth, or advancement; or feels the role doesn't fit.

Prototypes are a way of making men and women more comfortable, but they do not really help them face the threatening issues connected with their new roles: those of power, competition, sexuality, and intimacy. By relying on prototypes the tension connected with their new roles becomes diffused. "These roles return to the familiar, provide labels, set boundaries, and define behavior," writes psychologist Linda Moore in *Beyond Sex Roles.* "There is no demand for new ways of handling relationships."[8] It is only recently, as women entered the professions and corporations in increasing numbers, that men have been asked to change.

Men and women need a broader range of behaviors for the workplace. The best way to lessen collusion is first to expand the number of women in prominent positions and then to increase the interaction between men and women. The more men and women work together and are given cultural approval for it, the less anxious they will feel and the more comfortable they will become in their new roles. "It may seem surprising in an era sometimes labeled post feminist," writes Jaclyn Fierman in *Fortune* magazine, "but working closely with the opposite sex continues to make many male executives uncomfortable."[9] Men will then relate to women as authentic individuals and women can treat men in the same way. Today women tend to respond to men as power figures, and that can still carry a sexual connotation.

Change is difficult considering the newness of the situation, male-female dynamics, and the cultural milieu. We live in a society that is both sexist (in its attitudes toward women) and sexually charged (in its advertisements, media, and attitudes). Peggy Noonan, a speech writer in the Reagan White House, poignantly expresses some of the ambiguities in this new cultural milieu and the difficulty men and women have in relating to each other, in her book *What I Saw at the Revolution.* "People ask me, Do you ever get crushes on the men you work with? And the truth, which I usually find ways not to say, is yes, often, don't you? All these men and women running around America in their gray suits in the board room, in the television commercials where the woman in the meeting utters the topper. I think they're all half in love with each other and have trouble recognizing it, never mind admitting it, because it is potentially dangerous, and awkward, or painful, never mind politically incorrect. And the only thing to do, because men and women are going to keep working side by side, is: take that tension and turn it into creativity. Harness that electricity, turn it into the TVA. Or, rather, tenant ownership of public housing. Thank you."[10]

Increasing admissions was a priority, so Ed and Janice spent more and more time together. Since she didn't have her own office at that point, she'd often come into his office to use his phone, and then they'd talk about the new applicants, the parents, and the interviews.

Janice began by testing the children for admission and setting up appointments for them to visit the school. Once she felt comfortable with that, Ed asked her to sit in on his interviews with the parents. In the beginning Janice didn't say a word; she was too nervous. Afterward they would rehash the interview. It was difficult for them to talk with teachers walking in and out of Ed's office, so Ed closed his door—for the first time.

Feeling insecure in her new role, Janice seemed to need a lot of stroking, and Ed was always available. They talked over lunch, before school, and chatted in the halls between classes. Although their discussions always centered on "business," the other teachers wouldn't have known it from their affect and body language. They'd see a slim, handsome young couple engrossed in conversation, enjoying each other's company. Janice felt an excitement about her job and couldn't wait to get to work. "There was definitely a spark there," she recalls. "I really enjoy spending time with him. I see him as a friend as well as a boss, and I think he sees the same thing—as dangerous as it's been over the years."

After about six months Janice began conducting the parental interviews while Ed sat in, and in another month she was doing them herself. The admission decisions remained mutual, and there were always nuances and problems to iron out before an acceptance was given.

One night they decided to go out for a drink, taking the folders of several prospective students with them. Janice told him that there were rumors that they were having an affair and then said, "If it were another time and place, there might be something for them to worry about."

Ed was taken aback, "Are you kidding?" he said. "I'd never shake things up like that."

Janice and Ed's brief conversation changed their relationship. It was what psychiatrist Peter Rutter, author of *Sex in the Forbidden Zone*, calls "a healing moment." A healing moment is the inevitable turning point in the relationship that "determines whether the sexuality will be contained psychologically or acted upon physically.''[11] According to Rutter, this moment is in the hands of the man, who holds the power. With a mentor and protégé we feel they are both responsible for changing the course of the relationship, although a mentor may feel more responsibility. Until that point Janice and Ed were both carried along by an excitement, a danger, as Janice said. They both felt a spark and weren't sure where the relationship was going. Although sex was never discussed, a sexual aura surrounded their relationship. This excitement motivated Janice; she wanted to impress Ed both professionally and personally.

After the healing moment some of the excitement disappeared, but there was also relief. Janice remembers thinking, "Okay, now we can just be really businesslike and enjoy each other for who we are, without having the confusion of other issues. Somehow the edge, the danger, wasn't there. But that was the relief too." There was relief also because neither wanted to endanger the future of the school or of their respective marriages. (They were both happily married. Janice had a toddler, and Ed had three girls of school age.)

Since mutual liking, respect, and attraction formed the foundation of Janice and Ed's mentoring relationship, it is not surprising that intimate and sexual feelings were aroused. The conditions that generate attraction—similarity, proximity, and intensity—are all present in mentoring relationships.[12] In addition the protégé must be open and vulnerable in order to learn.

Rachel Hoffman, a flutist, talked about how the nonsexual intimacy she felt with her mentor-teacher energized her to learn. "It was like living in a dream for a couple of years. That somebody would care so much about me. I think he actually told me that he loved me, but he made it very clear that it was a real sensitive kind of love. 'I love you as a person. But don't worry,' he said. 'I'm never going to take it anywhere.' That was very nice actually, because I knew that he did, and he knew that I loved him. But it was never a sexual thing. It never went anywhere. It was just that very deep regard.''

She goes on, "That transfer of love has to take place if you're really learning something that you want to learn so deeply. For somebody else to take such an interest in having you learn and put that kind of time and energy into you, they've got to love you."

Because Rachel's mentor was gay, the intimacy was nonthreatening—she never had to worry about crossing the boundary and having sex. She could use the intimacy as a positive source of energy and creativity. For most heterosexual people, however, an intimate situation creates anxiety and stress. They are ambivalent and fearful about extending the boundaries of their relationship into the sexual arena. They fear if they do, they will lose the positive value of the mentoring. An affair can be very destructive for everyone involved, but the protégé has the most to lose because society still has a double standard and stigmatizes and punishes women more. The mentoring pair is also concerned about its ramifications on their personal relationships outside of work and on each of their careers.

These feelings, which are inevitable when men and women work together, can be handled in different ways. Some will discuss their attraction openly and decide not to get involved sexually. Others will test the boundaries and become involved in a sexual liaison. Still others will withdraw and limit the amount of time they spend alone or the frequency of their contacts. Some pairs may revert to the father-daughter pairing, in which they deny their sexual feelings and any kind of a sexual liaison becomes taboo.

One writer dealt with the sexual issue by keeping the door to sexual involvement open but never acting on it. Her motto was "Never say yes. Never say no. Always say maybe." This created tremendous stress for her because she felt she had to flirt with all the men with whom she worked, even though she had no intention of having sex with any of them. According to psychologist Anne Alonso, assistant clinical professor of psychology at Harvard Medical School and director of the Treatment Center at Boston Institute of Psychotherapies, "That kind of sexualization has very little to do with sex and much more with power and keeps a woman very much disempowered, which foils the whole point of a mentoring relationship."

Some male-dominated industries are very chauvinistic: the men hold the power and the women feel powerless. One way women feel they can gain power is by manipulating men through giving or withholding sex. When males give up stereotypes and begin using their power benevolently and authentically, women will feel less pressured to be manipulative.

For the female protégé, sexual dynamics are also linked to power dynamics.[13] "As a lot of women will tell you," notes one protégé, "power is an aphrodisiac." A man becomes attractive just because of the position he holds. Another protégé said her mentor, the president of the company, was "just charismatic. He has a personal magnetism that's very powerful. He is not good-looking. He's bald, overweight, graying at the temples. He wears glasses."

It is stimulating to be around a powerful person. There's an air of tension and excitement around him. Therefore when a protégé receives personal attention from him, she feels grateful. Being open, vulnerable, *and* grateful can put the protégé in a compromising position.

Dealing with feelings of intimacy is a special problem for people in the helping professions. Psychiatrists, psychologists, and people in helping roles hold tremendous power over their patients, who come to them at a time when they are vulnerable. "Day after day, men sit in inviolable privacy with women who trust, admire and rely upon us. There is a constant pull toward greater intimacy," writes Peter Rutter.[14] How easy it would be to betray that trust. Almost 80 percent of the women he spoke with had been approached sexually by a man who was her physician, therapist, pastor, lawyer, or teacher. In about half of the cases a sexual relationship occurred, with devastating results for the woman.[15]

Patients have fantasies about getting sexually involved with their therapists. One psychiatrist we interviewed told of an incident when he went to the movies with a date and ran into a patient, whom he greeted briefly. She missed her next appointment; when she next came in, she told him she had been "absolutely crazy" for a whole week after seeing him in a social situation. "I asked, 'How come?' and she said, 'Well, first, I saw you.' Which seemed to explain it all, because clearly to see me outside of my role as a therapist and outside of an office implied that I had some life in the real world, which was not expected by her. Secondly, not only did she see me but she saw me with someone other than herself, and clearly there was no one else that was permitted to be in my life other than her, a patient. And thirdly, she made it very clear to me that the someone that she saw me with was all wrong for me. My date wasn't the kind of person that I should be with. Clearly the person I should be with was herself."

This patient's distortion of reality makes her particularly vulnerable, especially with someone in a powerful position whom she trusts. (This sense of distortion can happen to a lesser degree with a student and teacher or protégé and mentor.) If both the parties agree on the boundaries of the relationship, there should be no problem. But if the patient is particularly vulnerable, as in this instance, and the psychiatrist did press her for sexual relations, she would have difficulty turning him down. In this case the psychiatrist held firmly to the professional boundaries, recognized the patient's vulnerabilities, and did not take advantage of her.

Another psychiatrist, a woman, spoke of the love she felt for her male psychiatric supervisor-mentor and of her appreciation that he adhered to professional boundaries. "I came to respect just about everything about him. It grew from feeling that he was very competent and professional to feeling that I absolutely loved him completely and at times I wanted to crawl up in his lap and have him be daddylike to me. I felt very grateful that he had a good sense of boundary, because I probably would have gotten involved sexually if he didn't have his good boundaries in place. Somehow there was, unconscious maybe, the message that we love each other but we love each other in these parameters."

These parameters, the boundaries of the relationship, make it safe for both the mentor and the protégé to continue being intimate without having sex. The psychiatrist goes on, "It wasn't even that much sexual as it was sort of infantile. That I wanted him to hold me and he did, without touching me. He held me with his mentoring."

In therapeutic situations the therapist is trained to look for transference, when a patient transfers her feelings about an earlier significant figure (such as a parent) to the therapist. He has a professional responsibility to keep the boundaries nonsexual. But the situation between the mentor and the protégé is somewhat different; neither party is trained to look for intimacy problems. Mentoring is an intimate relationship in which theoretically either person can set the boundaries. But because the mentor wields more power by virtue of his position and status, the protégé can feel very conflicted if the mentor wants sex.

The experts agree that it is unwise for a mentor and protégé to get involved sexually. Of course it does happen. Few protégés were willing to discuss this with us. Rutter believes that once a sexual relationship has been established, the original helping relationship has been forever compromised and cannot be restored.[16]

When a woman invests her professional, emotional, and sexual energy in the same person, he becomes far too important and powerful. He can exert influence on every aspect of her life, and if he withdraws any part of it, the protégé can feel devastated. Denise Beyer, a free-lance writer who was married to her mentor, a newspaper editor, learned this the hard way. Initially she was attracted to her mentor-husband because of his position and their common interest in journalism. As she got to know him, she learned he needed to be on a pedestal and wanted her to be on her knees, groveling for help. The more her writing improved and she got better assignments, the more he criticized her. "There was something wrong with every magazine story that I turned in, especially those that got on the cover—according to him," Denise remembers. He controlled her and kept her dependent by criticizing her work. Not having much confidence in herself, she then thought something must be wrong with her writing too.

Denise eventually divorced him because she needed a more equal relationship. "I had to get out from under that pressure," she continues. "I should be loved and accepted whether I was doing well or not. But he had a tier system. I liked it at first; I thought it was very stimulating, very challenging. Then I just had to get out of it. What is more challenging than trying to meet the approval of somebody every day? It was really exhausting." Even after her divorce she still felt him "reading over my shoulder." That took a while to shake. Now remarried to someone out of the field, Denise advises women to keep their personal and professional relationships separate.

When the mentor is a husband or lover, a power struggle can develop. He can try to control her by criticizing her performance, as Denise's husband-mentor did. He can discourage her from progressing in her career because she will need him less. He may be threatened by her advancement and fear the ramifications of her career strides on their family or marital relationship. If he believes succeeding is a "male" thing to do, he may feel emasculated by her success. The couple's sex life may suffer. She, on the other hand, may hold herself back from surpassing him because she feels uncertain of how her success will affect him and their marriage.

The competition between husband and wife is similar to that found between a middle-aged mentor and a young protégé or a clinical supervisor and a supervisee. In *The Quiet Profession* Anne Alonso writes, "On a conscious level, the supervisor needs to feel in control, to be more competent than the supervisee, in order to be helpful and for his/her own sense of self-worth. . . . There is a danger that the relationship will lapse into a struggle for dominance and control."[17]

When the protégé is involved in a sexual relationship with her mentor, she can also lose her credibility as a professional. People will continue to wonder whether she is advancing because of her own abilities or because she is sleeping with her mentor. If she has a sexual relationship at work, other powerful men may see her as a sex object, and she can lose whatever strides she has made as a professional woman.

A lawyer who had an affair with her mentor-professor and called it "the greatest love of our respective lives" talks of how she worried about losing her credibility. "At that point he wasn't my teacher anymore, but I was his teaching assistant and I worried about whether I would lose credibility. That was something in my mind that you don't do because then you're screwing up the whole thing. But I had some confidence in myself also and, given the timing of it, the teaching relationship was coming to an end, and there really was not going to be a whole lot more involvement from a professional standpoint." In spite of her concerns about losing her credibility, she continued with the relationship for six years and ended it, not because of her professional concerns but because of its ups and downs, which took an emotional toll on her life.

Although the sexual tension had disappeared between Ed and Janice, the other teachers wouldn't have known it because the pair still spent a lot of time together. The teachers continued to feel she was the favored one and were jealous of her access to Ed. They grew hostile toward Janice: they would pass her in the hall and not say hello, and at staff meetings they would ignore her suggestions. They didn't treat Ed any differently, because he was their boss. His position insulated him from their anger.

The low point for Janice occurred when the school was moving to larger quarters. Janice came in one Saturday to work on her classroom and found a team of teachers in one of the other rooms. When she walked in, they looked up briefly and went back to work. A huge lunch was spread on one of the desks, and some of the teachers were eating. No one said a word or offered her anything to eat. Finally Janice forced the issue. "Is there a scraper I can use?" she asked. After a long silence one of them pointed to their tools and said, "Use that one if you want."

Janice was crushed. She remembers, "We were supposed to be a small, caring family. They were being such hypocrites. It drove me crazy."

When they moved the school, Janice received the first office and got her own phone because the admission process, crucial to the expanded school, need to be conducted in privacy. The teachers were told of the necessity for confidentiality in talking with prospective students and their parents, but they did not believe it. None of the other teachers was given a private office or phone. Their resentment and jealousy grew.

Janice and Ed often discussed the other teachers' reaction to her. They decided to spend less time together, but Ed also chose not to react publicly to the situation. "Just do a good job and make me satisfied. The rest of it will eventually disappear," he told her, reminding her that she had to learn to deal with all sorts of people. He felt that if he told the teachers to back off, it would make matters worse.

Feeling isolated from the other teachers and from Ed, Janice sought out the school counselor, who was a good sounding board. She toyed with the idea of leaving, but didn't want to give the teachers the satisfaction. Besides, she didn't know where she'd find another boss like Ed.

Like many mentoring pairs, Janice and Ed learned that a mentoring relationship between members of the opposite sex is highly visible. In this setting, a school with a predominantly female staff, their special relationship stood out even more. Because far more men are mentored than women, when women *are* mentored, the relationship receives more attention. The standards and expectations are higher, and the success or failure of the experience becomes widely known.[18]

Because of this visibility the relationship is subject to public scrutiny. Not only must the mentoring pair resolve the relationship between them, but they must consider how they are perceived by others in the organization. Because of the male-female pairing, others look at the relationship with interest and at times with suspicion. Coworkers want to know, "Why is she being mentored?" They often suspect that her sponsorship is the result of favoritism or sexual involvement, not competence.[19]

In Janice's case the other teachers, who suspected sexual involvement, felt it was blatant favoritism when she received her own office and phone. Even when Ed explained to them Janice's need for confidentiality and privacy, they assumed that that was just an excuse. The faculty was jealous of the special attention Janice received from Ed and they resented that he was no longer as accessible to them. As the school got bigger and he took on more responsibility, he was busier and had to delegate more. When the school moved to larger quarters, all the classrooms were spread out. They were no longer a close-knit family in the old Victorian mansion. Although many factors created the changes in the school and in the teachers' relationship with Ed, the teachers held Janice responsible. They believed that if she hadn't had such a special relationship with Ed, everything would have remained the same.

If the relationship is truly open and intimate, the mentor and protégé can discuss how to handle any resentment from others and reach a mutual decision. When Janice discussed these concerns with Ed, he listened and sympathized but chose to let the situation resolve itself rather than intervene. This is common mentoring behavior: The mentor may pull strings magically but does not appear to do so. However, the mentor remains the protector, as Ed did. Even though they agreed to spend less time together and be less visible, Ed never felt the teachers' resentment in the same way Janice did. Because he was the headmaster, the other teachers had to be cordial to him. They targeted their resentment and jealousy at Janice.

To combat the public scrutiny, many cross-gender pairs make a conscious decision to spend less time together, as Ed and Janice did. They may decide not to talk behind closed doors or to be less visible as a pair at work. Many male mentors told us they would not go out with their female protégés to discuss business over drinks or dinner because of the fear of gossip about their relationship. Others choose to see the mentoring relationship as a father-daughter pairing. This enables them to keep the sex out of the picture, and it allows both mentor and protégé to fall into comfortable, familiar roles. Modifications of any sort may soften the reaction of others to the mentoring relationship, but in each instance the amount of teaching, coaching, and sponsorship that can occur may also be curtailed. This is a trade-off for cross-gender pairs.

In addition to concerns about how coworkers perceive the cross-gender mentoring relationship, many mentors and protégés told us of concerns about how their spouses would react to a close relationship at work with a member of the opposite sex. Often protégés made a special attempt to get to know their mentor's spouse, in order to reassure her that the relationship was above-board and to create a sense of familiarity. A corporate manager talks of how she dealt with this issue. "I'm a pretty straight shooter and my mentor's a real straight shooter. He knows my husband very well, and I know his wife very well. All four of us like all of us, and I think that's the key. From a woman's point of view, you have to be just somewhat guarded in the way that you talk to a wife about her husband because I don't ever want to plant a seed, a perception that something is different than it is. I've been a little bit cautious about that. I never have felt in any sense that sexual involvement was a question in her mind. It's not a question in my husband's mind either."

Janice and Ed's relationship became less intense as she needed less supervision. They thought so much alike that it was not necessary for her to check with him about admission decisions unless there was a problem. As they saw each other less, the gossip subsided. As time went on, many of the original faculty left the school, including some of the people who had spread rumors about Janice and Ed.

Nevertheless Ed bent over backward not to favor Janice in an effort to prove that she was not receiving special treatment. He assigned her a full teaching load in addition to her job as director of admissions, all at a time when she was contemplating having a second child. She fought him on it, telling him she was overworked. He felt he couldn't change the schedule because a change would be perceived by the other teachers as favoritism. Since Janice complained the entire year, Ed made small improvements in her workload the next two years.

On his own Ed educated the faculty about the complexity of the admission process. He wanted to dispel the "cushy" image the job had. He tried to involve the teachers by asking them to rate prospective students when they visited their classrooms.

Today Janice still sees Ed as her mentor and her friend. "I don't need him for my growth as much as I did before," she says. "I'm much more independent at accomplishing what I need to accomplish, and he's been very helpful in setting long-term goals." She also feels that now he is learning from her, although she doubts that he would admit it. "I'm juggling my family and my career and he's never had to deal with something like that before. His wife deals with those things." They spent the past year discussing these issues. Janice feels that if she can raise his consciousness about the difficulties dual-career families face, all the faculty will benefit by having more realistic workloads. That will be her gift to him.

She concludes by saying, "There aren't people at the school with whom I feel really comfortable and can really relax, but I do feel support. I feel as if people there enjoy working with me, enjoy my company, and value what I have to say and do. So it's very different than it has been."

Janice struggled to cope with the other teachers' resentment and jealousy about her relationship with Ed. Although she felt that she stayed out of weakness—she says that she was afraid to risk going to a new school and starting over—her endurance and perseverance were strengths. She did not give in to idle gossip and survived with a strong, though different, mentoring relationship.

In discussing what she taught Ed—how to cope with dual careers and families—Janice illustrated one of the pitfalls of cross-gender mentoring: Role modeling is limited. Because of the difference in gender, identification may be curtailed. Women cannot look to their male mentors as models for dealing with the personal and professional dilemmas they face today, as Janice found out. For example male mentors cannot help female protégés cope with managing multiple roles, surviving as a female and minority professional, and handling those professional conflicts that arise precisely because of gender.[20] One protégé spoke for many women when she said of her mentor, "As a man I don't think he understood the other pulls." For this reason we need to stress once more that in addition to a male mentor, a woman needs a female mentor, sponsor, coach, or peer with whom to share these concerns. Symbolic mentors can also serve as role models for juggling multiple roles and coping as a woman in a male-dominated environment.

Despite the problems associated with mentoring someone of the opposite sex, there are benefits for both the mentor and the protégé. They can both learn from each other, gaining understanding and insight into how the other gender thinks, acts, and feels in a work context. Some women who are aware of the sexual tensions at work may choose to distance themselves from men and limit their contacts. While this behavior may help them cope with the male-female tension in the workplace, it also limits the potential for developing authentic mentoring relationships. Our hope is that women will learn to manage the sexual tensions—rather than avoid them—so that they will be in a better position to thrive in the workplace in the 1990s.

As more women are promoted through their own efforts and those of their male mentors, men will have greater opportunities to work with women. As their exposure increases and they feel more comfortable working together, our hope for men is that tokenism, stereotypes, and prototypical ways of relating will be broadened to include authentic relationships with women as colleagues as well as mentors.

We also look forward to the time when men and women will experience a different kind of cross-gender mentoring: women mentoring men. This is fairly rare these days, but as more women move up the ranks and attain the higher status and rank associated with mentorship, we believe that female mentoring of men will become more common. Perhaps those male protégés who are mentored by powerful and supportive women will bring a fresh male perspective to the work world.

As men and women gain personally and professionally from cross-gender mentoring, the organization also benefits. When men and women work together, they bring different strengths, approaches, and perspectives to a project. They solve problems in different ways and may follow different processes to arrive at the same, similar, or different solutions. This mixing of styles and strengths brings a richness to the organization that cannot be achieved in a predominantly male environment.[21]

✧   ✧   ✧

CHAPTER NINE

The Life Mentor

Sally Enright sat back in her leather chair in her carefully appointed office and reflected on her life. At thirty-nine she was pleased that her name and her reputation as a labor attorney were impeccable all over Boston. She was married to one of the middle-aged partners of her mentor, Sam Fishbine. (Sam had fixed her up.) They had a satisfying life together, eating out frequently, traveling when both their busy schedules permitted. Since her husband had children from his first marriage, he did not want more children when they married. She understood his feelings and went along with him, but as she approaches forty, this decision has been gnawing away at her. "The bottom line is there's nothing left when the case is decided," she muses. "You move on to something else. You may tell some war stories later when you go out to dinner with the client, but when you've helped somebody become a whole lot more than they were when they started, that's like having a kid.

"You've got to do something to leave a tangible trail, or else it begins to wear a little thin at the end of the line. If I decide not to have children, I've got to be sure I build some alternatives, that I put the nurturing and building energy into something else. I'd like to do more of what Sam does. It's one of the things that's left when you're seventy years old. I think he's just as proud of the people he's mentored as he is of his own kids."

Sally Enright has reached a point in her life when she is considering becoming a mentor. Mentoring would fill a need for her, an alternative to what she calls "the nurturing energy" that usually goes into childrearing for women. As a woman who chose to follow the individualistic (typically male) path, she is at the same point that men often reach when they begin to mentor. Mentoring is a way for career-oriented women and for men to regenerate themselves and leave a legacy. (Many women achieve this by having children.)

Sally Enright is a harbinger of a new breed of female mentors. Like most of the women in this book, she had a positive experience with a mentor. She wants to give back some of what she has reaped, passing on what she has learned to a young attorney. This is partly altruistic and partly selfish. It is her way of finding meaning for herself at midlife. At this stage of her life she is realizing that having a career alone is not enough. After fifteen years of practicing law, case after case can wear thin, as she says. Involvement in a close, intimate relationship, such as mentoring, would fill a gaping hole in her life.

Carol Woodman, the surgeon we met in chapter 2, "The Anatomy of Mentoring," felt the same need when she took a young male resident under her wing. Although she had two children of her own, she had progressed to a point in her career when she was feeling restless and wanted a new challenge. Mentoring provided that challenge, as well as the intimacy she sought.

Because Sally Enright had learned so much from her mentor, she feels compelled to mentor others. Her mentor was a superb teacher, and she looked at him as a guru with high ideals and high ethics—something that she felt was becoming less common as law became more of a business than a profession. In addition, Sam Fishbine became for Sally what we call a *life mentor*. The work of the life mentor extends beyond the workplace into the protégé's personal life. For example, Sam influenced Sally's choice of a husband, where she lived, and how she lived. He helped her form both a professional identity and a personal identity, and now she wanted to help another young woman form hers.

Developing a professional identity is a complicated process for a woman—with or without a role model or mentor. She must learn the skills and techniques of a particular profession and she must also learn its values and behaviors—all within the context of being a woman. This task is more difficult for women because to succeed at work, they must go against the cultural proscriptions with which they were raised. Until recently most women were taught that it was unfeminine to be aggressive, think of their own needs, and go after what they want. But from the time men are little boys, they learn that these so-called masculine qualities are what makes them men. These qualities, which are congruent with a man's sense of himself, are revered in the work world.

To develop her professional identity, then, a woman must find a way to combine her work identity with her identity as a woman. Kathy Kram thinks the most critical developmental task for a woman is to find an image of herself that is both attractive (sexual) and viable in the work world.[1] This task is easier when a young woman has a female mentor as a role model. When the woman has a male mentor, she must internalize what feels right to her and reject those behaviors and values that are not consonant with her self-image as a woman. Another option is to look for women as secondary mentors who can serve as intensive role models and provide support and nurturing for blending roles and surviving in a man's work world. Peer mentors, female peers, and colleagues at work can also do this, but the relationship may have a different emphasis.

As we will see, Sally Enright used her mentor as a role model for developing her professional identity; she did not have women as secondary mentors or peers for support. Because of her mentor's prominence in her life, he became more than a career mentor to her. As she modeled other parts of his life, he became a life mentor as well.

Sally met Sam Fishbine the summer after her first year of law school when a friend told her to call him, because he knew all the labor people in town and might have a position. "Sam said, 'Look, I can't pay you anything, but if you want to come and follow me around, I've done that in the past.' That is a very accepted and traditional thing: Labor arbitrators take young people who may want to become labor arbitrators.

"I didn't fall into that category. I wanted to be a union-side labor lawyer, but I became an apprentice to Fishbine," says Enright. "I wrote decisions that Fishbine was able to use. I ultimately got paid for it, but they would be first drafts for him. Then, when it got to the point that he felt he was going to use them, he would tell me in advance what position to take, and we would talk it through. He was a very good teacher."

That whole summer Sally Enright followed Sam Fishbine around. She didn't literally carry his briefcase, but wherever Sam went, Sally was at his side. They made a striking pair: a young woman with shoulder-length auburn hair and the portly, respected barrister with thirty-four years of practice under his belt. He knew everyone in the labor-management bar in Boston, and through him Sally met them all.

When Fishbine negotiated contracts or grievances between labor and management, Sally would sit in the corner of the negotiating room, quietly taking notes on a yellow legal pad. She'd observe what he did, what he said, and how he handled witnesses and attorneys. "You learn the analytic stuff in law school, but you don't learn how to interact with clients, the procedural details," she notes. "You don't learn how to be, how to act, the role of humor, how casual to be, how formal. I got a real good grounding in all of that by going to hearings with Sam over the summer."

Sally Enright describes a time-honored tradition: learning a profession from an older, more experienced person. A cub newspaper reporter in a newsroom, a young scientist in a laboratory, an intern in a teaching hospital: They all want to learn to become professionals. They've completed their book learning, and now comes the time for hands-on learning: their apprenticeship to a master.

Throughout this book we've seen how a mentor frequently plays the master role; he becomes a teacher, and the protégé, an eager student.

This process is more complicated for a woman because she doesn't have the tradition of learning a profession from other women. The knowledge women have learned from their mothers and grandmothers for generations has usually been domestic: how to tend a sick child, roast a turkey, make a bed, or hem a skirt. But up until recently the professional/vocational apprenticeships have been male to male.

How, then, does a woman learn to become an attorney or a psychotherapist or a teacher? Each profession has its own substantive or technical skills, its body of knowledge and values. While the content varies, the process by which a woman learns the profession is the same across the board. Once she has acquired the necessary education, a woman learns by watching and mimicking, by observing and doing, by modeling her mentor's behavior and skills—just as an apprentice learned a trade from a master in the Middle Ages.

The early guilds were associations of craftsmen and merchants who taught young men a trade. Tailors, weavers, silversmiths, and blacksmiths all learned their trade or craft from a master. The apprentice worked for the master without pay for seven years—about the time it takes to become a partner in a law firm or receive tenure at a university today. The master's function was practical and work focused, and the apprentice learned by watching and doing. In the early days of law and medicine young doctors and lawyers also worked in an apprenticeship system. This is how they learned the ethics of their profession—the humanitarianism, the bedside manner, the interest in pro bono cases. This type of knowledge, which cannot be found in books or school, is the crux of what the mentor teaches today.

This is both a conscious, rational process and an unconscious one. It is similar to the identification that occurs between a woman and her psychotherapist. The apprentice watches, weighs the consequences, and uses his own judgment to decide which parts of the

observation to make his own. In the beginning he may copy everything until he has the confidence to say, "No, this is not for me"
or "This does not feel right to me." In the same way a woman must
temper what she learns from a man.

As we saw in chapter 5, Brenda Marks learned the advertising
business this way. She talks about how she observed and modeled
her boss-mentor's behavior. "For about three years I spent at least
seventy percent of each day, in one way or another, in his company.
I sat in his office while all the phone calls got made. I sat in his office
while we figured out what to do. I went with him on calls and visits
and meetings. In the very beginning I carried his briefcase. I made
coffee, I saw to it that his secretaries were hired, that the flowers
were on the desk, that the tapes were in the microcassette re-
corder."

Some women might refuse to make coffee or keep fresh flowers
on the desk because they feel it is demeaning. Brenda didn't. She
saw the tasks as necessary, as a way of paying her dues. While she
was doing these jobs, she was observing and learning and becoming
more comfortable in her mentor's presence. He in turn was also
observing how bright and creative she was.

While we're certainly not advocating that women start making
coffee in the office, any action—note taking, listening to phone
calls—in the corporation must be analyzed as part of the big picture. If a woman feels it's necessary—if it brings her closer to the
powerful and if it makes a potential mentor aware of her presence—it's worth considering. On the other hand, we saw in chapter
3 how Shawn Campbell, the fact checker who eventually became a
writer, stayed within her cubby, rarely talking to the rest of the
magazine staff. If she had been more pleasant and open to others,
she might perhaps have developed a network and found a mentor
sooner.

Brenda told us more about the process of learning by her boss's
side. "It was pedagogy all the way. He was the teacher and I was
the student. He didn't say, 'If you sit in my office and listen to me
handle this sensitive phone call, you'll learn how to do it.' It was

not didactic. It was implicit, and I was a sponge.

"I was an excellent observer and I had a need to absolutely soak up and emulate everything. I read every manila folder in every file drawer. I watched, I made notes, I memorized. I imposed the methodology on myself. I kept saying to myself, 'Now that I've seen how he did that, I can do that' or 'I'll know how to do that next time.' "

What Brenda learned is not something that can be learned by rote or done in isolation. This educational process works because it's within the context of a personal mentoring relationship. The mentor and protégé identify with each other and often share values. Each feels the other is special. The protégé wants to learn what the mentor knows, and the mentor enjoys teaching such a willing pupil.

Over the years Sam Fishbine had supervised several interns who had been placed in his law office through formal programs, but none of those relationships was as special as his relationship with Sally. "I can't remember ever not feeling comfortable with him," Sally says. "I can never remember being afraid of him or being intimidated by him. That was from day one. He is very gregarious and talkative. He taught all the time. That's what makes him a good mentor: he's so interested in what he does for a living that he likes to talk about it."

Sam intrigued Sally. A middle-aged Jew born and bred in Boston, he was like no one she had ever met. Though their backgrounds were different—she had grown up in Bettindorf, Iowa—their values were very similar. "We both have a sense of justice, of fairness in human rights, of decency. We both like good books, good music, good food, and the theater. And she had the kind of feistiness I think I had, ready to take on anything or anybody," Sam says.

He saw more than his own feistiness in Sally. He saw himself thirty-four years before: young, vigorous, and ambitious. He continues, "Yes, there was a big image reflection there, and so I was enticed. Ego—male ego—got involved. Hey, this is me all over again."

Sam was more than an entrée into the labor-law community. He introduced Sally to a whole new way of living. Sam's sophisticated townhouse, with its original artwork and interior-designer touches, dazzled her. "I think the whole concept of living in downtown Boston and what that would be like was something I got from Sam too. There was a whole lifestyle modeling going on," recalls Sally.

Sally soon moved a block away from Sam. Boston's Back Bay section of Boston was a far cry from provincial Bettindorf. Although she spent her formative years there, she never became a midwesterner at heart. Her mother, a transplanted easterner who agreed to live in Iowa to please her husband, raised Sally to reject everything midwestern. Growing up, Sally always felt different. Her mother dressed her in striking outfits that made her stand out from the other kids.

"I was taught that there's a whole world beyond the little church-based society in Bettindorf and that not being like them is all right," Sally says. Her mother, a professional social worker with a strong individualistic streak, gave her a commitment to hard work and a social consciousness. Her father, "the sweetest, most easygoing guy in the world," who never completed high school and worked as a manager of a used-car dealership, gave her an appreciation of being a woman.

Since she had been encouraged by her mother to seek out new worlds, going to college in the East was not a difficult transition for Sally. When Sam later initiated her into his world, she devoured it wholeheartedly—the labor-union movement, big-city living, even his ethos.

Sam enjoyed playing the role of teacher and life mentor, particularly because Sally was such a model student. "She was extremely bright and personable, pleasant to be with and have around," remarks Fishbine. "What teacher doesn't like a student who drinks from his cup?"

Sally drank from his cup with gusto. She respected him and viewed him as an ego ideal, a person she would like to become. Sam taught more than skills; he imparted a value system and represented someone Sally admired. Men can be life mentors for women, but they cannot model all the roles that women want to learn. We have seen how men can be career mentors and teach women a profession and help them understand the power structure; they can also give women the male insider's point of view. But men cannot present a woman's viewpoint on how to survive and succeed as a woman in a male-dominated organization. Nor can they teach them how to juggle their lives, to have time and energy for their careers as well as their personal relationships. Women want the best of both these worlds. Therefore women need—and yearn for—women mentors to serve as life mentors, to teach them how to live their lives as women professionals.

In Sally's case Sam could be her life mentor because she chose the individualistic path, the same path Sam chose. She identified with him professionally and personally. Because she had no children, she did not feel the conflicts over dividing her energy between family and career that many married women felt with their mentors. Perhaps if she had had a secondary mentor who was a woman or a close female peer, she would have felt support for other paths besides the male track. For example surgeon Carol Woodman looked to her mentor's wife as a domestic role model. Her mentor and his wife in combination became her life mentor: Woodman modeled her life on a blend of her mentor's professionalism and his wife's domesticity.

Sally looked to Sam alone for advice and role modeling. She internalized his behavior, took it in, and made it her own. This part of learning is unconscious and emotional. The protégé's idealizing of the mentor not only helps her learn but also distinguishes her from other subordinates.

Two other factors, respect and trust, distinguish the mentoring relationship from other learning relationships, according to James Clawson, an assistant professor of organizational behavior at the Harvard Business School.[2] "The recognition that another person has some skill that one desires is the beginning of respect and of the motivation to become, in part at least, like that person," he writes.[3] Wanting to be like that person forms the basis of identification.

"Identification is one of the most important aspects of the teaching situation," explains psychologist Harry Levinson in his book *Executive*.[4] "Successful teachers must be good identification figures and learners must be able to learn from them by identification. Identification is not simple imitation. For identification to succeed, children must first love, then imitate, then assert their relative independence to practice the behavior they have learned."[5]

This is exactly what happens with protégés and mentors. As respect for each other grows and trust develops, the identification deepens. A pediatrician describes her mentor, twenty years her senior: "He was considered one of the best private physicans in the city and was always at the hospital—I mean, twenty-four hours a day. All the house staff looked up to him, and he won the most-outstanding-teacher awards many years in a row from the house."

As she began to share a practice with him, she continued idealizing him, but it became more personal. "I always thought he was kind and gentle, never thinking of himself, but always being there for the families of the patients that he took care of and coming in all times of day or night. A totally nondemanding, giving type of person." This idealization formed the basis of her identification with him and allowed her to learn how to be a physician in private practice.

After they were partners for fifteen years, she took a year off and went to India as a missionary physician, something she had been yearning to do. It was as though her mentor had modeled the role of guru and now she played it out—her way. When she returned, her values had changed and the material benefits of the practice were less important to her. If she had to do it over, she's not sure she would choose private practice again.

This pediatrician drank from her mentor's cup but after years of working together, she realized that not everything she had imbibed did fit comfortably in her own mug. To become her own professional and develop her own professional identity as a doctor of charity, she needed to reject some of his ways and develop her own.

What the pediatrician learned from her mentor differs from what a university researcher or a corporate manager learns from her mentor. Nevertheless *how* a woman learns a profession and gains a professional identity is the same for all professions. She learns by idealizing the mentor, identifying with him, and then internalizing the parts that fit for her. The end result is different: being a doctor feels different from being a writer; being an accountant does not feel the same as being an attorney. But the process is the same across the board.

Sally identified strongly with Sam; she admired his skills, his contacts, his knowledge, and his professionalism. She learned by observing and imitating. After she watched Sam function as an arbitrator, they'd talk things out. He loved to teach with the Socratic method. He'd ask questions, draw her into a dialogue, and they'd argue back and forth. "You spin out a theory, and somebody says, 'Yeah, that's right. That makes sense or that makes sense but . . .' That's how you begin to develop self-confidence," Sally explains. "He'd let me go through what I saw that morning or what I thought the settlement should be and he'd tell me things he knew from prior dealings with those parties."

He didn't teach her content, though; he taught what she couldn't learn in law school or from books. During the last two years of law school they met or talked by phone at least once a week. When she began practicing, their contact tapered off, but Sam was always a phone call away. Sally could go to him with almost any kind of problem. As their relationship evolved, so did her professional identity. She had to take what she was learning about this tough, aggressive field and make it jibe with her image of herself as a woman.

Actually her concepts of herself as a woman and as a lawyer were not that far apart. Sally never saw herself as a quiet, shrinking violet. Her mother had taught her to stand up for what she believed, and Sally constantly defended her unconventional stands while growing up. Although Sally feels her mother seemed uncertain about her femininity and how to act as a woman, she served as a role model for a strong, competent professional. Interestingly Sally feels she received her positive feelings about being a woman from her father, a warm, outgoing man who liked to dance and appreciated having a daughter.

Sally has developed her own style as a woman lawyer. Her determination and core of steel are respected by the toughest union bosses, yet she always behaves with class. If she walks into a negotiating room a few minutes late and someone comments about how she looks, she does not confront him in a room full of people. Instead she says, "I try to be graceful. I never act as if I resent it." Later she will take the man aside and educate him about how to treat women.

Developing a professional identity may be more difficult for women in certain situations. In corporations it is necessary to learn the "corporate culture." Each corporation has its own unique culture, based on shared values and basic beliefs. Some of these informal rules are fairly clear-cut; they tell people how to behave. Is it all right to swear in public? What's the dress code? Are there clear rules about socializing?[6] Other things are more subtle: they define success, establish standards of achievement, and clarify how much deviance will be tolerated. A woman must be part of the culture for a while to discern how women and minorities are treated and how the informal communication network works.[7] The mentor also functions as a teacher of the corporate culture. The protégé must decide whether she is willing to buy into the corporate culture.

In the 1970s some women tried to get ahead by acting and dressing like men. It was easy to spot the striving corporate woman by her serious dark suit and floppy bow tie. Today businesswomen, feeling more secure, dress more femininely, and it's not unusual to see a highly placed woman wearing a dress. However, women still receive mixed messages today. We saw how Ann Hopkins, the CPA at Price Waterhouse, was denied partnership because she acted too much like a man. Even though she brought in more business than any other candidate for partnership, the other partners voted against her because she cursed, smoke, drank beer, and did not wear makeup. It sounds as if she would have fit in with the dominant male corporate culture, yet the men criticized her for not being feminine enough.

"Analyzing a company's corporate culture doesn't guarantee landing a job or a promotion, career experts and managers agree," writes reporter Carol Hymowitz in the *Wall Street Journal.* "But it can illuminate why achievements and a sense of belonging come easier in some settings than in others."[8] The match between a woman's personality and the corporate culture will determine how easily she develops a professional identity there.

An attorney who has worked in a number of corporate settings says, "If you are going to survive in a corporate world, you have to learn how to play the game." Yet she refuses to do that. "If somebody asked my opinion, I'd tell them my true opinion. I was told that I was too direct. In the corporate world they want you to beat around the bush and be sneaky. That is how I interpret it." Although this attorney has excellent credentials, she usually lasts only a year in each corporation. While she reads the corporate culture correctly, she refuses to play according to their rules. Ironically she found private practice, which would seem to mesh better with her personality, too isolating.

A director of marketing and communications, an attractive blonde with an artsy-creative bent, felt her femininity and her creativity were stifled by the corporate culture of the pharmaceutical company for which she works. "I'm such a creative person that I find a lot of stress in playing the corporate role. As I move higher and higher, I must sell myself as a corporate type—that's corporate prostitution. I wear the pin-striped suits and the pumps and the hair in a bun, but that's not really me."

This woman understands the corporate culture but is not sure she wants to buy into it. For a free spirit who likes to dress as she pleases, wear her hair loose, and curse freely, the rigid corporate environment can feel stifling. It will be difficult for her to keep her own personal and feminine identity intact if she stays at this corporation. She doesn't have a mentor, so she alone will have to sort out the issue of whether this corporation is the right place for her.

Women who work alone, such as writers and artists, often have a different problem in developing a professional identity. They work in an isolated setting and must create their own culture. Often they develop professional identities by studying others' works and fantasizing about symbolic mentors or role models. While it is difficult to maintain a personal relationship with a more established writer or artist, the careers of these symbolic mentors can be inspirational.

Identifying with a symbolic mentor helps a woman who works alone feel supported. A woman writer feels a kinship with a symbolic mentor through their writing. The writing process and the writing life give her a bond, a sense of comradeship, with the accomplished writer. Even though each writer works alone at her own word processor or typewriter, there is a sense of shared experience. This identification gives a writer the support necessary to be creative. Artists often have similar experiences when they view works by their symbolic mentors, the artists they admire. In fact professionals in private practice go through a similar process. These symbolic mentors serve as powerful teachers for women who work alone.

* * *

Sam Fishbine feels proud of his protégé. The Boston labor-law community regards Sally Enright as a strong negotiator, and she's made her mark. Many people told her that a woman couldn't make it with the building trades, but that did not stop Enright. Recently one of the largest construction unions in the city asked her to represent them. "That feels wonderful," she says. "Especially when my partners—even the most progressive, reasoned, enlightened, and honestly nonsexist—warned me about how difficult they would be for a woman to deal with."

Although Enright and Fishbine's relationship is less intense today, they still keep in touch. Their relationship has mellowed over its fifteen-year duration. The teacher and student roles have blurred; they have become peers. Her work has become her life's passion. She says, "I don't do this just because I make a living at it. I do it because it's what I want my life to stand for. It's part of the world that I want my life to contribute to."

That world is very different from the parochial world she grew up with. It is Sam's world: a world of interest and grievance arbitrations, of union halls and liberal causes, of concerts and dining out, and of Passover seders and Chanukah celebrations. It is the world and the life that Sally Enright has chosen and made her own.

Sam Fishbine became Sally Enright's life mentor. She modeled both his stance as a lawyer and his lifestyle as a person. He taught her how to become a professional and how to live her life. Sally felt comfortable modeling her life after a man's; most women wouldn't. But because she had chosen a typically "male" path, it worked—until she approached her fortieth birthday. Then she couldn't deny her yearning for a child and some of her regrets that she would never be a mother.

With Sally Enright's story the book comes full circle. We began in chapter 1 with Pearl Brown, a dissatisfied housewife who yearned to do more with her life. She had four children, a supportive husband, and a comfortable life in the suburbs—but it wasn't enough. Sally Enright, on the other hand, has the career every woman dreams of. She has challenging work, high prestige, her peers' respect, and a hefty salary; but she, too, is dissatisfied. In a sense they each want what the other has. (After much struggling, though, Pearl was able to find a satisfying career without sacrificing her family.) In fact most women want both: a satisfying career and gratifying personal relationships.

Can women have both or have it all? We believe they can't do everything well at the same time. We're pleased to see that women in the 1990s have given up striving to be Superwoman and have more realistic goals. The more women realize this, the more they can pace their goals and use one decade to give their children a good start, another for focusing on their career, and so on. Nor can women reach their achievements by themselves. Women need mentors, role models, sponsors, coaches, and peers to show them the way, to teach them how to juggle their responsibilities and keep their sanity, and to model how to be women in the fullest sense of the word. Women are the best life mentors for other women, but until more women reach the professional positions of a Sally Enright and a Pearl Brown, women must take whatever kind of mentoring and role modeling they can get and temper it to fit their own individual needs.

◇   ◇   ◇

CHAPTER TEN

How to Find a Mentor

Finding a mentor is an active process, requiring vision, planning, and sensitivity. You must be at the right place at the right time. Having talent and potential are important, but women cannot wait to be chosen. That's too passive an approach for the business and professional world.

This chapter offers a blueprint to help you find a mentor. We've developed two series of questions to give you an opportunity to assess yourself and the people with whom you work. The first set of questions, "Self-Assessment," explores your past experience with relationships, your strengths and weaknesses, and your goals for the future. The next set of questions, "Assessing Your Potential Mentors," will help you understand the women and men with whom you work, the organizational hierarchy, and where you fit in. By the end of the chapter, you should have reached a realistic assessment of yourself, your current network, and the direction and initiative you need to take to approach and attract a mentor.*

Self-Assessment

1. What age and developmental stage am I in in my career?

A middle-aged woman in a second career, a divorcée or widow entering the work force for the first time, a working mother with

*For purposes of clarity in this section we continue to use the pronoun he for the mentor and she for the protégé. We encourage you to read "she" for the mentor also.

school-age children, a young single woman right out of college—
these women all have different needs and different expectations
from their careers and their mentors. When choosing a mentor,
keep in mind what you need at this particular stage of your career
and what kind of support you may need in terms of child care. This
is not static. Your needs will change as there are changes in your
goals or in your marital status and as your children become more
independent.

Remember that mentors often play important roles at crisis
periods or turning points in protégés' careers: a young physician
deciding on a specialty, a mature woman making a career change,
or a female manager on the verge of a promotion. The presence of
a mentor can make the difference between success and failure.[1]

2. What are my career goals?

Your career goals are closely connected to the age and stage of
your career. It's important to assess them as you choose a mentor.
Look at where you are now, where you want to be at the end of this
year, in five years, and then in ten years. It's crucial to keep the big
picture in mind when choosing a mentor, because if you have
clearly focused goals, a mentor can help you achieve them.

3. What are my strengths and weaknesses professionally?

Women tend to have difficulty taking credit for their accomplishments, but take an honest look at yourself. Consider your
training and education, your vocational and interpersonal skills,
your past work record and your achievements and accomplishments. What have been the peaks and the valleys in your career?
Which areas do you need to develop or fine-tune, and in which do
you feel most competent? This analysis will help you focus on the
areas you can develop with a mentor's guidance and on the
strengths you bring to a mentoring relationship.

4. What has been my pattern in dealing with intimacy?

Mentoring is an intimate relationship. How you have fared in
other intimate relationships—marriage, friendships, family—will

give you a clue about how you will probably relate in a mentoring relationship. Consider whether you have a lot of acquaintances or a few good, close friends. Look at your patterns in initiating, maintaining, and ending relationships. Consider the quality of your relationships, the amount of closeness or distance you're comfortable with, and whether you relate better to a man or a woman and why.

5. Where's my job in the organizational hierarchy?

Try to analyze where your job fits in in the overall organizational hierarchy. Are you in a line position (these traditionally have been male, and the way one moves up the ranks), or are you in a staff position? Did you choose this position and are you satisfied with it? Is your position exempt or nonexempt, and do you know how to get from there onto the management track? Look at yourself in relation to female and male peers and see how you compare with them.

6. What are the signals that someone may be observing me as a potential protégé?

There are verbal and nonverbal cues that someone may be interested in you as a protégé. In addition to their showing interest in you professionally and asking questions about your career and your goals, notice whether someone also takes a personal interest in you. Sharing advice and information and teaching you what the potential mentor knows are also ways of showing interest in you as a potential protégé. Be aware of nonverbal cues too; these include expressions and gestures, the amount of eye contact, and listening carefully.

7. What relationships do I have now at work that I might develop into mentoring relationships?

The best place to start building relationships is within your own immediate network. This includes your boss, supervisor, or manager. Your peers, indirect bosses or supervisors, and other professionals are people who could serve as guides, coaches, or sponsors.

Analyze the work relationships you already have and ask yourself what you are currently getting and what you miss. Try to be as specific as possible. If you feel supported and nurtured but do not have the access to the powerful, then you may want to look for a person who wields power as a mentor. If you have the ear of the manager but feel isolated and alone, then you need a more nurturing relationship to balance your network.

8. What type of relationship am I looking for at work?

Before you enter a work relationship that *might* fit your needs, you need to figure out what kind of relationship you are looking for and what your goals are. Do you want a coach: someone to counsel you on your current assignments, give you positive feedback, and appraise your progress? Or maybe you're looking for a sponsor, a person to promote you within the organization, get you on the right committees, give you visibility with the big bosses? Perhaps you want a guide, someone who is one step ahead of you who can share a wealth of information about moving up to the next rung of the ladder. Or maybe you just want a peer, a colleague at your organizational level who can provide support.

"An Abbreviated Guide to Matching Your Needs," the chart on the next page, will help you focus on the type of relationship you want. Read through the statements in the boxes along the bottom and check the numbers that apply to you (choose as many as you like). Then see under which number most of your numbers are clustered. That will help you pinpoint what type of relationship you are looking for.

You do not need to choose *between* these relationships. At one point in your career you may have a coach, a sponsor, and a boss who is a facilitator. At another point you may have a male mentor and a close female peer. Each of these relationships is valuable in its own right, and each can enhance your career. You can learn from many different people.

If you are looking for a true mentor, however, that means you

An Abbreviated Guide to Matching Your Needs

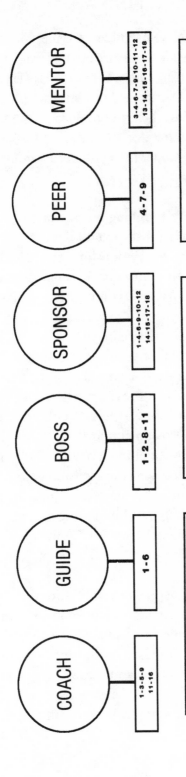

COACH   GUIDE   BOSS   SPONSOR   PEER   MENTOR

COACH: 1-3-5-9 11-16

GUIDE: 1-6

BOSS: 1-2-8-11

SPONSOR: 1-4-6-10-12 14-15-17-18

PEER: 4-7-9

MENTOR: 3-4-6-7-9-10-11-12 13-14-15-16-17-18

1. I want to be in the right place at the right time.

2. I don't like to ask for help or make mistakes.

3. I just want to develop my skills.

4. I need encouragement and support for my goals.

5. I just need someone to help me through with the next project.

6. I need more information on how my profession works.

7. I want a friend to listen to me; I need a shoulder to cry on.

8. I just want to do my job and keep a low profile.

9. I need more positive feedback.

10. I want to be on the fast track. I want to be the CEO.

11. I'm the kind of person who needs a kick in the pants, but I do good work.

12. I need someone to help me actualize my goals.

13. I need a brain to pick; I need vision.

14. I'd like advice on my career path; I don't know what to do next.

15. I'd like a chance to develop my talents.

16. I need someone to "love" and admire.

17. I'm in lower management. How do I crack the next level?

18. I want to be more of a risk taker.

are seeking an intensive one-on-one relationship that has elements of all of the above roles as well as the intimacy of a personal relationship. How will you know if it is true mentoring? Agnes Missirian's research suggests that true mentoring has three elements that distinguish it from other supportive relationships: *the power or access to power the mentor has, the level of identification, and the intensity of emotional involvement.*[2]

9. Am I willing to pay my dues if I find a mentor?

A mentor may be willing to enter a relationship with you, but he will want something in return. As we have stressed throughout this book, mentoring is reciprocal. Mentors may want you to work long hours on one of their projects in return for their teaching, coaching, and support. These are all ways for your mentor to feel comfortable with you, and for you to get your foot in the door and achieve your long-term goals. These are especially necessary for women, who are often excluded from outings or sporting events where deals are made. Think hard about whether you're willing to pay your dues in exchange for the opportunity to work with the mentor.

Assessing Your Potential Mentors

1. Where do I look for a mentor?

Mentors and protégés meet everywhere. Although the most common meeting ground is the workplace, many women meet their mentors through leisure activities or at community or business groups. Usually the relationship evolves as two people work together and develops because of shared interests, admiration, or job demands that require teamwork.[3]

The logical place to begin is with your own network, which you identified in question 7 of the Self-Assessment. Keep in mind that not every boss and supervising manager is a mentor. Mentors and superiors differ in their objectives, their self-interest, their roles, and their tasks.[4] Mentors are more future and developmentally oriented, teaching generic tasks, while bosses often just want to get the present job done as efficiently as possible.

If the opportunity presents itself, you may be lucky enough to choose someone outside your immediate network, someone who is much higher up than you. Nancy Collins, author of *Professional Women and Their Mentors,* suggests aiming for the CEO, the chairman of the board, the dean, or the head of the department. This is the person with power or access to power.[5]

A mentor a level or two above you will provide different benefits from someone at the top. Which you choose will depend on whether you want someone who is accessible and who can provide ongoing support or whether you prefer to have the ear of a powerful person—even if it's only for a few minutes a week or a few times a year. Consider your own personality too: Some women have no difficulty approaching high-level executives or heads of companies; others are not gutsy or comfortable enough to approach a powerful person.

2. How can I attract a mentor?

Women can increase their chances of attracting a mentor by exhibiting the qualities that mentors look for in a protégé. According to Michael Zey, these include intelligence, ambition, loyalty, commitment to the organization, the ability to form alliances, and the desire and ability to accept power and take risks.[6] Mentors also value assertiveness, independence, and competence in their protégés.[7]

To let others know you have these qualities, you must be highly visible. A high profile is easier to achieve in a small company; in a larger organization you must create situations where you can toot your own horn.[8] (This is not something women do comfortably, because they are brought up to believe it is selfish and unfeminine to draw attention to themselves or their accomplishments.) Successfully completing a project is only part of the task; others must know about it for you to reap the benefits. You need a high profile without appearing to be arrogant.

Take risks. Risk taking shows others that you are willing to take the initiative, put your head or maybe your job on the line, and accept a challenge.[9] Volunteer for the task that no one else wants and then handle it creatively. Take a stand that may be unpopular if you believe in it. Others will respect you for your beliefs and actions.

Show a desire to learn. Mentors are interested in people who want to grow. When you show curiosity and interest in expanding your knowledge, behavior, or skills, you signal to others that you are receptive to new ideas and open to changing. It's also important to accept criticism constructively.

Learn to read signals correctly.[10] Develop a political savvy so that you can understand body language, read between the lines, and gain insight into the shadow organization. As you move up the corporate ladder, communication is much more subtle. You must understand the organization's nonverbal cues.

3. How much initiative should I take in my pursuit of a mentor?

Staying in your office, working hard, and waiting to be discovered is not a good idea. On the other hand, we agree with author Nancy Collins, who discourages women from approaching a potential mentor in a blunt, mechanical way by asking, "Will you be my mentor?"[11] We believe this question is a turnoff.

Try to put yourself in a position of working with the person you'd like to be your mentor. This can be difficult if he is in another department or company. Perhaps you could get on a committee he chairs or work on an all-company project together. Then ask for his help. Good questions to ask a potential mentor are: "Will you help me learn such-and-such skills?" "Will you teach me the value system of this corporation?" "Will you help me learn more about the organization?" Another good question to ask is, "I'd really like to learn more about your speciality in the profession. How can I do it?"

4. What if I get rebuffed by the mentor?

It's not enough to find a mentor; the mentor must be responsive and willing to take on the mentoring role. If the person you approach is *not* responsive, try to find out tactfully why he is not interested in helping you. It could be that the timing is bad; maybe he is overloaded with his own work and has little energy left. Perhaps the person is thinking of leaving the company and doesn't want to begin any new relationships. Or he may be overwhelmed with personal problems at this time. You may ask whether his interest may change in a few months when his situation has stabilized or whether he can recommend someone else who could help you.

There's also the possibility that you may not be his type, which is something he probably cannot verbalize. For informal mentoring to work, the chemistry—that ephemeral but necessary quality that draws mentor and protégé together—must be right.

5. Who makes a good mentor for a woman?

All good mentors share certain qualities. They are competent and successful, respected for their knowledge. They are good teachers and good motivators. They inspire confidence and are empathic. But as a minority, women must be especially careful not to ally themselves with the wrong person. It's important to identify with the mentor over a broad range of attitudes and behaviors and to understand the mentor's attitudes toward women and minorities.

6. Should I look for a male or female mentor?

Whether you seek a male or a female mentor will depend on who is available and how responsive he or she is. You must also consider whether you want someone who wields power or someone who offers intimacy. Unfortunately these two qualities typically break along gender lines. Our research has shown that male mentors offer more in terms of advancement, whereas female mentors give more support and teaching. The study of women physicians and their mentors (see page 29) also supports our findings.[12]

Again, we stress that for women the mentoring relationship must be supplemented with other relationships. To avoid getting enmeshed in a relationship such as Brenda Marks and Bert Paley did in chapter 5, it is necessary to develop other connections. This also prevents you from becoming too linked politically with one person. That way if your mentor falls out of favor, you won't necessarily be severed from the other power holders.

7. How can I find a mentor if I work alone?

If you work alone—as a writer, artist, or consultant or in a private practice—it is much more difficult to find a mentor. The professional organizations to which you belong are a source; for instance the officers and committee chairs are potential mentors. Writing for journals and taking courses and seminars are other avenues to increase your contacts while you learn about a new subject. (You might also apply these ideas if you work in an organizational culture that does not foster mentoring relationships.)

Since it is more difficult to find a primary mentor if you work alone, consider using your colleagues and peers for support. Writers and artists, for example, often form support groups. These groups help break the isolation of working alone and provide much-needed moral support. Members also critique each other's work, discuss their craft, and share marketing tips. Psychotherapists and consultants can form similar support groups. Joining networking groups of men and women from *different* professions can also put you in touch with potential mentors.

8. How can I help my career if I can't find a mentor?

If you can't find a mentor, don't despair. Many other types of relationships can advance your career and help you develop personally. There is an array of options open to women today. Although many women spoke to us of one significant relationship, scores of others talked about having a series of relationships or a constellation of relationships with varying degrees of intimacy and power.

Peer relationships, for example, are becoming increasingly important for women. In addition to using peers informally for support and networking, some women are developing small groups of contemporaries who can be helpful to them, such as the writers' and artists' support groups mentioned above.

Brief sponsorships can also be helpful. A telephone call or an occasional lunch with an influential and experienced person can provide critical information at key points in your career. (Remember to follow up with a thank-you note or call.) Networks and business and professional organizations also serve a mentoring function. Like corporations, many professional organizations are now starting formal mentoring programs that match young women with older, more experienced professionals within their fields. This is another way to become acquainted with experienced and powerful people in your profession.

Lastly, don't underestimate the power of a symbolic mentor. For some women they serve as substitute mentors; for others they are secondary mentors when the primary mentor is a man. Although you may never meet these mentors, they can provide role modeling and motivate and inspire you.

Mentoring is not a one-time opportunity. If you haven't found a mentor yet, don't give up. There will be many chances through your lifetime to form relationships that will advance and enhance your career. Don't make finding a mentor your driving purpose in life. Remember, the worst way to attract a mentor is to become so obsessed with the pursuit that you alienate potential mentors and lose sight of everything else. If you follow the advice in this chapter, you will find that whether you land a mentor or not, you will have enhanced your professional status and gained a greater understanding of your position in the organization. Even if you don't find someone who wants an intense mentoring relationship, you will most likely attract others to your network who can be helpful to you.

To review our recommendations:

- Assess yourself: the age and stage of your career, your strengths and weaknesses professionally, and your pattern in dealing with intimacy, as well as your place in the organizational hierarchy and your career goals.
- To find a mentor you must take the initiative and plan for it. Most relationships develop slowly out of working together for a while.
- Examine the relationships in your current network. Start with your boss and study your relationship with him. Then decide what kind of relationship you are looking for at work—mentor, sponsor, coach, guide, facilitator, or peer—and actively pursue it. Remain open to all relationships at work and in your professional organizations. Relationships with varying levels of intimacy, learning, and power can provide different experiences. You can benefit from all kinds of people and many types of relationships.
- Look for people who are competent at what they do, who are good teachers, active motivators, and powerful and secure in their positions. But don't rule out the iconoclast who may have less to lose (by mentoring a minority) but who can teach you a lot.
- To attract a mentor, keep a high profile, take risks, show a desire to learn, and develop a political savvy to understand the shadow organization.
- Your career will not suffer if you can't find one significant mentor. Surround yourself with a network of people who can support, nurture, sponsor, promote, and teach you. Then try to give back some of what you have received. The process will regenerate itself.

Conclusion

That women must redefine the mentoring relationship in their own terms to meet their unique needs is a bold, new idea. Rather than struggle to make the male model fit, women must create a new model if they are to fulfill their own potential.

Women possess within themselves the strength to be mentors. They have an affinity for building relationships that allows them to define themselves as well as to grow within a relationship. They have an ability to reach consensus and conciliation while nurturing and supporting others. Women's developmental paths are complex; their roles and their lives are complicated. In addition, each woman brings her own individual experience, creativity, and talents to the workplace. For women the mentoring experience must reflect all of these facets of existence.

Since most of the previous work on mentoring has been done on men by men, we used the traditional, old boys' kind of mentoring as the base of our study. Most of the protégés we profiled were mentored by men, as are the majority of mentored women today. While women *do* advance professionally without mentors, we believe many of the women we interviewed would not have achieved their prestigious positions without their male mentors, and so do they. Law professor Gina Carbone would not have made tenure as quickly without her three mentors. Carol Woodman developed her reputation as a surgeon from her association with her mentor. Sally Enright learned labor law from her mentor and developed self-confidence as well as the endorsement of the labor-law community because of this relationship. Account executive Susan Richards would not have advanced as fast or as far without her mentor. The list goes on and on.

But cross-gender mentoring is complicated. Men and women are not used to working closely together as colleagues. Sexual issues and innuendo add to their discomfort. Some women avoid these issues by seeing their mentors as father figures, as did law professor Gina Carbone. This does work even as it prevents both men and women from facing the very real, threatening issues connected with their new roles: issues of power, competition, sexuality, and intimacy. The identification in cross-gender mentoring is limited too. Women can identify with their male mentors as professionals and colleagues and they can model some of their skills, attitudes, and behaviors but they can't identify on the most basic level of gender.

At some point in the cross-gender mentoring process each protégé had to confront her femininity. It is at this juncture that she often rejects the male model, finding it narrow and limiting. Kathie Long, for example, got no support from her mentor, Richard Hendricks, when she told him she wanted to scale back her career and lead a more balanced life—that is, marry and have children. Janice Celica reached a turning point in the mentoring relationship with the principal when they acknowledged that they were sexually attracted to each other but did not want to act on their feelings.

In these examples and many more we found that the male model did not mesh with the contemporary woman's needs or with her unique place in the work force. Women wished for a female perspective on surviving and thriving in the predominantly male work environment. They longed for a female role model to show them how to combine their career and family responsibilities. In essence they yearned for a broader, more eclectic perspective on mentoring. Our synthesis of the mentoring relationship, which has evolved after analyzing interviews with 106 protégés, recognizes women's unique developmental paths, their affinity for relationships, and their minority status in a predominantly male work environment.

Because of their unique developmental paths and the developmental differences between men and women, women can have mentors in their twenties, thirties, forties, or even their fifties, depending on when they enter the work force and when they start their families. (About half of our sample had their initial mentoring relationship after age thirty.) Having mentors at different times in their adult lives means that mentors will serve different purposes in different decades.

A young woman in her twenties who has not started her family would benefit from a powerful older, male mentor to help her launch her career. For instance, Kathie Long was single and twenty-four when she met her mentor, Richard Hendricks. He was an ideal mentor for someone just starting out who had dreams of becoming partner. However, Long and Hendricks clashed as she approached thirty because illness compelled her to face female developmental issues. Men are not usually conflicted about having a career *and* a family; women often are.

A working woman in her midthirties with young children could relate better to another working mother as a mentor, rather than a man. Similarly, a single or divorced woman could relate well to a woman in the same circumstances. When writer Bonnie Philpott served as a role model for Shawn Campbell, she showed her that a woman could have a social life and a successful career. Shawn feared becoming "a magazine widow" but by using Bonnie's life as a model, she saw that she didn't have to be married to her career to succeed. On the other hand a woman in her mid-forties who has already raised her family or is divorced or widowed and is entering the work force for the first time may have a mentor the same age—male or female—who has been working for fifteen years. Pearl Brown, the corporate officer who had gone back to school for her MBA in her thirties after raising her family, had several male mentors when she was in her forties. They served a purely instrumental role. She was not interested in an intense personal relationship; she wanted to learn the skills needed to succeed in the corporate world.

In our new model a woman will probably not have one traditional male mentor for her lifetime; instead she'll have a number of mentoring relationships spanning her career. At one point she may have a strong primary male mentor and a secondary female mentor or peer. At another she may have a male coach or sponsor and a female peer. Or she may benefit from a series of relationships: a mix of male and female mentors, sponsors, coaches, bosses, and peers. The permutations are endless, as long as women are open to relationships. The more relationships a woman has, the more her career will benefit and the more she will grow personally.

One goal of this book has been to raise the consciousness of women so that they are more cognizant of their position in the workplace. We are not content with women's minority status nor are we satisfied with the status quo. We want to see women earn the same dollar men earn, not 71.8 cents. Since women make up almost half of the work force, we want to see them represented more equally in leadership positions. They are a minority in the upper echelons of power in practically every business, professional, and corporate setting.

However, some women don't see themselves as a minority. A black woman, whose minority status is more obvious, understands that she needs to ally with the powerful to advance politically. She also recognizes that another underdog can be a powerful ally and mentor, as Susan Richards did with recovering alcoholic Budd Churninsky. But most (white) women, whether through denial or naiveté, don't comprehend this. They tell their mentor or boss, "I want to be treated like a man," which is a way of denying their gender in order to be accepted in a man's world. Women need to accept that *for now* they are politically disadvantaged and that a mentor (who is typically male) can be their political ally.

Mentoring can help women crack the old boys' network. While it's not the only way to get ahead, having an important political relationship can make a significant difference in penetrating the hierarchy of the power elite. An associate professor speaks about how her mentor, a revered professor, sponsored and promoted her. "He introduced me to an amazing number of extraordinary people.

I had lunch with the president of the National Academy of Sciences. There were twenty august people, most of whom were gentlemen, and three women. And he made a point of saying, 'Dr. So and So, I'd really like you to sit with X, Y, and Z (the three women), because you haven't had a chance to talk with them in your stay at the university.' That was followed by a meeting with the head of a certain division of an international organization, who asked if we might collaborate on research."

A woman must work hard to overcome discrimination and combat the isolation she feels in a predominantly male environment. She must also choose her associations carefully and develop political savvy. A mentor can open doors for her, introduce her to the power holders, promote her within the corporation, and help her understand the subtleties of the corporate culture.

When a woman is a protégé, she finds ways of accepting the male model and tempering it to suit her needs. Being a protégé is one way to become a mentor. Women who receive good mentoring want to give that back to others. Many of our protégés, in fact, have since become mentors; this phenomenon is bound to help the women of the future. As we have seen, surgeon Carol Woodman became a mentor to one of her male residents. He is the same age as she but is about six years behind her in his training. She says, "I can see so many parallels with my own mentor. We'll meet in the hallway and talk. I'll invite him over with his wife, just kind of keeping in mind where he is, what's going on, how he's doing, and how his residency is working out."

Law professor Gina Carbone, who is now undergraduate dean, has also become a mentor to two women on her staff; she says they "see me as a role model and would like to do what I'm doing." She consciously looks for women employees with potential to mentor. "Once you've been on the receiving end," she says, "you want to be on the giving end."

Brenda Marks now works for a large advertising agency and has four women under her, who look at her as a mentor. She remembers how she learned the advertising business from her mentor, Bert Paley; now she sees the same scenario replayed with her own protégés. "Bert was a cinematic experience. I watched and I remembered. That's because he let me spend so much time with him," she says. "Bert became a huge success largely through the function of personality. We are in a business that entitles us to do that—almost demands it. That's what I watched and that's what I now put into play. So now I see how I am watched and I see some imitative behaviors. I realize that I'm going to mentor pretty much the way Bert did it. I want to, and it works. That's the nicest tribute I can pay him."

As more women move into positions of power, we are confident that more women will become mentors. And what a difference it will make! Consider Kathie Long's relationship with Richard Hendricks. He was the ideal political mentor as long as Kathie was willing to put in twelve-hour days and put her career before anything else in her life. But when she chose to lead a more balanced life, after her serious bout with bleeding ulcers, Hendricks lost interest in her; he felt she settled for being a "7" when she could have been a "10" (or his idea of a "10").

Fast forward ten years. Imagine that a woman like Kathie Long has a powerful *female* mentor, a woman in her late forties with two college-aged children. How would she react to Kathie's desire to marry and have children *and* strive for partnership? Since the mentor herself has struggled with raising her own family and pursuing her career, she could empathize with Kathie's conflicts. Their identification would deepen. Her mentor would support her in balancing her life and do whatever she could to accommodate her at the office. In this case it would be in her mentor's interest for her protégé to succeed as a mother as well as a partner.

We'd like to think that female mentors are as interested in their protégé's parenting as in their career, but of course that's an ideal. There are plenty of women who don't behave this way and who would not be nurturing or supportive of other women. They may feel insecure themselves or threatened by another competent woman. Others may not feel political themselves or may not truly understand women's minority status, since they themselves may have had little difficulty advancing. Any of these reasons hold some women back from giving to other women.

Nevertheless most women desperately need and yearn for women mentors to help them cope with the issues they face today. As they struggle with new demands on themselves and their families, they are experimenting with new ways of coping. For most women whether or not to work is no longer a choice. However, for married women the needed second income comes with a second shift—of housework, child care, and cooking. In her book *Second Shift* author Arlie Hochschild found that the average working woman puts in an extra month of work at home each year.[1]

Flextime, job sharing, and the family track are ways businesses and industry are trying to cope with new demands on families in the 1990s. We commend corporations with formal mentoring programs because developing such programs shows a recognition of the need to help women and minorities move ahead. All of these ideas need further consideration and exploration.

Women need other women as role models to teach them how to live their lives as professionals, wives, and mothers. Women also need other women as supporters and nurturers; only another woman can understand the conflicts and struggles a woman experiences. A manager spoke of how she helped her young protégé: "She's even asking when the best time to be pregnant is. There was no one to talk to about those kinds of issues—about affordable child care and how do I manage. These are real issues for females in corporations." These are issues for women in academia, in law firms, and in private practices as well.

Women also need other women as advocates. "I make damn sure that any committee I serve on has a good number of women, including younger ones," stresses a prominent psychotherapist. "I'm also in a position now of being much in demand as a speaker, and I won't go unless there is another woman on the panel itself." As advocates, as role models, and as supporters, women can inspire each other to dream their wildest dreams and then go after them.

What else would it take for more women to mentor other women? Reality factors aside, it would require women to think about themselves differently and then act differently. This will not be easy, because society still punishes women for acting in "unfeminine" ways. Women must try to accept all parts of themselves, the aggressive along with the nurturing. Women need to realize that it is not unfeminine to be assertive, to satisfy their own needs and goals, or to dream their own dreams. Female mentors may help facilitate these realizations. Woman-to-woman mentoring, at its best, encourages the younger woman to aspire to what the older woman has achieved.

Recognizing that jealousy from others is natural and that they may feel guilty when they try new, more "masculine" behaviors, women must learn to take credit for their accomplishments, not to attribute them to luck or happenstance.

Lastly women must learn to feel comfortable with power (they are just as capable of handling it as men). But women need more encouragement and more opportunity to see themselves as the holders of power. Psychologist Pamela Enders, associate director of training at Boston Institute of Psychotherapies and instructor in the Department of Psychiatry at Harvard Medical School, talks about women's difficulty in accepting the power implicit in the mentor's role. "Women have been traditionally less willing to acknowledge their power, the power of their influence over others. They might shy away from that. I think a good mentor needs to acknowledge the power that she has. Men do that very easily. I see women's reluctance to acknowledge and use the power they have in many ways. For example, they might say, 'I'm not a mentor,' 'I'm not this,' 'I just work here.' "

If women in all fields begin perceiving power in a healthy, productive way, as men do, women's perceptions and roles will change. At first there will probably be a certain amount of discomfort and conflict for women and men, as well as for the culture, but out of it will come women's leadership and then their mentorship.

Mentors can give women permission to be whole people, to

accept the "feminine," nurturing sides of themselves as well as their "masculine," aggressive feelings—Carl Jung's anima and animus. If women spend their early adult years traditionally, by raising a family and supporting a husband, their mentor's support for their professional side is tantamount to saying, "Yes, it's all right for you to be an aggressive woman and go after what you want in your career." On the other hand if women devote their twenties and early thirties to their career, a mentor who is a working mother can affirm their decision to have children later and can serve as a role model for juggling family and career.

Although women did not say it in so many words, they yearned for life mentors who would teach them how to live their lives, not just how to advance in their careers. Attorney Sally Enright found such a figure in Sam Fishbine: He taught her how to live her life as well as how to advance her career. But he presented a male perspective, even though he was in touch with his nurturing side, as are many men who mentor at midlife.

What might Sally's experience have been like if her life mentor had been a woman, or if she had had a secondary female mentor or even a close woman colleague? There's a better chance a woman would understand the emptiness she felt because her nurturing needs had not been satisfied. Although Sally might not necessarily have chosen a different path, she would have had a balance to the male perspective. Even if she had made the same decision in the end, she would have selected it from a broader range of options.

It is not surprising that women yearn for female life mentors, considering the pressures they face today. Such a mentor would understand the angst a woman feels, which a male has not experienced in our society. Women want a meaningful career yet most also want meaningful personal relationships: a husband and children.

Juggling work and family made many competent women stammer and stutter when we asked them to define success. No matter how prestigious their position, they told us that they couldn't feel successful unless they felt good about their personal relationships.

More often we heard that they felt tired, overworked, overstressed, and underpampered from the strain of coping with so many roles. "I never had a day where I didn't feel guilty about something." Pearl Brown says. "It's just part of life. Feeling guilty about either my children or my work is something that is part of the natural terrain for me." It seems clear that women don't feel successful unless they can master both the job and the home front.

A life mentor is reminiscent of the very first mentor from Greek mythology: the goddess Athena, who was disguised in the body of Mentor, a close friend of Odysseus. When she entered his body, the male and female personas merged, and together they guided Telemachus in his search for his father, Odysseus.[2] Mentor/Athena served as a teacher, parent substitute, friend, coach, support, and guru—all roles mentors play today. He/she guided Telemachus developmentally to help him become a full person. This androgynous figure contains the roots of the contemporary mentor. Ideally mentors behave "femininely": They nurture, love, care, teach, listen, and protect; they show kindness and empathy and share their wisdom. By means of their "masculine" nature they are also authority figures who set standards, lead, initiate, and even at times give their protégés a kick in the pants.

Such an ideal is rarely found in contemporary society. In reality mentors and protégés relate to each other just as they do to all others with whom they are intimate. They bring their gender baggage and their own personal baggage to mentoring, just as they do to other close relationships. For example, ad executive Bert Paley and his protégé, Brenda Marks, became enmeshed because they brought unresolved issues from their families of origin into the office.

An ideal mentor, such as Mentor/Athena, is more fantasy than reality. Reading about the very real women we profiled can nonetheless be a powerful mentoring experience in itself. It can inspire and teach women how to be mentors. Each protégé who has been profiled can serve as a role model or a symbolic mentor. She has struggled with many of the same issues all women face each day. The type of success she attained is something most of us can strive for. Each of these protégés, like every woman, has the potential to become a mentor herself.

Women possess within themselves the strength to become mentors. They know intimacy well from their personal relationships. If women use their power and their understanding of intimacy, they can restructure the mentoring relationship to keep pace with women's evolving position in our changing society. Women bring valuable experience, expertise, and talents to the workplace. By sharing these with other women—and with men—women can contribute to others and to themselves.

Women must have an honest and accurate understanding of their unique place in society and in the work force, but they must also have dreams and a vision of the future, which the mentoring process may help to provide. From this knowledge women must create their own mentors and their own mentoring situations. Salvaging what fits from the traditional male model, women must move on to fashion a blend of intimacy and power that works for them. By utilizing their facility for relationships and expanding their network professionally, women can develop an evolving constellation of relationships to support and empower them. Women *can* dream their own dreams and mold their own future.

As women shatter the glass ceiling, move into leadership positions, and serve as mentors for other women (and for men), they can transform the workplace. Their talents, their experience, and their sensitivities can humanize professions, corporations, and businesses across the country. As women become more confident of their gifts and share them with others, both women and men will benefit, and the corporate and professional climate will change to reflect women's influence. We look forward to the day when women will not be discriminated against for their gender but valued for their competence, their humanity, and their femininity. These changes may take decades to accomplish, but they are clearly a possibility within reach. We hope the voices of the women in this book will inspire others to pass on what they have learned. Thus the new mentoring process may regenerate itself and so begin the future.

APPENDIX A

❖ ❖ ❖

Addressing Your Ability to Mentor

Becoming a mentor is the last step in the mentoring process. It requires a woman to see herself in a leadership role, something with which many woman are not yet comfortable. To find out if you are a good candidate to become a mentor, take the following quiz. It will help you evaluate if you are ready for this important responsibility, and it will help you begin the process of seeing yourself in a new way and in a new position: as a mentor and a leader. After taking the quiz, if you feel that you do not have enough of the qualities necessary to become a mentor, work on developing them; then take the quiz again in six months or a year.

Except for No. 1, check as many items that apply to you. The rating system follows the quiz.

1. What is my age? ＿＿ under 30 ＿＿ 30–35 ＿＿ 35–40 ＿＿ 40–45 ＿＿ 45–50 ＿＿ 50–60 ＿＿ over 60

2. What is my stage?
   ＿＿ experienced veteran
   ＿＿ high level of responsibility
   ＿＿ plateaued on career
   ＿＿ on the fast track
   ＿＿ independent professional/businesswoman
   ＿＿ mommy track
   ＿＿ bored with job, looking for a challenge
   ＿＿ potential role model

3. I enjoy educating younger or less experienced people by:
   ＿＿ teaching them a specific skill

_____ helping them clarify business/professional goals
_____ introducing them to my organization
_____ introducing them to my values
_____ giving them specific information
_____ demonstrating to them that their roles and responsibilities have changed

4. I get a feeling of satisfaction developing others by:
_____ recognizing potential in an average, satisfactory, or high-level performer
_____ providing support and encouragement
_____ teaching a set of skills
_____ encouraging them to rise to the challenge
_____ asking them to "surprise" themselves
_____ giving recognition to improve confidence and self-esteem
_____ discussing and promoting certainty in their own values

5. I feel rewarded when coaching others by:
_____ assessing technical ability within a team
_____ developing teamwork within an organization for common goals
_____ assessing leadership ability within a team
_____ improving others' skills
_____ improving others' performance

6. I enjoy counseling/nurturing others by:
_____ giving advice as necessary
_____ holding back advice when experience would be a better teacher
_____ recognizing when they have reached developmental or organizational milestones
_____ recognizing indirect offers for my help
_____ providing encouragement
_____ providing admiration
_____ recognizing when a performance is not up to par and supporting them even when their performance is at a lower level
_____ recognizing when education/information has not been effective
_____ helping them recognize "stuck points"
_____ helping them understand their limitations and compensate for them
_____ standing by even when they don't follow my advice

_____ encouraging them to find other models and have other relationships

_____ discussing fear of success because of gender

7. I am able to confront others by:

_____ first exhausting education, development, and counseling tools

_____ labeling (fairly) a mismatch between expectation and performance

_____ helping them understand consequences of "failed" performance

_____ recognizing and labeling deteriorating performance in neutral terms

_____ asking them to take a challenge although they are negative about it

_____ pushing them when they are afraid

_____ recognizing and minimizing an individual's disruptiveness to team effort

8. I enjoy promoting others by:

_____ clarifying goals related to their skills and abilities

_____ assigning them difficult tasks and helping them succeed

_____ matching skills and abilities to future goals

_____ matching goals to promotions and higher job responsibilities

_____ recognizing privately and publicly their roles and responsibilities

_____ recognizing privately and publicly their leadership at prescribed tasks

_____ recognizing privately their business leadership ability

_____ understanding the ladder of success and showing others how to get there

_____ being interested in grooming others for my job

9. I am able to guide others through our corporation/organization by:

_____ clarifying values of the organization

_____ showing how to contribute better to the corporation

_____ clarifying and changing ambiguous values of the organization

_____ explaining the "shadow organization" and what it really means in terms of promotion

_____ promoting business/professional ethics

10. I value myself and know that protégés will help with:

_____ helping take over my work load

___ assuming responsibilities I should delegate

___ demonstrating fine performances that reflect well on me

___ spreading my credibility and reputation in the organization

___ providing me with interpersonal satisfaction

___ increasing my self-esteem through their improvement and maturation

___ showing admiration and recognition to me as a leader/person

___ spreading my values

Rating System for Potential-Mentor Quiz

1. You can be any age, but the typical mentor age is thirty to forty-five years old.

2. You can be in any stage, but the most classic mentor is usually an experienced veteran who is in a position to help.

3–10. It is difficult to give an exact profile for a potential mentor. But if you have checked at least half the items in questions 3–10, you are very likely a good potential mentor. That is, if you have checked thirty-three items or more (remember, at least half in each category), you are probably prime material for becoming a mentor.

APPENDIX B

❖ ❖ ❖

Sample Survey Results

The purpose of our study was to investigate whether successful women had mentors and how the mentors helped them. We interviewed 106 successful women. Our primary criteria for success were such common norms as education and income.* Other less quantifiable measures included job responsibility, job title, and position within a given organization. Recognition and reputation within the women's particular profession or industry were also considered.

Our sample was not drawn using statistical (random) sampling methods. In fact we were looking for an atypical sample of successful women. The women selected were intentionally an elite group because we intended to study the relationship between success and informal mentoring. Although Gerald R. Roche had done a study on successful male executives and their mentors,[1] research solely on women as protégés with either male or female mentors is relatively recent. In particular we found two studies on females, one by Nancy Collins, which surveyed them as protégés over a broad range of professions,[2] and one by Agnes Missirian, which described women as protégés in the managerial/corporate structure.[3]

We began by considering traditionally male fields that had been virtually closed to women until the mid 1970s: law/accounting partnerships, medicine, academia, and corporate/business management. We wondered how women advanced in these fields once they had overcome "starting gate" discrimination.

We also considered the traditionally female fields of nursing and

*Figure 1 shows the educational level of our sample, and figure 2 shows their income at the time we interviewed them.

207

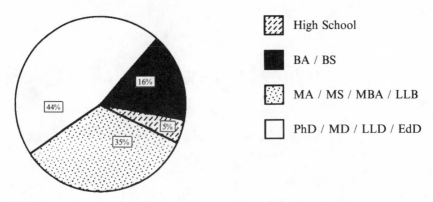

Figure 1.   Distribution of Educational Level

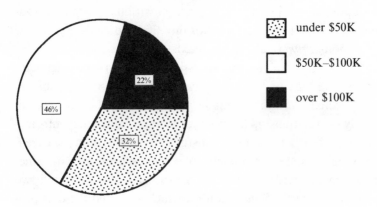

Figure 2.   Yearly-Income Distribution of Sample

teaching, seeking out those women who had left clinical nursing or class-room teaching to move into administration. In teaching, such roles as principal, curriculum coordinator, or vice principal had typically been restricted to males, even though teaching is traditionally a female profession. Had mentors been helpful to those women?

The last two occupations, psychotherapy and writing, were selected because they were our own. We wanted to survey women at a variety of levels within each of these specialties. In the former field we interviewed psychiatrists, psychologists, and social workers. Our writers were free-lance journalists, feature writers, and nonfiction book authors. All were considered talented and on the rise.

Individuals for our sample were located through a snowball sampling technique: Women in various parts of the country were contacted after they had been identified through one or more sources. We then asked the women we interviewed for other names. We screened these and selected some of them and in turn asked these individuals for more names (and so on).

After telephone screening, the women selected were interviewed starting early in 1989. In order to gain insight into the mentoring process and its relationship to advancement and intimacy, we used a semistructured interview with a prescribed set of questions. In the interviewing process we combined the skills of journalism and psychotherapy, attempting to listen with objectivity, acceptance, and empathy while maintaining human interest and the excitement of a good story. However, as the interview progressed, we felt free to deviate from our formal questions in order to gain better rapport and thus elicit more open responses about the nature of the woman's particular mentoring relationship.

Of the 106 protégées we initially interviewed, we selected fourteen to look at more deeply as part of the developmental protégé-mentor relationship. We therefore interviewed many of the men who had been identified by the female protégés as their mentors. (The lengthy case studies described in chapters 3 through 10 were chosen from these fourteen relationships.) We were interested in both the protégés' and the mentors' stories because we wanted to explore the dynamics of these relationships from each individual's point of view.

The initial interviews with the 106 protégés lasted from one to two hours, and follow-up interviews of similar length were conducted with the women in our sample who formed part of a protégé-mentor pair. Each interview was tape-recorded and transcribed.

Since we each interviewed roughly half of the 106-woman sample, we discussed the content of our respective interviews with each other. In this manner we were able to gain different perspectives. Occasionally we joined forces and interviewed together. For the lengthy case studies in each chapter we also listened to each other's tapes to get the nuances of speech and inflection.

After we had completed all our interviews, we created a questionnaire to quantify our mentoring data more solidly and to test our hypothesis that success and mentoring for women were indeed correlated. We sent the questionnaire to the same 106 women whom we had interviewed.

Approximately 60 percent of our sample responded. From these responses we distilled some interesting data, which have been organized into the bar graphs and pie charts presented in the figures in these pages. We have also drawn a number of conclusions from these data.

There was indeed a relationship between success and mentoring. Seventy-seven percent of our sample had one or more mentors. Figure 3 shows the mentor population by gender. It is significant to note that 19 percent of the protégés had had only female mentors. Figure 4 shows the number of mentoring relationships that women had had. Of significance here is the fact that more than three-quarters had had more than one mentor.

The above-mentioned figure of 77 percent actually correlates fairly well with Missirian's figure of 86 percent in her survey of successful female executives.[4] This reflects our belief that in order to get ahead in the system, women need more instrumental and psychosocial support. Those who do get such support do climb the corporate ladder higher and faster.

The women we interviewed were from twenty-four to seventy years old (see figure 5). The women who had mentors were either presently in

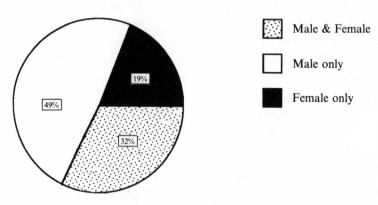

Figure 3.   Mentor Gender Profile
(of Those Who Had Mentors)

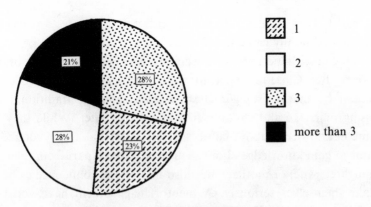

Figure 4.   Mentor Multiplicity Profile
(of Those Who Had Mentors)

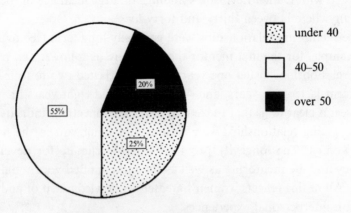

Figure 5.   Age Distribution of Sample

a mentoring relationship or were looking back on the mentoring process that had occurred at different adult developmental stages. We were especially curious about the age that a woman experienced her initial mentoring relationship. The process started at different ages, although, as might be expected, for well over half of our sample that process began before the age of thirty (see figure 6). These women followed what we have discussed earlier in the book as the individualistic model (closer to the male path). That is, they started out with a plan to have a career first; marriage and family came later.

On the other hand 18 percent were protégés between the ages of thirty and thirty-five. Close to 10 percent were forty years old and above when they first became a protégé. These women took the traditional path, stressing marriage and children first and career later. While they were mature in knowledge about family and other life issues, they looked to a mentor to gain knowledge about their profession. Apart from their roles as daughter, wife, or mother, they also needed the confidence to be able to take themselves seriously. A mentor helped them have vocational aspirations, "a dream," and a belief that they could succeed.

Figure 7 shows the ages of the mentors, both male and female, at the time the mentoring began. About 30 percent were under forty; approximately 42 percent were between forty and fifty; and roughly 30 percent were over fifty. The ages of the mentors, who were predominantly male, correlated with Daniel Levinson's findings that the ideal age of the mentor is anywhere between thirty and forty-five.[5]

The mentoring relationships were generally long term (see figure 8). For example, for the first mentor the data were as follows: Ten percent of the relationships lasted one year; 30 percent lasted two to four years; 10 percent lasted five years; and 42 percent lasted eight years or more.

It seems clear to us that the length of these connections indicates that the mentoring relationships were serious and significant in the lives of these women. The longevity provided a fertile climate for developing intimacy and life mentoring as well as the more limited vocational mentoring. All of this reflects women's greater acknowledgment of and comfort with interpersonal experiences.

Women were asked to identify one or more of the mentoring functions that had been most helpful to them (see figure 9). What had they gained most from their mentor? Significantly 85 percent of the women stated that "advice and information" had been an important ingredient of the mentoring relationship, whereas 80 percent cited "personal support" as a key contributor. This reveals how crucial it is for women to interact with their working environment through an interpersonal relationship. Rather than be outsiders they must become insiders in order to overcome the closed environment of the old boys' network.

In terms of vocational and personal satisfaction, 99 percent of those

Percentage of
Total

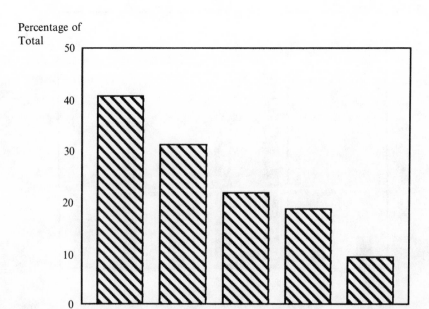

Figure 6.   Age of Protégé at Beginning of Mentoring Process

Percentage of
Total

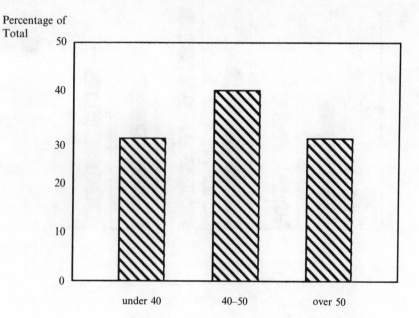

Figure 7.   Age of Mentor at Beginning of Mentoring Process

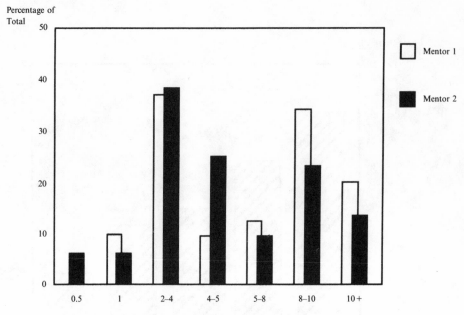

Figure 8. Length of Mentoring Relationship (years)

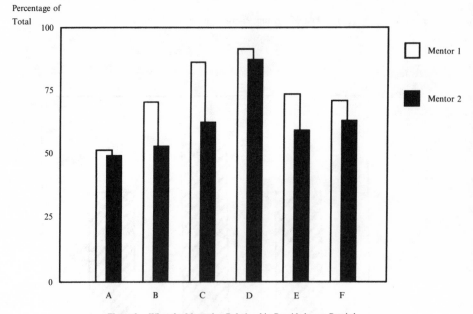

Figure 9. What the Mentoring Relationship Provided to te Protégé

A - Advancement
B - Role model
C - Personal support
D - Advice and information
E - Values and ethics
F - Technical knowledge

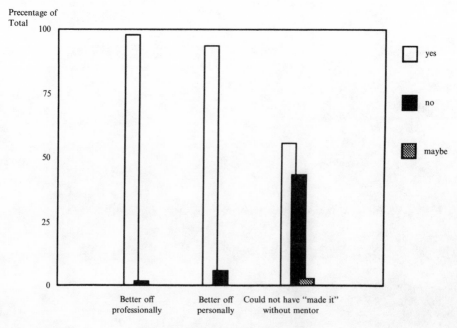

Figure 10. Satisfaction / Advancement Profile

women who did have mentors felt they were better off professionally, and 95 percent felt they were better off personally (see figure 10). These findings correlate with Gerald Roche's study of 1,250 successful executives. Those executives who were mentored reported better job satisfaction and more pleasure in their work.

We asked the women whether they agreed with the statement "I would never be where I am without my mentor." Of those in our sample who were protégés, 66 percent agreed without qualification. Thus they gave their mentors a great deal of credit for their own advancement and career satisfaction.

One of our initial goals was to discover the prevalence of mentors for women and the impact on their protégés' careers and lives. From our study it is clear that mentors helped their female protégés climb the career ladder. In the process, mentor and protégé shared experiences and intimacy that were important to both. These relationships did much to offset the isolation and discrimination often experienced by women in the workplace.

Notes

INTRODUCTION

1. Marilyn Loden, *Feminine Leadership or How to Succeed in Business Without Being One of the Boys* (New York: Times Books, 1985), p. 20.
2. Margaret Hennig and Anne Jardim, "Women Executives in the Old-Boy Network," *Psychology Today,* Jan. 1977, p. 76.
3. Robert E. Seiler and Jerome S. Horovitz, "The Partnership Decision—The Hishon Case," *CPA Journal,* Jan. 1985, p. 18.
4. Jaclyn Fierman, "Why Women Still Don't Hit the Top," *Fortune,* 30 July 1990, p. 50.
5. Ibid., p. 42.
6. U.S. Department of Labor, Bureau of Labor Statistics, tabulations from "Current Population Survey of Women Who Usually Work Full-Time, 1989 Annual Averages," unpublished, table 26.
7. Claudia Wallis, "Onward, Women!" *Time Magazine,* 4 Dec. 1989, p. 85.
8. Ibid.
9. Walecia Konrad, "Welcome to the Women-Friendly Companies," *Business Week,* Aug. 1990, p. 50.

CHAPTER 1: DEVELOPING AS WOMEN

1. Wendy Ann Stewart, "A Psychosocial Study of the Formation of the Early Adult Life Structure in Women," Unpublished Ph.D. diss., Columbia University, 1977, p. 55.
2. Ruth Halcomb, *Women Making It: Patterns and Profiles of Success* (New York: Atheneum, 1979), p. 128.

3. Ibid., p. 126.
4. Emily Hancock, *The Girl Within* (New York: Dutton, 1989), p. 24.
5. Pamela Daniels and Kathy Weingarten, *Sooner or Later: The Timing of Parenthood in Adult Lives* (New York: Norton, 1982), p. 5.
6. Daniel J. Levinson, et al., *The Seasons of a Man's Life* (New York: Ballantine Books, 1978), p. 237.
7. Priscilla Roberts and Peter M. Newton, "Levinsonian Studies of Women's Adult Development," *Psychology and Aging* 2, no. 2 (1987): 154.
8. Levinson, et al., p. 109.
9. Stewart, p. 60.
10. Carol Gilligan, *In a Different Voice* (Cambridge, Mass.: Harvard University Press, 1982), p. 73.
11. Ibid., p. 12.
12. Betty Friedan, *The Feminine Mystique* (New York: Dell, 1963), p. 11.
13. Ruth Droge, "A Psychosocial Study of the Formation of the Middle Adult Life Structure in Women," Unpublished Ph.D. diss., California School of Professional Psychology, Berkeley, 1982, p. 175.
14. Friedan, *The Feminine Mystique,* p. 72.
15. Betty Friedan, *It Changed My Life: Writings on the Women's Movement* (New York: Random House, 1976), p. 304.
16. Diane Johnson, "The Life She Chose," Review of *Simone de Beauvoir* by Deirdre Bair, *New York Times Book Review,* 15 April 1990, p. 24.
17. Friedan, *It Changed My Life,* p. 304.
18. Roberts and Newton, p. 158.

CHAPTER 2: THE ANATOMY OF MENTORING

1. Daniel J. Levinson, et al., *The Seasons of a Man's Life* (New York: Ballantine Books, 1978), p. 333.
2. Ibid., p. 97.
3. Kathy E. Kram, *Mentoring at Work: Developmental Relationships in Organizational Life* (Glenview, Ill.: Scott Foresman, 1985), p. 33.
4. Woodlands Group, "Management Development Roles: Coach, Sponsor and Mentor," *Personnel Journal,* Nov. 1980, p. 918.
5. Kram, pp. 28–29.
6. Woodlands Group, p. 919.

7. Ibid.
8. Richard L. Ochberg, Gail M. Barton, and Alan N. West, "Women Physicians and Their Mentors," *Journal of American Medical Women's Association* 44, no. 4 (July–Aug. 1989): 123.
9. Agnes K. Missirian, *The Corporate Connection: Why Executive Women Need Mentors to Reach the Top* (Englewood Cliffs, N.J.: Prentice-Hall, 1982), p. 88.
10. Levinson, et al, p. 100.
11. Kram, p. 32.
12. U.S. Department of Labor, Bureau of Labor Statistics, tabulations from "Current Population Survey of Women Who Usually Work Full-Time, 1989 Annual Averages," unpublished, table 26.
13. Kram, p. 153.
14. Ruth Halcomb, "Mentors and Successful Women," *Across the Board* 17 (Feb. 1980): 18.
15. Kram, p. 3.
16. Harry Levinson, *Executive* (Cambridge, Mass., and London: Harvard University Press, 1981), p. 55.

Chapter 3: The Mother-Daughter Pair

1. Grace Baruch, Rosalind Barnett, and Caryl Rivers, *Lifeprints: New Patterns of Work and Love* (New York: McGraw-Hill, 1983), p. 204.
2. Wendy Ann Stewart, "A Psychosocial Study of the Formation of the Early Adult Life Structure in Women," unpublished Ph.D. diss., Columbia University, 1977, p. 12.
3. Toni Bernay and Dorothy W. Cantor, eds. *The Psychology of Today's Woman* (Hillsdale, N.J.: The Analytic Press, 1986), p. 66.
4. Ibid.
5. Stewart, p. 13.
6. Carol Gilligen, *In a Different Voice* (Cambridge, Mass.: Harvard University Press, 1982), p. 12.
7. Francine Prose, "Confident at 11, Confused at 16," *New York Times Magazine,* 7 Jan. 1990, p. 23.
8. Ibid., p. 45.
9. Luise Eichenbaum and Susie Orbach, *Between Women,* (New York: Viking Penguin, 1987), p. 94.

10. Nancy Friday, *My Mother, My Self* (New York: Delacorte Press, 1977), pp. 175–176.
11. Eichenbaum and Orbach, p. 114
12. Ibid., p. 117.
13. Friday, p. 138.
14. Eichenbaum and Orbach, p. 126.
15. Ibid., p. 33.
16. Murray H. Reich, "The Mentor Connection," *Personnel Journal* 63, no. 2 (Feb. 1986), p. 53.
17. Eichenbaum and Orbach, p. 122.
18. Richard L. Ochberg, Gail M. Barton, and Alan N. West, "Women Physicians and Their Mentors," *Journal of American Medical Women's Association* 44, no. 4 (July/Aug. 1989), p. 123.
19. Walecia Konrad, "Welcome to the Women-Friendly Companies," *Business Week,* Aug. 1990, p. 52.
20. Raymond A. Noe, "Women and Mentoring: A Review and Research Agenda," *Academy of Management Review* 13, no. 1 (1988): 66.
21. Linda Russman, "Getting Hotter: Women, Men and Media Update," *Professional Communicator,* Summer 1989, p. 10.
22. Sheila J. Gibbons, ed., "NFPW Study: Women Grossly Underrepresented in Newspaper Content, Editorial Decisions," *Media Report to Women* 18, no. 4. (July–Aug. 1990): 2.
23. Nancy Campbell-Heider, "Do Nurses Need Mentors?" *Image: Journal of Nursing Scholarship* 18, no. 3 (Fall 1986): 110.
24. U.S. Department of Health and Human Services, "The Registered Nurse Population: Findings from the National Sample Survey of Registered Nurses, March 1988," p. 44.
25. C. Emily Feistritzer, *Profiles of School Administrators in the U.S.* (Washington, D.C.: National Center for Educational Information, 1988), p. 13.
26. Ada Lewis Keown and Charles F. Keown, "Factors of Success for Women in Business," *International Journal of Women's Studies* 8, no. 3 (May–June 1985): 280.
27. Ruth Halcomb, *Women Making It: Patterns and Profiles of Success* (New York: Atheneum, 1979), p. 135.
28. Agnes K. Missirian, *The Corporate Connection: Why Executive Women Need Mentors to Reach the Top* (Englewood Cliffs, N.J.: Prentice-Hall, 1982), p. 31.

29. Margaret Hennig and Anne Jardim, *The Managerial Woman* (Garden City, N.Y.: Anchor/Doubleday, 1977), p. 28.
30. Margaret Hennig and Anne Jardim, "Women Executives in the Old-Boy Network," *Psychology Today,* Jan. 1977, p. 76.
31. Halcomb, p. 135.
32. Eichenbaum and Orbach, p. 94.

CHAPTER 4: THE FATHER-DAUGHTER PAIR

1. Kathy E. Kram, *Mentoring at Work: Developmental Relationships in Organizational Life* (Glenview, Ill.: Scott Foresman, 1985), p. 122.
2. Grace Baruch, Rosalind Barnett, and Caryl Rivers, *Lifeprints: New Patterns of Work and Love* (New York: McGraw-Hill, 1983), p. 204.
3. Margaret Hennig and Anne Jardim, *The Managerial Woman* (Garden City, N.Y.: Anchor/Doubleday, 1977), p. 125.
4. Kram, p. 29.
5. Ibid., p. 30.
6. Hendrie Weisinger, "How Tough Critics Can Be Mentors in Disguise," *Working Woman Magazine* 14 (June 1989): 102.
7. Kram, p. 56.
8. Ibid., p. 57.
9. Harriet Goldhor Lerner, *The Dance of Anger* (New York: Harper and Row, 1985), pp. 1–3.
10. Colette Dowling, *The Cinderella Complex* (New York: Summit Books, 1981), p. 32.
11. National Center for Educational Statistics, "The Salaries, Tenure and Fringe Benefits of Full-time Instructional Faculty," Higher Education General Information Survey, 1985–86, unpublished.
12. Nadya Aisenberg and Mona Harrington, *Women in Academe: Outsiders in the Sacred Grove* (Amherst, Mass.: University of Massachussets Press, 1988), p. 5.
13. Ruth Halcomb, *Women Making It: Patterns and Profiles of Success* (New York: Atheneum, 1979), p. 134.
14. Daniel J. Levinson, et al., *The Seasons of a Man's Life* (New York: Ballantine Books, 1978), p. 253.
15. Ibid., p. 29.

Chapter 5: The Enmeshed Pair

1. Maggie Scarf, *Intimate Partners: Patterns in Love and Marriage* (New York: Random House, 1987), p. 45.
2. Ibid., p. 50.
3. Althea Horner, *Being and Loving* (New York: Schocken Books, 1978), p. 51.
4. Harry Levinson, *Executive* (Cambridge, Mass., and London: Harvard University Press, 1981), p. 179.
5. Horner, p. 47.
6. Anne Alonso, *The Quiet Profession: Supervisors of Psychotherapy* (New York: Macmillan, 1985), p. 28.
7. Lawton Wehle Fitt and Derek A. Newton, "When the Mentor Is a Man and the Protégé a Woman," *Harvard Business Review*, March–April 1981, p. 48.
8. Levinson, p. 206.
9. Donald W. Myers and Neil J. Humphreys, "The Caveats in Mentorship," *Business Horizons*, July–Aug. 1985, p. 12.
10. Levinson, p. 236.
11. Gail Sheehy, "The Mentor Connection: The Secret Link in the Successful Woman's Life," *New York Magazine*, 5 April 1976, p. 39.
12. James G. Clawson and Kathy E. Kram, "Managing Cross-Gender Mentoring," *Business Horizons*, May–June 1984, p. 22.
13. Daniel J. Levinson, et al., *The Seasons of a Man's Life* (New York: Ballantine Books, 1978), p. 99.

Chapter 6: The Interracial Pair

1. D. A. Thomas and C. P. Alderfer, "The Influence of Race on Career Dynamics: Theory and Research on Minority Career Experiences," in *Handbook of Career Theory*, ed. Arthur, Hall, and Lawrence (Cambridge, Eng., and New York: Cambridge University Press, 1989), p. 135.
2. David A. Thomas, "The Impact of Race on Managers' Experiences at Gaining Mentoring and Sponsorship: An Intra-Organizational Analysis," to appear in *Journal of Occupational Behavior*, p. 16.
3. Thomas and Alderfer, p. 144.
4. Ibid.

5. All studies are cited in Ibid., p. 141.
6. David A. Thomas, "The Influence of Racial Differences on the Structure and Process of Developmental Relationships" unpublished, p. 200.
7. Ibid., p. 201.
8. Ibid., p. 196.
9. Ibid., p. 169.
10. Ibid., p. 187.
11. Ibid., p. 160.
12. Ibid.
13. Ibid., p. 166.
14. Thomas, "The Impact of Race," p. 16.
15. Thomas and Alderfer, p. 143.
16. Thomas, "The Impact of Race," p. 33.
17. Ibid., p. 17.
18. Thomas, "The Influence of Racial Differences," p. 167.

CHAPTER 7: THE POLITICAL PAIR

1. Jaclyn Fierman, "Why Women Still Don't Hit the Top," *Fortune,* 30 July 1990, p. 42.
2. Darrell Sifford, "The 'Glass Ceiling' May Be Cracking," *Philadelphia Inquirer,* 22 March 1990, p. 11-D.
3. "Lawyerly Harassment," *Newsweek,* 11 Dec. 1989, p. 10.
4. U.S. Department of Labor, Bureau of Labor Statistics, tabulations from "Current Population Survey of Women Who Usually Work Full-Time, 1989 Annual Averages," unpublished, table 26.
5. Claudia Wallis, "Onward, Women!" *Time Magazine,* 4 Dec. 1989, p. 85.
6. Ibid.
7. Allan J. Cox, *The Cox Report on the American Corporation* (New York: Delacorte Press, 1982), p. 297.
8. Ibid., p. 286.
9. Ibid., p. 198.
10. Srully Blotnick, *The Corporate Steeplechase* (New York: Viking, 1984), p. 92.
11. Alice G. Sargent, ed., *Beyond Sex Roles* (St. Paul, Minn.: West Publishing, 1985), p. 218.

12. Michael Zey, *The Mentor Connection* (Homewood, Ill.: Dow Jones Irwin, 1984), p. 164.
13. Ibid.
14. Ada Lewis Keown and Charles F. Keown, "Factors of Success for Women in Business," *International Journal of Women's Studies* 8, no. 3 (May–June 1985): 281.
15. Zey, p. 126.
16. Rosabeth Moss Kanter, *Men and Women in the Corporation* (New York: Basic Books, 1977), p. 182.
17. Woodlands Group, "Management Development Roles: Coach, Sponsor and Mentor," *Personnel Journal,* Nov. 1980, p. 919.
18. Kanter, p. 166.
19. Ibid., p. 174.
20. Agnes K. Missirian, *The Corporate Connection: Why Executive Women Need Mentors to Reach the Top* (Englewood Cliffs, N.J.: Prentice-Hall, 1982), p. 31.
21. Zey, p. 31.
22. Raymond A. Noe, "Women and Mentoring: A Review and Research Agenda," *Academy of Management Review* 13, no. 1 (1988): 65.
23. Nancy Collins, *Professional Women and Their Mentors* (Englewood Cliffs, N.J.: Prentice-Hall, 1983), p. 127.
24. Ibid., p. 122.
25. Missirian, p. 31.
26. Murray H. Reich, "The Mentor Connection," *Personnel Journal* 63, no. 2 (Feb. 1986): 50.
27. Zey, p. 137.
28. Ibid., p. 153.
29. Ibid., p. 195.
30. Michael Zey, "A Mentor for All Reasons," *Personnel Journal,* Jan. 1988, p. 47.
31. Arthur Bragg, "Is a Mentoring Program in Your Future?" *Sales and Marketing Management,* Sept. 1989, p. 54.
32. Raymond A. Noe, "An Investigation of the Determinants of Successful Assigned Mentoring Relationships," *Personnel Psychology* 41, no. 3 (Autumn 1988): 474.
33. Ibid., p. 458.

Chapter 8: The Intimate Pair

1. Gail Sheehy, "The Mentor Connection: The Secret Link in the Successful Woman's Life," *New York Magazine,* 5 April 1976, p. 34.

2. U.S. Department of Labor, Bureau of Labor Statistics, tabulation from "Current Population Survey of Women Who Usually Work Full-Time, 1989 Annual Averages," unpublished, table 26.

3. C. Emily Feistritzer, *Profiles of School Administrators in the U.S.* (Washington, D.C.: National Center for Educational Information, 1988), p. 13.

4. Kathy E. Kram, *Mentoring at Work: Developmental Relationships in Organizational Life* (Glenview, Ill.: Scott Foresman, 1985), p. 105.

5. Ibid., p. 110.

6. Ibid.

7. Ibid., p. 111.

8. Alice G. Sargent, ed., *Beyond Sex Roles* (St. Paul, Minn.: West Publishing, 1985), p. 217.

9. Jaclyn Fierman, "Why Women Still Don't Hit the Top," *Fortune,* 30 July 1990, p. 42.

10. Peggy Noonan, *What I Saw at the Revolution* (New York: Random House, 1990), p. 332.

11. Peter Rutter, *Sex in the Forbidden Zone* (New York: St. Martin's Press, 1989), p. 215.

12. Lisa A. Mainiero, *Office Romance: Love, Power and Sex in the Workplace* (New York: Rawson Associates, 1989), p. 154.

13. Kram, p. 121.

14. Rutter, p. 6.

15. Ibid., p. 11.

16. Ibid., p. 31.

17. Anne Alonso, *The Quiet Profession: Supervisors of Psychotherapy* (New York: Macmillan, 1985), p. 93.

18. Elizabeth Lean, "Cross-Gender Mentoring: Downright Upright and Good for Productivity," *Training and Development Journal,* May 1983, p. 62.

19. Kram, p. 124.

20. Ibid., p. 114.

21. Lean, p. 62.

CHAPTER 9: THE LIFE MENTOR

1. Kathy E. Kram, *Mentoring at Work: Developmental Relationships in Organizational Life* (Glenview, Ill.: Scott Foresman, 1985), p. 71.
2. James G. Clawson, "Mentoring in Managerial Careers," in *Work, Family and the Career: New Frontiers in Theory and Research,* ed. C. Brooklyn Deer (New York: Praeger, 1980), p. 156.
3. Ibid., p. 155.
4. Harry Levinson, *Executive* (Cambridge, Mass., and London: Harvard University Press, 1981), p. 163.
5. Ibid., p. 164.
6. Terrence E. Deal and Allan A. Kennedy, *Corporate Cultures: The Rites and Rituals of Corporate Life* (Reading, Mass.: Addison-Wesley, 1982), p. 79.
7. Ibid., p. 15.
8. Carol Hymowitz, "Which Corporate Culture Fits You?" *Wall Street Journal (Marketplace),* 17 July 1989, p. B1.

CHAPTER 10: HOW TO FIND A MENTOR

1. Ruth Halcomb, "Mentors and Successful Women," *Across the Board* 17 (Feb. 1980): 13.
2. Agnes K. Missirian, *The Corporate Connection: Why Executive Women Need Mentors to Reach the Top* (Englewood Cliffs, N.J.: Prentice-Hall, 1982), p. 88.
3. Raymond A. Noe, "An Investigation of the Determinants of Successful Assigned Mentoring Relationships," *Personnel Psychology* 41, no. 3 (Autumn 1988): 458.
4. Richard Tyre, "Mentoring Seminar: Reaching Fullest Potential," unpublished.
5. Nancy Collins, *Professional Women and Their Mentors* (Englewood Ciffs, N.J.: Prentice-Hall, 1983), p. 38.
6. Michael Zey, *The Mentor Connection* (Homewood, Ill.: Dow Jones Irwin, 1984), p. 183.
7. Nina L. Colwill, "Mentors and Protégés, Women and Men," *Business Quarterly* 49, no. 2 (Summer 1984): 19.
8. Jacqueline Thompson, "Patrons, Rabbis, Mentors—Whatever You Call Them, Women Need Them Too," *BMA* 10 (Feb. 1976): 35.

9. Ibid.

10. Thompson, p. 35.

11. Collins, p. 40.

12. Richard L. Ochberg, Gail M. Barton, and Alan N. West, "Women Physicians and Their Mentors," *Journal of American Medical Women's Association* 44, no. 4 (July–Aug. 1989): 123.

APPENDIX B: WOMEN, MENTORS, AND SUCCESS

1. Gerald R. Roche, "Much Ado about Mentors," *Harvard Business Review,* Jan.–Feb. 1979, p. 14.

2. Nancy Collins, *Professional Women and Their Mentors* (Englewood Ciffs, N.J.: Prentice-Hall, Inc., 1983), p. 118.

3. Agnes Missirian, *The Corporate Connection: Why Executive Women Need Mentors to Reach the Top* (Englewood Cliffs, N.J.: Prentice-Hall, Inc., 1982), p. 29.

4. Ibid.

5. Daniel Levinson, et al., *The Seasons of a Man's Life* (New York: Ballantine Books, 1978), p. 99.

CONCLUSION

1. Arlie Russell Hochschild, *The Second Shift* (New York: Viking, 1989), p. 129.

2. Anne Alonso, *The Quiet Profession: Supervisors of Psychotherapy* (New York: Macmillan, 1985), p. 7.

Glossary

Boss is a woman's direct supervisor. He is involved at the job at hand, but not necessarily committed to developing potential. Not all bosses become mentors; some are coaches and others are sponsors. Some are even guides or facilitators, removing obstacles and making it easier for the woman to move ahead.

Coach shares information about key players and the political process. Like the athletic coach, the career coach works on building skills but also suggests strategies and moves. Coaching is usually a short-term, results-oriented relationship.

Guide is a more experienced individual who gives the woman important information and advice. This is a short-term, temporary relationship.

Mentor is someone who is more experienced, more powerful and who may be older than the protégé. The mentor embodies both traditional masculine and traditional feminine qualities, "the kick in the pants" and "the shoulder to cry on." The mentor teaches, guides, sponsors, advises, supports, promotes, and protects the protégé. Mentoring is a complementary relationship, built on both the mentor's and protégé's needs for intimacy and power.

Peer is a colleague at work. She has as much power as the protégé and is at the same organizational level. She can be a sounding board and provide political information and feedback.

Peer mentor is a colleague at work whose expertise complements the protégé's expertise, experience, or knowledge. Each can compensate for and learn from the other, helping both to advance or reach personal and professional goals.

Sponsor is a powerful figure several ranks above the woman who uses his power to publicly support her, promote her within the organization, and put her in the limelight.

Symbolic mentor is a historical, mythical, or famous person who provides inspiration and motivation. The relationship is imaginative, rather than interpersonal.

Bibliography

Aisenberg, Nadya; and Mona Harrington. *Women in Academe: Outsiders in the Sacred Grove.* Amherst, Mass.: University of Massachusetts Press, 1988.

Alderfer, C. P.; C. J. Alderfer; L. Tucker; and R. Tucker. "Diagnosing Race Relations in Management," *Journal of Applied Behavioral Science* 16 (1980): 135–66.

Alleman, Elizabeth. "Mentoring Relationships in Organizations: Behaviors, Personality Characteristics, and Interpersonal Perceptions." Unpublished Ph.D. diss., University of Akron, 1982.

Alleman, Elizabeth; John Cochran; James Doverspike; and Isadore Newman. "Enriching Mentoring Relationships." *Personnel and Guidance Journal,* Feb. 1984, pp. 329–32.

Alonso, Anne. *The Quiet Profession: Supervisors of Psychotherapy.* New York: Macmillan, 1985.

"Are Partnerships Immune to Sex-Bias Laws?" *Business Week,* 7 Nov. 1983, p. 52.

Bailyn, Lotte; and Edgar Schein. "Life/Career Considerations as Indicators of Quality of Employment." In *Measuring Work Quality for Social Reporting,* edited by A. D. Biderman and T. F. Drury, pp. 151–68. New York: Russell Sage, 1976.

Baird, L.; and K. Kram. "Career Dynamics: Managing the Superior-Subordinate Relationship." *Organizational Dynamics,* Summer 1983, pp. 46–64.

Baker-Miller, Jean. *Toward a New Psychology of Women.* Boston: Beacon Press, 1986.

Baruch, Grace; Rosalind Barnett; and Caryl Rivers. *Lifeprints: New Patterns of Work and Love.* New York: McGraw-Hill, 1983.

Bell, Carolyn Shaw. "Alternatives for Social Change: The Future Status of Women." In *Women in Their Professions,* edited by Laurily Keir Epstein, pp. 123–36. Lexington, Mass.: Lexington Books, 1975.

Bernay, Toni; and Dorothy W. Cantor. *The Psychology of Today's Woman.* Hillsdale, N.J.: The Analytic Press, 1986.

Blotnick, Srully. *The Corporate Steeplechase.* New York: Viking, 1984.

Bowen, Donald D. "The Role of Identification in Mentoring Female Protégés." *Group and Organization Studies* 11, nos. 1–2 (March–June 1986): 61–74.

———. "Were Men Meant to Mentor Women?" *Training and Development Journal,* Feb. 1985, pp. 30–34.

Bragg, Arthur. "Is a Mentoring Program in Your Future?" *Sales and Marketing Management,* Sept. 1989, pp. 54–63.

Bureau of Labor Statistics. "Employment and Earnings (1988 Annual Averages)." U.S. Department of Labor, 1989.

———. "Tabulations from Current Population Survey, 1989 Annual Averages." Unpublished.

Bushardt, Stephen C. "Role Ambiguity in the Male/Female Protégé Relationship." *Equal Opportunities International* 7, no. 2 (1988): 5–8.

Campbell-Heider, Nancy. "Do Nurses Need Mentors?" *Image: Journal of Nursing Scholarship* 18, no. 3 (Fall 1986): 110–13.

Carmody, Deirdre. "Secrecy and Tenure: An Issue for High Court." *New York Times (Education),* 6 Dec. 1989, p. B14.

Carsrud, Alan L.; Connie Marie Gaglio; and Kenneth W. Olm. "Entrepreneurs—Mentors, Networks, and Successful New Venture Development: An Exploratory Study." *American Journal of Small Business* 12, no. 2 (Fall 1987): 13–18.

Carter, Betty, and Monica McGoldrick, "Women and the Family Life Cycle." In *The Changing Family Life Cycle,* edited by Betty Carter and Monica McGoldrick, pp. 31–69. New York and London: Gardner Press, 1989.

Chodorow, Nancy J. *Feminism and Psychoanalytic Theory.* New Haven: Yale University Press, 1989.

Clawson, James G. "Is Mentoring Necessary?" *Training and Development Journal,* April 1985, pp. 36–39.

———. "Mentoring in Managerial Careers." In *Work, Family and the Career: New Frontiers in Theory and Research,* edited by C. Brooklyn Deer, pp. 144–65. New York: Praeger, 1980.

Clawson, James G.; and Kathy E. Kram. "Managing Cross-Gender Mentoring." *Business Horizons* 27, no. 3 (May–June 1984): 22–32.

Clift, Jean Dalby; and Wallace B. Clift. *Symbols of Transformation in Dreams.* New York: Crossroad, 1987.

Collins, Elizabeth G. C.; and Patricia Scott. "Everyone Who Makes It Has a Mentor." *Harvard Business Review* 56, no. 4 (July–Aug. 1978): 89–101.

Collins, Nancy. *Professional Women and Their Mentors.* Englewood Cliffs, N.J.: Prentice-Hall, 1983.

Colwill, Nina L. "Mentors and Protégés, Women and Men." *Business Quarterly* 49, no. 2 (Summer 1984): 19–21.

Cox, Allan J. *The Cox Report on the American Corporation.* New York: Delacorte, 1982.

Daniels, Pamela; and Kathy Weingarten. *Sooner or Later: The Timing of Parenthood in Adult Lives.* New York: Norton, 1982.

Davidson, Jeffrey P. "The Case for Multiple Mentors." *Personnel Development,* March 1988, p. 51.

Deal, Terrence E., and Allan A. Kennedy. *Corporate Cultures: The Rites and Rituals of Corporate Life.* Reading, Mass.: Addison-Wesley, 1982.

Deutsch, Claudia H. "When Feuding Goes Too Far." *New York Times,* 18 Feb. 1990, sec. 3, p. 25.

Diamond, Helen. "Patterns of Leadership." *Image* 11, no. 2 (June 1979): 42–44.

Dowling, Colette. *The Cinderella Complex.* New York: Summit, 1981.

———. *Perfect Women.* New York: Simon and Schuster, 1988.

Droge, Ruth. "A Psychosocial Study of the Formation of the Middle Adult Life Structure in Women." Unpublished Ph.D. diss., California School of Professional Psychology, Berkeley, 1982.

Ehrlich, Elizabeth. "The Mommy Track." *Business Week,* 20 March 1989, pp. 126–32.

Eichenbaum, Luise; and Susie Orbach. *Between Women.* New York: Viking Penguin, 1987.

———. *Understanding Women: A Feminist Psychoanalytic Approach.* New York: Basic Books, 1983.

Epstein, Aaron. "One Woman's Seven-Year Fight for a Partnership." *Philadelphia Inquirer,* 18 May 1990, p. 3E.

———. "Partial Win for Women in Bias Case." *Philadelphia Inquirer,* 1 May 1989, p. 1.

Epstein, C. F. "Encountering the Male Establishment: Sex-Status Limits on Women's Careers in the Professions." *American Journal of Sociology* 75 (May 1980): 965–82.

Epstein, Laurily Keir. "Success, Motivation and Social Structure: Comments on Women and Achievement." In *Women in Their Professions,* edited by Laurily Keir Epstein, pp. 1–13. Lexington, Mass.: Lexington Books, 1975.

Erickson, E., ed. *Adulthood.* New York: Norton, 1980.

Evans, Martin G. "Reducing Control Loss in Organizations: The Implications of Dual Hierarchies, Mentoring and Strengthening Vertical Dyadic Linkages." *Management Science* 30, no. 2 (Feb. 1984): 156–68.

Fagin, Claire. "Claire Fagin." In *Making Choices, Taking Changes: Nurse Leaders Tell Their Stories,* edited by Thelma Schorr and Anne Zimmerman, pp. 94–104. St. Louis: C. V. Mosby, 1988.

Fast, Julius. *Body Language.* New York: M. Evans and Co., 1970.

Feistritzer, C. Emily. *Profiles of School Administrators in the U.S.* Washington, D.C.: National Center for Educational Information, 1988.

Fierman, Jaclyn. "Why Women Still Don't Hit the Top." *Fortune,* 30 July 1990, pp. 40–62.

Fitt, Lawton Wehle; and Derek A. Newton. "When the Mentor Is a Man and the Protégé a Woman." *Harvard Business Review* March–April 1981, pp. 56–60.

Forbes, Benjamin; and James E. Piercy. "Rising to the Top: Executive Women in 1983 and Beyond." *Business Horizons* 26 (Sept.–Oct. 1983): 38–47.

Freedman, Sara M.; and James S. Phillips. "The Changing Nature of Research on Women at Work." *Journal of Management* 14, no. 2 (1988): 231–51.

Friday, Nancy. *My Mother, My Self.* New York: Delacorte Press, 1977.

Friedan, Betty. *The Feminine Mystique.* New York: Dell, 1963.

———. "The Good News About Women and Work and the '90s." *Glamour Magazine,* March 1990, pp. 260–65, 302.

———. *It Changed My Life: Writings on the Women's Movement.* New York: Random House, 1976.

———. "Not for Women Only." *Modern Maturity,* April–May 1989, pp. 66–71.

Furst, Kathryn Ann. "Origins and Evolutions of Women's Dreams in Early Adulthood." Unpublished Ph.D. diss., California School of Professional Psychology, Berkeley, 1983.

Gaillard, Frye. "Fossils Among the Oaks." *Progressive,* April 1983, p. 18.

Gibbons, Sheila J., ed. "NFPW Study: Women Grossly Underrepresented in Newspaper Content, Editorial Decisions." *Media Report to Women* 18, no. 4 (July–Aug. 1990): 2–3.

Gilligan, Carol. *In a Different Voice.* Cambridge, Mass.: Harvard University Press, 1982.

Gornick, Vivian. "Who Says We Haven't Made a Revolution?" *New York Times Magazine,* 13 April 1990, pp. 24–53.

Gould, Roger. "The Phases of Adult Life: A Study in Developmental Psychology." *American Journal of Psychology* 129 (Nov. 1972): 5.

———. *Transformations: Growth and Change in Adult Life.* New York: Simon and Schuster, 1978.

Grant, Jan. "Women as Managers: What They Can Offer to Organizations." *Organizational Dynamics* 16, no. 3 (Winter 1988): 56–63.

Halcomb, Ruth. "Mentors and Successful Women." *Across the Board* 17 (Feb. 1980): 13–18.

———. *Women Making It: Patterns and Profiles of Success.* New York: Atheneum, 1979.

Hamilton, Edith. *Mythology.* New York: New American Library, 1940.

Hancock, Emily. *The Girl Within.* New York: Dutton, 1989.

Harragan, Betty Lehan. *Games Mother Never Taught You.* New York: Warner Books, 1977.

Harree, Rom; and Roger Lamb, eds. *The Encyclopedic Dictionary of Psychology.* Cambridge, Mass.: MIT Press, 1983.

Harrison, Pat. ed. *America's New Women Entrepreneurs.* Washington, D.C.: Acropolis Books, 1986.

Hayes, Linn Spencer. "The Superwoman Myth." *Social Casework: The Journal of Contemporary Social Work,* Sept. 1989, pp. 436–41.

Hennig, Margaret; and Anne Jardim. *The Managerial Woman.* Garden City, N.Y.: Anchor/Doubleday, 1977.

———. "Women Executives in the Old-Boy Network." *Psychology Today,* Jan. 1977, pp. 76–81.

Hermanson, Roger, and Tad D. Runsopher. "What the Hishon Case Means to CPA Firms." *Journal of Accounting,* Feb. 1985, pp. 78–80.

Hochschild, Arlie Russell. "Inside the Clockwork of Male Careers." In *Woman and the Power to Change,* edited by Florence Howe, pp. 47–80. New York: McGraw-Hill, 1975.

———. *The Second Shift.* New York: Viking, 1989.

Homer. *The Odyssey,* translated by E. V. Riev. Baltimore; Penguin, 1946.

Horner, Althea. *Being and Loving.* New York: Schocken Books, 1978.

Horner, Martha. "Toward an Understanding of Achievement Related Conflicts in Women." *Journal of Social Issues* 28, no. 2 (1972): 157–75.

Hunt, David Marshall; and Carol Michael. "Mentorship: A Career Training and Development Tool." *Academy of Management Review* 8 (Nov. 1983): 475–85.

Hurley, Dan. "The Mentor Mystique." *Psychology Today,* May 1988, pp. 41–43.

Hymowitz, Carol. "Which Corporate Culture Fits You?" *Wall Street Journal (Marketplace),* 17 July 1989, p. B1.

Jacobs, Deborah L. "Smile When You Say That, Partner." *Ms. Magazine,* Jan.–Feb. 1989, p. 137.

Jacobson, Sheryl. Review of *The Psychology of Today's Woman: New Psychoanalytic Visions.* by T. Bernay and D. W. Cantor. *Sex Roles* 18, nos. 1–2 (1988): 116–18.

Johnson, Diane. "The Life She Chose." Review of *Simone de Beauvoir,* by Deirdre Bair. *New York Times Book Review,* 15 April 1990, pp. 1, 24.

Johnson, Miriam. "Fathers, Mothers and Sex Typing." *Sociological Inquiry* 45, no. 1 (1975): 15–26.

Jung, Carl G. *Memories, Dreams, Reflections.* New York: Pantheon, 1961.

———. *Modern Man in Search of a Soul.* New York: Harcourt Brace, 1933.

Jung, Carl G.; M. L. von Franz; Joseph Henderson; Jolande Jacobi; and Aniela Jaffé. *Man and His Symbols.* Garden City, N.Y.: Doubleday, 1964.

Kanter, Rosabeth Moss. *Men and Women of the Corporation.* New York: Basic Books, 1977.

———. "Why Cowboy Management Is Bad for American Business." *Working Woman,* April 1987, pp. 134–36, 166.

Kantrowitz, Barbara; and Pat Wingert. "Advocating a 'Mommy Track.'" *Newsweek,* 13 March 1989, p. 45.

Keele, Reba L.; Kathy Buckner; and Sheri J. Bushnell. "Formal Mentoring Programs Are No Panacea." *Management Review,* Feb. 1987, pp. 67–68.

Keown, Ada Lewis; and Charles F. Keown. "Factors of Success for Women in Business." *International Journal of Women's Studies* 8, no. 3 (May–June 1985): 278–85.

Kerr, Michael E. "Obstacles to Differentiation of Self," chap. 5 in *Casebook of Marital Therapy,* edited by Allen S. Gurman. New York and London: Guilford Press, 1985.

Konrad, Walecia. "Welcome to the Women-Friendly Companies." *Business Week,* 6 Aug. 1990, pp. 49–55.

Korda, Michael. *Power.* New York: Random House, 1975.

Kram, Kathy E. "Improving the Mentoring Process." *Training and Development Journal,* April 1985, pp. 40–43.

———. *Mentoring Processes at Work: Developmental Relationships in Managerial Careers.* Ph.D. diss., Yale University, 1980.

———. *Mentoring at Work: Developmental Relationships in Organizational Life.* Glenview, Ill.: Scott Foresman, 1985.

———. "Phases of the Mentor Relationship." *Academy of Management Journal* 26, no. 4 (1983): 608–625.

Kram, Kathy E.; and L. Isabella. "Mentoring Alternatives: The Role of Peer Relationships in Career Development." *Academy of Management Journal* 28 (1985): 110–32.

"Lawyerly Harassment." *Newsweek,* 11 Dec. 1989, p. 10.

Lean, Elizabeth. "Cross-Gender Mentoring: Downright Upright and Good for Productivity." *Training and Development Journal,* May 1983, pp. 60–65.

Lees, Susan. Review of *The Campus Troublemakers: Academic Women in Protest,* by Athena Theodore. *Sex Roles* 18, nos. 1–2 (1988): 113–15.

Lerner, Harriet Goldhor. *The Dance of Anger.* New York: Harper and Row, 1985.

———. *The Dance of Intimacy.* New York: Harper and Row, 1989.

Levinson, Daniel J.; et al. *The Seasons of a Man's Life.* New York: Ballantine Books, 1978.

Levinson, Daniel J.; Charlotte M. Darrow; Edward B. Klein; Maria H.

Levinson; and Braxton McKee. "Growing Up With the Dream." *Psychology Today,* Jan. 1978, pp. 20–31, 89.

————."Periods in the Adult Development of Men: Ages 18 to 45." *The Counseling Psychologist* 6, no. 1 (1976): 21.

Levinson, Harry. *Executive.* Cambridge, Mass., and London: Harvard University Press, 1981.

————. "On Being a Middle-aged Manager." *Harvard Business Review,* July–Aug. 1969, pp. 51–60.

Loden, Marilyn. *Feminine Leadership or How to Succeed in Business Without Being One of the Boys.* New York: Times Books, 1985.

London, Manuel; and Edward M. Mone. *Career Management and Survival in the Workplace.* San Francisco: Jossey-Bass Publishers, 1982.

Mainiero, Lisa A. *Office Romance: Love, Power and Sex in the Workplace.* New York: Rawson Associates, 1989.

Manley, Rebecca Oxford. "Parental Warmth and Hostility as Related to Sex Differences in Children's Achievement Orientation." *Psychology of Women Quarterly* 1, no. 3 (Spring 1977): 229–46.

McLaughlin, Patricia. "The Feminine Critique." *Philadelphia Inquirer Magazine,* 15 July 1990, p. 35.

"Mentors for Women: Like It or Not, It's a Two-way Street." *Management Review* 69, pp. 14–16 (June 1989): 6.

"The Merits of Mentors: Myth or Reality?" *Training,* April 1985.

Miller, Annetta; and Pamela Kruger. "The New Old Boy." *Working Woman,* April 1990, pp. 94–96.

Missirian, Agnes K. *The Corporate Connection: Why Executive Women Need Mentors to Reach the Top.* Englewood Cliffs, N.J.: Prentice-Hall, 1982.

Moore, Linda L. "Issues for Women in Organizations." In *Beyond Sex Roles,* edited by Alice G. Sargent, pp. 215–25. St. Paul, Minn.: West Publishing, 1985.

Myers, Donald W.; and Neil J. Humphreys. "The Caveats in Mentorship." *Business Horizons,* July–Aug. 1985, pp. 9–14.

National Center for Educational Statistics, "The Salaries, Tenure and Fringe Benefits of Full-time Instructional Faculty." Higher Education General Information Survey, 1985–86, unpublished.

Nelson-Horchler, Joan. "Women's Mentor Changes Careers." *Industry Week,* 9 Feb. 1987, p. 54.

Noe, Raymond A. "Women and Mentoring: A Review and Research Agenda." *Academy of Management Review* 13, no. 1 (1988): 65–78.

———. "An Investigation of the Determinants of Successful Assigned Mentoring Relationships." *Personnel Psychology* 41, no. 3 (Autumn 1988): 457–79.

Noonan, Peggy. *What I Saw at the Revolution*. New York: Random House, 1990.

Ochberg, Richard L.; Gail M. Barton; and Alan N. West. "Women Physicians and Their Mentors." *Journal of American Medical Women's Association* 44, no. 4 (July–Aug. 1989): 123–26.

Odiorne, George S. "Mentoring an American Management Innovation." *Personnel Administrator* 30, no. 5 (May 1985): 63–70.

Pert, Candace. "First Word." *Omni Magazine,* Sept. 1985, p. 6.

Phillips-Jones, Linda. "Establishing a Formalized Mentoring Program." *Training and Development Journal,* Feb. 1983, pp. 38–42.

———. *Mentors and Protégés*. New York: Arbor House, 1982.

Piontek, Stephen. "Protégés and Mentors Share Joys and Pains." *National Underwriter* 89, no. 14 (6 April 1985): 2, 30.

"The Power of a Mentor: Protégés' and Nonprotégés' Perception of Their Own Power in Organizations." *Group and Organizational Studies* 13, no. 1 (June 1988): 182–94.

Price, Margaret. "Corporate Godfathers: By Appointment Only." *Industry Week,* 20 June 1981, pp. 71–74.

Prose, Francine. "Confident at 11, Confused at 16." *New York Times Magazine,* 7 Jan. 1990, pp. 22–25, 37–39, 45–46.

Public Health Service, Health Resources and Services Administration. "The Registered Nurse Population: Findings from the National Sample Survey of Registered Nurses, March 1988." U.S. Department of Health and Human Services, June 1990.

Reich, Murray H. "The Mentor Connection." *Personnel Journal* 63, no. 2 (Feb. 1986): 50–56.

Roberts, Priscilla; and Peter M. Newton. "Levinsonian Studies of Women's Adult Development." *Psychology and Aging* 2, no. 2 (1987): 154–63.

Roche, Gerald. "Much Ado About Mentors." *Harvard Business Review,* Jan.–Feb. 1979, pp. 14–28.

Rosch, Leah. "Modern-Day Mentors: Five Lessons in Success." *Working Woman Magazine,* August 1987, pp. 55–59.

Rubin, Lillian B. *Women of a Certain Age: The Midlife Search for Self.* New York: Harper and Row, 1979.

Russman, Linda. "Getting Hotter: Women, Men and Media Update." *Professional Communicator,* Summer 1989, pp. 8–10.

Rutter, Peter. *Sex in the Forbidden Zone.* New York: St. Martin's Press, 1989.

Sargent, Alice G. *Beyond Sex Roles.* St. Paul, Minn.: West Publishing Co., 1985.

Scarf, Maggie. *Intimate Partners: Patterns in Love and Marriage.* New York: Random House, 1987.

———. *Unfinished Business: Pressure Points in the Lives of Women.* New York: Doubleday, 1980.

Schaef, Anne Wilson. *Women's Reality: An Emerging Female System in a White Male Society.* San Francisco: Harper and Row, 1981.

Schein, Virginia Ellen. "The Relationship Between Sex Role Stereotypes and Requisite Management Characteristics." *Journal of Applied Psychology* 57, no. 2 (1973): 95–100.

Schwartz, Felice N. "Management Women and the New Facts of Life." *Harvard Business Review,* Jan.–Feb. 1989, pp. 65–76.

Seiler, Robert E.; and Jerome S. Horvitz. "The Partnership Decision: The Hishon Case." *CPA Journal,* Jan. 1985, pp. 12–18.

Settle, Mary E. "Developing Tomorrow's Managers." *Training and Development Journal,* April 1988, pp. 60–64.

Shapiro, Eileen C.; Florence P. Haseltine; and Mary P. Rowe. "Moving Up: Role Models, Mentors, and the 'Patron System.'" *Sloan Management Review* 19, no. 3 (Spring 1978): 51–58.

Sheehy, Gail. "The Mentor Connection: The Secret Link in the Successful Woman's Life." *New York Magazine,* 5 April 1976, pp. 33–39.

———. *Passages: Predictable Crises of Adult Life.* New York: Dutton, 1976.

Shreve, Anita. *Remaking Motherhood.* New York: Viking, 1987.

———. *Women Together, Women Alone.* New York: Viking, 1989.

Sifford, Darrell. "The 'Glass Ceiling' May Be Cracking." *Philadelphia Inquirer,* 22 March 1990, p. 11-D.

Smelser, Neil J.; and Erik H. Erikson, eds. *Themes of Work and Love in Adulthood.* Cambridge, Mass.: Harvard University Press, 1980.

Sternhell, Carol. "The Women Who Won't Disappear." *Ms. Magazine (Campus Times),* Oct. 1984, pp. 94–98.

Stewart, Wendy Ann. "A Psychosocial Study of the Formation of the Early Adult Life Structure in Women." Unpublished Ph.D. diss., Columbia University, 1977.

Thomas, David A. "The Impact of Race on Managers' Experiences at Gaining Mentoring and Sponsorship: An Intra-Organizational Analysis." To appear in *Journal of Occupational Behavior.*

————. "The Influence of Racial Differences on the Structure and Process of Developmental Relationships." In unpublished book.

Thomas, D. A.; and C. P. Alderfer. "The Influence of Race on Career Dynamics: Theory and Research on Minority Career Experiences." In *Handbook of Career Theory,* edited by M. Arthur, B. Hall, and B. Lawrence. Cambridge, Eng., and New York: Cambridge University Press, 1989.

Thomas, David A.; and Kathy Kram. "Promoting Career-Enhancing Relationships in Organizations: The Role of the Human Resource Professional." To appear in *The Human Resource Professional and Employee Career Development,* edited by Manuel London and Edward M. Mone.

Thompson, Ann McKay; and Marcia Donnan Wood. *Management Stratagies for Women or Now That I'm Boss, How Do I Run This Place?* New York: Simon and Schuster, 1980.

Thompson, Jacqueline. "Patrons, Rabbis, Mentors—Whatever You Call Them, Women Need Them Too." *BMA* 10 (Feb. 1976): 27, 30, 35, 36.

Turkel, Ann Ruth. "The Impact of Feminism on the Practice of a Woman Analyst." *American Journal of Psychoanalysis* 36 (1976): 119–26.

Tyre, Richard. "Mentoring Seminar: Reaching Fullest Potential." Unpublished.

Viorst, Judith. *Necessary Losses.* New York: Random House, 1986.

Wachtel, Ellen F.; and Paul L. Wachtel. *Family Dynamics in Individual Psychotherapy.* New York and London: Guilford Press, 1986.

Wallis, Claudia. "Onward, Women!" *Time Magazine,* 4 Dec. 1989, pp. 80–89.

Waters, Harry F.; and Janet Huck. "Networking Women." *Newsweek* 13 March 1989, pp. 48–54.

Weisinger, Hendrie. "How Tough Critics Can Be Mentors in Disguise." *Working Woman Magazine* 14 (June 1989): 102–103.

Welch, Mary Scott. *Networking: The Great New Way for Women to Get Ahead.* New York: Warner Books, 1980.

Wheatley, Meg; and Marcie Schorr Hirsch. "Five Ways to Leave Your Mentor." *Ms. Magazine,* Sept. 1984, pp. 106–8.

Wilkins, Joanne. *Her Own Business: Success Secrets of Entrepreneurial Women.* New York: McGraw-Hill, 1987.

"Women Finally Get Mentors of Their Own." *Business Week,* 23 Oct. 1978, pp. 74–80.

Woodlands Group. "Management Development Roles: Coach, Sponsor and Mentor." *Personnel Journal,* Nov. 1980, pp. 918–21.

Zemke, Ron. "The Honeywell Studies: How Managers Learn to Manage." *Training,* Aug. 1985, pp. 46–51.

Zey, Michael. "A Mentor for All Reasons." *Personnel Journal,* Jan. 1988, pp. 46–51.

———. *The Mentor Connection.* Homewood, Ill.: Dow Jones Irwin, 1984.

———. "Mentor Programs: Making the Right Moves." *Personnel Journal,* Feb. 1985, pp. 53–57.

Index